STUDIES IN MEMORY OF JOHN JAY PARRY

John J. Parry

STUDIES

BY MEMBERS

OF THE ENGLISH DEPARTMENT

UNIVERSITY OF ILLINOIS

IN MEMORY OF

JOHN JAY PARRY

Essay Index Reprint Series

BOOKS FOR LIBRARIES PRESS

FREEPORT, NEW YORK

First Published 1955

Reprinted 1968 by arrangement with
The University of Illinois Press

LIBRARY OF CONGRESS CATALOG CARD NUMBER:
68-58798

PRINTED IN THE UNITED STATES OF AMERICA

CONTENTS

The following studies, dedicated to the memory of Professor John Jay Parry, have earlier appeared as part of a special memorial number of *The Journal of English and Germanic Philology* (October 1955), of which journal Professor Parry was General Editor from 1944 until his death. It was thought fitting, however, that the English Department of the University of Illinois, a department with which Professor Parry was associated as scholar and teacher for nearly forty years, should pay individual tribute under its own name. This desire of the Department has been given expression in the present volume.

The editors wish especially to thank Miss Rachel E. Anderson, assistant editor of the University of Illinois Press, for her valuable help in preparing these studies for publication.

HENNING LARSEN

ROBERT W. ROGERS

G. BLAKEMORE EVANS

IN MEMORIAM—JOHN JAY PARRY

THE DEATH of John Jay Parry, Professor of English, on October 8, 1954, closed a career of thirty-eight years of service to the University of Illinois. Professor Parry was born in Rome, New York, on September 30, 1889. He attended successively the Rome Free Academy, Hotchkiss School, and Yale University. From the last he received the degrees of B.A., 1912; M.A., 1914; and Ph.D., 1915. After one year of teaching in the University of California he came to Illinois as Instructor in English in 1916. During the years 1917–1919 he served as second lieutenant in the American Expeditionary Forces, after which he returned to the University and continued uninterruptedly his teaching career. He was appointed Professor of English in 1939. In 1921 he was married to Marion J. Austin who survives him along with their two children: John Jay of Schenectady, New York, and Anne Elizabeth of Urbana. There are two grandchildren, Susan and William, the latter born only a few days before his grandfather's death.

In the course of the years Professor Parry taught many courses in the department, notably those in Comparative Literature and Survey of English Literature, but his field of professional interest and teaching was the Middle Ages and in that large area, specifically, The Arthurian Legend. To the study of this longest-lived story material in English he brought not only his vast learning, but the warmth of his enthusiasm for the tales and language of Wales, which were his ancestral inheritance. He published in this field *The Vita Merlini* (1925), *A Bibliography of Critical Arthurian Literature*, vol. 1 (1931)— he was co-author of vol. 2 (1936)—and *Andreas Capellanus, the Art of Courtly Love* (1941). Since 1944 he had been busy and happy in the editorship of *The Journal of English and Germanic Philology*. He served on the Advisory Committee of the International Arthurian Society, for three years as councilor of the Medieval Society, and for six years on the advisory and editorial board of *Speculum*. He belonged to many learned and professional societies and was an active member of the Exchange Club of Champaign.

Professor Parry's encyclopaedic knowledge was that of the old-time humanist ever less frequently met with in this age of specialization in letters. In him the learning of the scholar blended with the citizen of the community, each enriching the other. His professional province of study, apparently so remote from contemporary life in time, in content, and even in language, focussed without confining his curiosity, which reflected, in the multifarious details it gathered and the scope of its interests, the universality of the great age in which he worked. Few men have found so much pleasure in their knowledge, and few have had so much to enjoy. His mind ranged over the world of literature in many languages and penetrated into remote corners, so that, like an experienced traveler, he had friends wherever culture had tarried and could illumine the most unlikely spot with a tale, glorious, or scandalous, or funny, or terrible of what had happened there. He was, in the good, old English sense of the word, a gossip of the ages. Perhaps this very range of association was one reason why he preferred, instead of traveling, to remain at home surrounded by family and books and familiar walks and faces.

His students found him understanding, helpful, exacting, and enormously informative. Even after failing health had delivered its warning, he found his courses too interesting to accept the proffered relief in load.

His friends knew him as a genial lover of company and conversation, who took a genuine delight in human intercourse without regard to academic interest or attainment. What many even of them did not know was his habit, gladly exercised over the years, of extending financial aid to needy graduate assistants. Only those who did the soliciting knew how generous he was to every call from a community campaign. As his generosity was unostentatious so his learning was modestly borne, and we shall remember him as one in whom knowledge, lovingly acquired, had ripened into that rich contentment with daily life which can be the supreme gift of humane letters.

PAUL LANDIS

A BIBLIOGRAPHY OF THE WRITINGS OF JOHN JAY PARRY

1917

The Poems and "Amyntas" of Thomas Randolph,
  ed., with an introduction and notes. Yale University Press, 1917.
"A New Version of Randolph's *Aristippus*,"
  Modern Language Notes, XXXII (1917), 351–54.

1920

"A Seventeenth Century Gallery of Poets,"
  Journal of English and Germanic Philology, XIX (1920), 270–78.

1921

"Dr. Johnson's Interest in Welsh,"
  Modern Language Notes, XXXVI (1921), 374–76.
Rev. of *Shakespeare and the Welsh*, by Frederick J. Harris:
  Journal of English and Germanic Philology, XX (1921), 410–12.

1922

"Modern Welsh Versions of the Arthurian Stories,"
  Journal of English and Germanic Philology, XXI (1922), 572–600.

1923

"Note on William Hemminge's *Elegy*,"
  London *Times Literary Supplement*, XXII (1923), 355.

1924

" 'Selling' English Literature to Non-Literary Students,"
  English Journal, XIII (1924), 10–22.
"An Arthurian Parallel,"
  Modern Language Notes, XXXIX (1924), 307–309.
Rev. of *The Romance of Tristram and Ysolt* by Thomas Britain, trans.
  by Roger Sherman Loomis:
  Journal of English and Germanic Philology, XXIII (1924), 609–10.
Rev. of *The Troubadours and England*, by H. J. Chaytor:
  Journal of English and Germanic Philology, XXIII (1924), 610–11.

1925

The Vita Merlini,
> University of Illinois *Studies in Language and Literature,* Vol. x,
> No. 3.
> University of Illinois Press, 1925.

"The Date of the *Vita Merlini*,"
> *Modern Philology,* xxii (1925), 413–15.

"Celtic Tradition and the *Vita Merlini*,"
> *Philological Quarterly,* iv (1925), 193–207.

1926

Rev. of *The Grail and the English Sir Percival,* by C. L. Brown:
> *Journal of English and Germanic Philology,* xxv (1926), 433–35.

Rev. of *Die Vier Zweige des Mabinogi,* by Ludwig Mühlhausen:
> *Journal of English and Germanic Philology,* xxv (1926), 575–78.

1927

"Geoffrey of Monmouth and Josephus,"
> *Speculum,* ii (1927), 446–47.

Rev. of *The Character of King Arthur in English Literature,* by E. Van
der Ven-Ten Bensel:
> *Modern Language Notes,* xlii (1927), 417–20.

1928

Rev. of *Celtic Myth and Arthurian Romance,* by Roger Sherman
Loomis:
> *Journal of English and Germanic Philology,* xxvii (1928), 246–51.

1929

"A Note on the Prosody of William Morris,"
> *Publications of the Modern Language Association,* xliv (1929), 308.

"The Chronology of Geoffrey of Monmouth's *Historia, Books I and
II*,"
> *Speculum,* iv (1929), 318–22.

Rev. of *Mediaeval Studies in Memory of Gertrude Schoepperle Loomis:*
> *Journal of English and Germanic Philology,* xxviii (1929), 550–51.

Rev. of *Melanthe, A Latin Pastoral Play of the Early Seventeenth
Century* by Samuel Brooke, ed. Joseph S. G. Bolton:
> *Journal of English and Germanic Philology,* xxviii (1929), 593.

Rev. of *The Drama in Modern Wales,* by Olive Ely Hart:
> *Journal of English and Germanic Philology,* xxviii (1929), 594.

1930

Bibliography of Modern Versions of Arthurian Stories (with C. S. Northup).
  Mimeo. ed., Urbana, Illinois, 1930.
"Abel Morgan,"
  Dictionary of American Biography, XIII (1930), 163–64.
"The Triple Death in the *Vita Merlini*,"
  Speculum, V (1930), 316–17.
Rev. of *Studies in English*, University of Texas, Nos. 6 and 7, 1926–27:
  Journal of English and Germanic Philology, XXIX (1930), 136–37.

1931

A Bibliography of Critical Arthurian Literature for the Years 1922–1929, ed. for Arthurian Group of the Modern Language Association of America.
  Modern Language Association, 1931.
"Further Comment on Randolph's Text,"
  Modern Language Notes, XLVI (1931), 510–12
Rev. of *The Mabinogion*, trans. by T. P. Ellis and John Lloyd:
  Speculum, VI (1931), 139–42.
Rev. of *The Historia Regum Britanniae of Geoffrey of Monmouth*, ed. Jacob Hammer:
  Journal of English and Germanic Philology, XXX (1931), 95–98.
Rev. of *Arthuriana*, in *Proceedings of the Arthurian Society*, Vol. I:
  Journal of English and Germanic Philology, XXX (1931), 98–99.
Rev. of *The Drinking Academy* by Thomas Randolph, ed. H. E. Rollins:
  Journal of English and Germanic Philology, XXX (1931), 439–440.
Rev. of *Lancelot and Guenevere*, by T. P. Cross and W. A. Nitze:
  Speculum, VI (1931), 482–83.

1932

"Ellis Pugh,"
  Dictionary of American Biography, XV (1932), 257.
"A Variant Version of Geoffrey of Monmouth's *Historia*,"
  A Miscellany of Studies in Romance Languages and Literatures.
  Cambridge, England, 1932, pp. 384–89.
Rev. of *Le Poème du Gral et ses Auteurs*, by Maurice Wilmotte:
  Speculum, VII (1932), 439–44.

Rev. of *The Relation of Golagros and Gawane to the Old French Perceval*,
by Paul J. Ketrick:
Journal of English and Germanic Philology, XXXI (1932), 426.
Rev. of *Le Haut Livre du Graal Perlesvaus*, ed. William A. Nitze and
F. Atkinson:
Speculum, VII (1932), 570–72.

1933

Rev. of *Arthurian Legend in the Seventeenth Century*, by Roberta
Florence Brinkley:
Modern Language Notes, XLVIII (1933), 267–68.
Rev. of *Mabinogi Cymru*, by Gan Timothy Lewis:
Journal of English and Germanic Philology, XXXII (1933), 403–406.

1934

Rev. of *Classical Mythology and Arthurian Romance*, by Charles
Bertram Lewis.
Speculum, IX (1934), 336–37.

1935

Rev. of *The Tale of Gargantua and King Arthur* by Francois Girault,
ed. Huntington Brown:
Journal of English and Germanic Philology, XXXIV (1935), 124.
Rev. of *Welsh Christian Origins*, by Arthur W. Wade-Evans:
Speculum, X (1935), 116–18.
Rev. of *Motif-Index of Folk Literature*, by Stith Thompson:
Journal of English and Germanic Philology, XXXIV (1935), 593–94.

1936

A Bibliography of Arthurian Critical Literature for the Years 1930–1935.
ed. (with Margaret Schlauch) for Arthurian Group of the Modern
Language Association of America.
Modern Language Association, 1936.
Brut y Brenhinedd (Cotton Cleopatra Version), edited and translated.
The Mediaeval Academy of America, 1937.

1938

"Geoffrey of Monmouth and the Paternity of Arthur,"
Speculum, XIII (1938), 271–77.

1939

Rev. of *Arthurian Legends in Mediaeval Art,* by Roger Sherman Loomis:
Journal of English and Germanic Philology, XXXVIII (1939), 156–57.

1940

"A Bibliography of Critical Arthurian Literature for the Years 1936–1939" (with Margaret Schlauch),
Modern Language Quarterly, I (1940), 129–74.

Rev. of *Bibliotheca Celtica,* New Series, Vol. I, 1929–1933:
Journal of English and Germanic Philology, XXXIX (1940), 141–44.

1941

The Art of Courtly Love by Andreas Capellanus, ed. with introduction, translation, and notes.
Columbia University Press, 1941.

"A Bibliography of Critical Arthurian Literature for the Year 1940,"
Modern Language Quarterly, II (1941), 293–305.

1942

"A Bibliography of Critical Arthurian Literature for the Year 1941,"
Modern Language Quarterly, III (1942), 307–16.

Rev. of *The Crusade of Richard Lion-Heart* by Ambroise, trans. by Norton Jerome Hubert:
Journal of English and Germanic Philology, XLI (1942), 377–78.

Rev. of *Das Haus Anjou und der Orient in Wolframs Parzival,* by William Snelleman:
Journal of English and Germanic Philology, XLI (1942), 543–44.

Rev. of *The Eighth Supplement to a Manual of the Writings in Middle English,* by John Edwin Wells:
Journal of English and Germanic Philology, XLI (1942), 568.

Rev. of *Saints and Sinners in Old Romance,* by Charles Maxwell Lancaster:
Journal of English and Germanic Philology, XLI (1942), 568–69.

1943

"A Bibliography of Critical Arthurian Literature for the Year 1942,"
Modern Language Quarterly, IV (1943), 225–31.

"Welsh Versification,"
Dictionary of World Literature, 1943, pp. 620–23.

1946

"A Bibliography of Critical Arthurian Literature for the Year 1945,"
  Modern Language Quarterly, VII (1946), 221–40.
"The Revival of Cornish: An Dasserghyans Kernewek,"
  Publications of the Modern Language Association, LXI (1946),
  258–68.
Encyclopedia of Literature, ed. J. T. Shipley. Philosophical Library,
  1946. See the following articles:
  "Cornish Literature, " pp. 176–77; "Welsh Literature," pp. 1001–
  25; "Aneirin," pp. 1059–60; "Cynddelw," p. 1081; "Dafydd ab
  Edmwnd," p. 1081; "Dafydd ap Gwilym," p. 1081; "Dafydd
  Namnor," pp. 1081–82; "Owen Morgan Edwards," pp. 1086–87;
  "William John Gruffydd," pp. 1099–1100; "John 'Ceirog'
  Hughes," pp. 1107–08; "Henry Jenner," p. 1112; "John Morris
  Jones," p. 1114; "Thomas Gwynn Jones," p. 1114; "Morgan
  Llwyd," pp. 1126–27; "Llywarch the Old," p. 1127; "Huw
  Morus," p. 1140; "Daniel Owen," p. 1146; "Goronwy Owen,"
  pp. 1146–47; "Rhys Prichard," pp. 1152–53; "Taliesin," pp.
  1172–73; "William Thomas, 'Islwyn,'" p. 1175; "Edward Wil-
  liams, 'Iolo Morganwg,' " p. 1186; "William Williams, 'Panty-
  celyn,'" p. 1186; "Ellis Wynne," p. 1187.
"Albert William Aron—In Memoriam,"
  Journal of English and Germanic Philology, XLV (1946), 123–24.
Rev. of *Geoffrey of Monmouth, 1640–1800*, by Ernest Jones:
  Modern Language Quarterly, VII (1946), 111–12.
Rev. of *Algemene Literatur Geschiedenis*, two chapters, by H. Sparnaay,
  "Het Hoofse Epos" (II, 204–57) and "De Germaanse Lyriek"
  (II, 360–80):
  Journal of English and Germanic Philology, XLV (1946), 121.

1947

"A Bibliography of Critical Arthurian Literature for the Year 1946,"
  Modern Language Quarterly, VIII (1947), 243–52.
"Arthurian Romance" [a bibliography],
  A Critical Bibliography of French Literature, Syracuse University
  Press, N. Y.: Vol. I, *The Medieval Period*, ed. U. T. Holmes,
  1947, pp. 101–23.
Rev. of *Anglica: Revista di Studi Inglesi e Americani*, ed. N. Orsini:
  Journal of English and Germanic Philology, XLVI (1947), 115.

Rev. of *Geoffrey of Monmouth and the Late Latin Chroniclers 1300–1500*,
by Laura Keeler:
Modern Language Quarterly, IX (1948), 1104–1105.

1948

'A Bibliography of Critical Arthurian Literature for the Year 1947,"
Modern Language Quarterly, IX (1948), 224–37.

1949

Rev. of *The Heresy of Courtly Love*, by Alexander J. Denomy:
Modern Language Quarterly, X (1949), 107–109.

1950

"A Bibliography of Critical Arthurian Literature for the Year 1949,"
Modern Language Quarterly, XI (1950), 217–36.

1951

"A Bibliography of Critical Arthurian Literature for the Year 1950,"
Modern Language Quarterly, XII (1951), 165–82.

1952

"A Bibliography of Critical Arthurian Literature for the Year 1951,"
Modern Language Quarterly, XIII (1952), 163–79.
"The Court Poets of the Welsh Princes,"
Publications of the Modern Language Association, LXVII (1952),
511–20.
Rev. of *Arthurian Tradition and Chrétien de Troyes*, by Roger S.
Loomis:
Modern Language Quarterly, XIII (1952), 99–101.

1953

"Arthur's Round Table and Bran the Blessed,"
Modern Language Quarterly, XIV (1953), 133.
"A Bibliography of Critical Arthurian Literature for the Year 1952,"
Modern Language Quarterly, XIV (1953), 163–83.

1954

"A Bibliography of Critical Arthurian Literature for the Year 1953,"
Modern Language Quarterly, XV (1954), 147–67.

ON POPE'S "HORTICULTURAL ROMANTICISM"

IN THE "Epistle to Richard Boyle, Earl of Burlington," the fourth of the *Epistles to Several Persons*, Alexander Pope's discussion of taste— or of false taste—includes a section on gardening which is his fullest expression of a theory he had developed during a period of almost twenty years. As a child at Binfield, Pope was exposed to his father's enthusiasm for gardening,[1] and when the poet leased his own tiny estate at Twickenham in 1718, he laid out a grotto and gardens with such success that friends seeking to improve their own grounds frequently sought his advice. To the end of his life, Pope continued to expand and embellish his grotto, to revamp his grounds, to plan gardens for his friends, and to advise such professional gardeners as Charles Bridgman and William Kent, two of a succession of notable designers who developed the famous gardens at Stowe. In addition, Kent was Burlington's protégé, so that he was chiefly responsible, apparently with some suggestions from Pope, for the grounds which the poet praised for their good taste in the fourth *Epistle*.

During the period of his interest in gardening, Pope made a number of statements which taken together constitute a reasonably consistent theory of the garden art. This theory called for the abandonment of the excessive artifice of the formal garden and for the adoption of a simpler, more "natural" style in gardening. Pope's precepts on the subject and his example at Twickenham have been credited with popularizing a revolution in garden design leading to the widespread growth of the natural landscape garden.[2]

More recently, a number of writers have considered Pope's gardening to be a romantic contradiction to the prevailing neoclassicism of his poetry. Thus Professor Bracher sees the grotto at Twickenham as an outlet for submerged romantic tendencies during the years of "moralized song."[3] This attitude parallels the tendency to label Pope's earlier, obviously more exuberant poetry "romantic," as against the later satiric and didactic work, which is presumed to be typically neoclassic.[4] Arthur O. Lovejoy, on the other hand, speaks of

[1] George Sherburn, *The Early Career of Alexander Pope* (Oxford, 1934), p. 35.

[2] Isabel Wakelin Chase, *Horace Walpole: Gardenist* (Princeton, N. J., 1943), pp. 28–29, 107; Christopher Hussey, "The Aesthetic Background of the Art of William Kent," in *The Work of William Kent . . .* by Margaret Jourdain (London, 1948), pp. 21–22.

[3] Frederick Bracher, "Pope's Grotto: The Maze of Fancy," *Huntington Library Quarterly*, XII (1949), 141–62.

[4] Émile Montégut, "Heures de lecture d'un critique: Pope," *Revue des deux mondes*,

the "horticultural romanticism" of Pope's later years as leading "to a revulsion against the strait-laced regularity and symmetry of the heroic couplet, to a general turning from convention, formality, artifice in all the arts."[5] While there is little room for doubt that Pope was influential in spreading the gospel of the naturalistic landscape garden, I believe that there is no real contradiction between his neoclassicism as a poet and his theory and practice as a gardener. This point of view can best be demonstrated by considering Pope's theory against the background of English gardening as it had developed to the time of his first comment on the matter.

Early in the seventeenth century, Inigo Jones, influenced by Palladio, the great sixteenth-century Italian neoclassic architect, had introduced into England a style of building emphasizing horizontal lines and perfect symmetry. The stateliness and formality of the Palladian style seemed to demand a comparable treatment of the grounds about the building. Like neoclassic architecture, formal gardening followed distinct principles. Its most prominent feature was an axial design reflecting the precise symmetry of the building and extending its vistas through the grounds. The garden axis was marked by an avenue cut through the woodland or by symmetrically planted trees or shrubs accurately spaced and trimmed to geometric precision. The distant end of the vista was often closed by a piece of statuary, a perspective scene painted on a wall, or even by artificial ruins.

The extreme of garden formalism was achieved in a number of artificial devices. "Knots," inherited from the English medieval garden and developed with great intricacy throughout the Renaissance, were symmetrical designs composed of interlaced bands of close-cropped cover plants such as carpet bugle. A French development of the same technique produced the *parterre de broderie*, an intricate pattern

---

LXXXVI (1888), 274–323; Robert K. Root, *The Poetical Career of Alexander Pope* (Princeton, N. J., 1938), pp. 69 ff.; Bracher, *op. cit.*

[5] "On the Discrimination of Romanticisms," *PMLA*, XXXIX (1924), 241. B. Sprague Allen, *Tides in English Taste* (Cambridge, Mass., 1937), II, 125: "It is ironic . . . that Addison and Pope, who from many points of view symbolized the age of classical authority in its more brilliant moments, were chiefly instrumental in dislodging from its position in popular esteem the garden of axial design, which impressively embodied the Renaissance ideal of order." Montague Summers, *The Gothic Quest* (London [1938]), pp. 20–21: "No whole-hearted or single-minded Classicist . . . could have conceived and builded that delicious 'Aegerian grot' at Twickenham. . . . Here we have a baroque romanticism no genuine Augustan would have tolerated for a moment." Chase, p. 171: "Pope, whose poetry represents the epitome of neo-classic polish, was a romantic in his garden at Twickenham."

worked out on a flat surface in colored earth or gravel. Small square or octagonal beds of low-growing flowers arranged in geometric patterns were duplicated at precise intervals throughout a regular area to give the scene all the natural wildness of a tile floor. And by the early years of the eighteenth century, formal gardening had reached a summit of absurdity in topiary work, sculpture representing animals and geometric figures, using yew, privet, or boxwood as a medium.[6]

Topiary work provided Pope with his first opportunity to comment on gardening, for in *The Guardian*, No. 173, September 29, 1713, he satirized the "various tonsure of greens." An eminent town gardener, Pope reported, planned to dispose of a collection of carved shrubs including such items as: " 'Adam and Eve in yew; Adam a little shattered by the fall of the tree of knowledge in the great storm: Eve and the serpent flourishing.' 'St. George in box; his arm scarce long enough, but will be in a condition to stick the dragon by next April.' "[7] More important for our consideration of Pope as poet is the comment with which he introduced this bit of whimsy:

There is certainly something in the amiable simplicity of unadorned nature that spreads over the mind a more noble sort of tranquility and a loftier sensation of pleasure, than can be raised from the nicer scenes of art. . . . I believe it is no wrong observation, that persons of genius, and those who are most capable of art, are always most fond of nature: as such are chiefly sensible, that all art consists in the imitation and study of nature.[8]

The idea that art is the imitation of nature persisted in Pope's utterances on gardening; in 1722, writing to Martha Blount, he described Robert Digby's estate at Sherborne in these terms:

The gardens are so irregular, that it is very hard to give an exact idea of them, but by a plan. Their beauty arises from this irregularity; for not only the several parts of the garden itself make the better contrast by these sudden rises, and falls, and turns of ground; but views about it are let in.

Yet Pope also noted a colonnade of lime trees, six terraces, and a

---

[6] For the foregoing discussion, I am largely indebted to Allen, *op. cit.*

[7] Thomas Babington Macauley, ed., *The Tatler and Guardian* (Cincinnati, 1884), p. 233.

[8] *Ibid.*, p. 231. Pope seems to be echoing here ideas advanced by Joseph Addison in *The Spectator*, No. 414, June 25, 1712, and No. 477, September 6, 1712. Addison summarized No. 414 in this manner: "Contents: The works of nature more pleasant to the imagination than those of art. The works of nature still more pleasant, the more they resemble those of art. The works of art more pleasant, the more they resemble those of nature. . . . " Addison then went on to praise French and Italian gardens for their "artificial rudeness" as against the trim neatness of English formal gardens. *The Spectator* (London, 1808), VI, 75–79.

T-shaped canal—all formal features—as beauties of the Sherborne scene. He suggested that the open courts between buildings of the ruined castle that adorned the grounds be "thrown into circles or octagons of grass or flowers," and a little temple, he thought, might well be built on a neighboring hill.[9] In the same vein is the remark attributed to Pope by Joseph Spence in 1728: "Arts are taken from nature; and after a thousand vain efforts for improvements, are best when they return to their first simplicity." Again Spence reports Pope to have said, "In laying out a garden, the first thing to be considered is the genius of the place." While this remark has sometimes been taken to mean that the gardener should make the most of the terrain by adapting his design to it, the rest of the sentence makes clear that this was not Pope's intention: "thus at Riskins, for example, Lord Bathurst should have raised two or three mounts; because his situation is all a plain, and nothing can please without variety."[10]

Later Pope made further specific suggestions which find an echo in the "Epistle to Burlington." The influence of the Italian landscape painters is evident in the comment reported by Spence for September, 1739:

The lights and shades in gardening are managed by disposing the thick grove work, the thin, and the openings, in a proper manner. . . . You may distance things by darkening them, and by narrowing the plantation more and more towards the end, in the same manner as they do in painting.[11]

Thus the landscape painter's techniques of chiaroscuro and perspective may be used by the gardener. Spence later reports a conversation of 1742 in which Pope expressed a summary and (as the date indicates) mature view of gardening: "All the rules of gardening are reducible to three heads:—the contrasts, the management of surprises, and the concealment of the bounds." Pope then quoted lines fifty-five and fifty-six of the "Epistle to Burlington" as a concise statement of

---

[9] *The Works of Alexander Pope*, ed. Rev. Whitwell Elwin and W. J. Courthope (London, 1871–89), IX, 300. This edition is hereafter referred to as *Works*.

[10] Joseph Spence, *Anecdotes, Observations, and Characters of Books and Men*, ed. S. W. Singer (London, 1820), pp. 11–12. I wish to express my thanks to Dr. James M. Osborn of Yale University, who has verified the dates of the quotations from Spence. This quotation will be part of item 609 in Dr. Osborn's forthcoming edition of Spence's *Anecdotes* enlarged from the original manuscript.

[11] *Ibid.*, pp. 209–10; item 610 in Dr. Osborn's text. See also Elizabeth Manwaring, *Italian Landscape in Eighteenth Century England* (New York, 1925). For the possible influence of Pope's experience as an amateur painter, see Robert J. Allen, "Pope and the Sister Arts," *Pope and His Contemporaries*, ed. James L. Clifford and Louis A. Landa (Oxford, 1949), pp. 78–88.

his aesthetic view: "He gains all points, who pleasingly confounds, /Surprises, varies, and conceals the bounds."[12]

What Pope objected to, then, was the artificiality of the formal garden. In the "Epistle to Burlington" Timon's offensive garden is bounded by a wall and patterned in tiresome symmetry. Topiary work and statuary abound, while the fountain and the summer house are placed without regard for the functions they might be expected to perform. Pope's remedies would consist of improving upon the natural beauties of the terrain, introducing intricate variety in design, and opening vistas into the natural landscape beyond the garden by "concealing the bounds," that is, by eliminating walls or hedges that marked the limits of the garden. Thus Pope undoubtedly advocated a garden design more natural than that of the seventeenth-century formal garden. After his time the relaxation of garden formality was carried even further by such professional designers as Kent and "Capability" Brown.[13] But that there is any serious split in Pope's mind on the subjects of gardening and poetry may be doubted. Several considerations show that the discrepancy is less serious than has been supposed.

First, I would suggest that the contrast between the poems before and after 1717 has been exaggerated. *An Essay on Criticism*, surely the English epitome of neoclassic poetics, belongs to the earlier period.[14] In addition, as Professor B. Sprague Allen points out, such a poem as "Windsor Forest" (1704, 1713), while it does discuss nature, does so in the rather formal conventions of neoclassicism rather than in the intimate, affectionate manner of the romantics, who drew on first-hand knowledge of field, river, and forest.[15] Pope is not approving the wildness of untamed nature here, for he describes the scene as

> Not chaos-like together crushed and bruised,
> But, as the world, harmoniously confused:
> Where order in variety we see,
> And where, though all things differ, all agree.[16]

---

[12] Spence, p. 260; item 612 in Dr. Osborn's text.

[13] Margaret Jourdain, "Landscape Gardening," *The Work of William Kent . . .* (London, 1928), pp. 74–81.

[14] Although published in 1711, *An Essay on Criticism* was written even earlier. Professor Root places the poem in the "maze of fancy" because it shows Pope's "power of terse and witty epigram"—a quality hardly lacking in the later satires—but he recognizes its neoclassic aesthetics. Root, *op. cit.*, p. 70.

[15] Allen, I, 129.

[16] *Works*, I, 340; ll. 13–16.

These lines are in accord with both the neoclassic view of the cosmos, and the view of nature as the model for poets expressed in *An Essay on Criticism*. If there was more exuberance and more outdoor scenery in the early work than in the later satires, there is, nevertheless, no need to label this tendency romantic, or to suppose that Pope suppressed romantic tendencies after he turned to the satires.

Secondly, too much has undoubtedly been made of Pope's "correctness" as a poet. It should be remembered that in *An Essay on Criticism*, Pope struck out not only at poetry "where nothing's just or fit; / One glaring chaos and wild heap of wit," but also at dullness in "such lays as neither ebb nor flow, / Correctly cold, and regularly low."[17] In addition, the endless variety of effect Pope achieved throughout his own poetry by variation in meter, tone color, caesura position, and weight of syllable, and by the imaginative daring of many of his lines suggests that for him there was nothing "strait-laced" about the regularity and symmetry of the heroic couplet. Indeed he would undoubtedly—and with justice, I think—have rejected the comparison between his verse and the monotonous orderliness of an unimaginative formal garden. The parterres, hedges, and topiary work which Pope ridiculed in Timon's Villa may more justly be compared to Euphuistic than to Addisonian prose, to the dull, rule-bound neoclassic poetry which Pope ridiculed than to his own.

Another matter that needs attention is the significance of the term "nature." The neoclassicists in poetry had appealed to nature as their ultimate authority, just as the rebels against formalism in gardening did after them. Pope had, in fact, counselled his readers to follow nature in both poetry and gardening. Professor Lovejoy holds that the ultimate effect of the advice was very different in the two cases, however, for Pope and others had shifted the "aesthetic connotation of 'conformity to nature' from simplicity to complexity and from regularity to irregularity."[18] Yet Pope's earliest extant comments on gardening, in the *Guardian* paper of 1713, referred to nature as the desirable norm in much the same way that *An Essay on Criticism* had used the term only a few years earlier. If the *Guardian* paper had found less regularity in nature than in the artificial garden, it had nevertheless found greater simplicity. And all of Pope's subsequent remarks on the garden art were essentially harmonious with this

[17] *Works*, II, 50, 48; ll. 291–92; 239–40.
[18] "The First Gothic Revival and the Return to Nature," *MLN*, XLVII (1932), 442.

earliest statement. In gardening and poetry alike, Pope recommended the emulation of nature by the use of surprise instead of monotony, variety instead of rigid regularity, and subtle concealment—but not overthrow —of the rules governing the composition.

A final body of evidence helps us evaluate both the extent of Pope's "romanticism" as a gardener, and the signification which he attached to such terms as "regular," "wild," "intricate," and "natural." His own garden, considered as an exemplification of his theories, shows him to be less a rebel than his manifestoes alone might indicate. The layout of Pope's grounds as they appeared at the time of his death has been preserved in a plan by John Searle, his gardener.[19] The design does not forget nature, but it seems to remember her through the mists of a dream. While some pleasing intricacy appears in the far corners of the plot, a symmetry of straight lines and a balanced arrangement of statuary dominates the central area. The main structural characteristic of the plan is an axial vista terminated by an obelisk in memory of the poet's mother. Several mounds with spiral walks leading to the apex improve on the genius of the place. Here is "nature methodized"; to find "nature to advantage dressed" we need only turn to Pope's beloved grotto. Pope's house was separated from his garden by the Hampton Court-London road, so that he found it advantageous to build a tunnel giving access to the garden. Expanding the tunnel and extending rock structures at each end, Pope developed a grotto in the style then popular in English gardens. Shells, minerals, bits of looking-glass, busts of poets, and an alabaster lamp contributed to what Pope conceived to be a garden ornament in the "rustic" or "natural" taste.[20] In his own garden Pope retained many of the characteristics of the earlier formal plan, and employed a sort of wildness which was at best "artful" indeed. The grounds at Twickenham represented not so much a reaction against the formal garden itself as against its excesses; Pope's garden was a half-way stage in the development toward the later landscape garden which became a fully developed reality only after the middle of the eighteenth century.

[19] John Serle [*sic*], *A Plan of Mr. Pope's Garden* (London, 1745).
[20] Pope's letter to Edward Blount dated June 2, 1725, from Twickenham gives the poet's own description of the grotto. See *Works*, VI, 383–84. A more detailed description is contained in Professor Bracher's article cited in Note 3, above. The perspective view of the grotto appearing in Searle's *Plan* may be more readily found by many readers in [Robert Dodsley], *A Collection of Poems . . . by Several Hands*, 5th ed. (London, 1758), III, [1], where it appears as a headpiece over Pope's "On a Grotto near the Thames, at Twickenham. . . . "

Pope was, then, neither the most strait-laced of neoclassic poets nor the most unbridled of romantic gardeners, so that there is no real discrepancy between his theories of the two arts. For Pope, poetry, gardening, painting, and architecture were all expressions of a whole mind.

The real difficulty, I believe, lies in our tendency to simplify the history of the arts by establishing arbitrary criteria for "periods" or "movements"—criteria to which sometimes even the most prominent figures of the time cannot be made to conform. The work of the cultural historian should be descriptive rather than normative, so that we need show neither delighted surprise nor irritation when we discover that Pope, of all people, does not fit our definitions of neoclassicism. Our understanding of neoclassicism should be broadened to accommodate the actual Pope, who will not fit an *a priori* idea of eighteenth-century rigidity. In addition, metaphorically representing the development of aesthetic standards as a series of revolutions or swings of the pendulum or alternations of the tides leads us to expect, without warrant, that all the standards of a previous age will be dislodged in an upheaval that wholly reshapes the cultural landscape. This aesthetic catastrophism needs to be modified, I think, by a concept which, while taking full account of those moments in history when tastes in all the arts are sufficiently in harmony to permit a description and a name, will recognize the essentially evolutionary character of aesthetic standards.

A. Lynn Altenbernd

IN HIS *Hero and Leander* Marlowe himself refers to Musaeus in connection with the story, and Musaeus is accepted, correctly, as his ultimate principal source. If so, in what kind of text did Marlowe use Musaeus? Professor Martin notes that the poem attributed to Musaeus "had been frequently printed in the Greek (beginning ?1484) and also in Latin, Italian, and French translation. It was included in *Poetae Minores Graeci* (H. Estienne) in 1566; and it seems worthy of mention that the Latin verse translation of F. Paulinus published in 1587 forms part of a volume entitled *Centum Fabulae ex Antiquis*, where, among the fables, is to be found 'Gallus et Gemma,' probably the fable referred to by Marlowe in II. 51."[1] As for Aesop's scratching rooster, every schoolboy met him not later than the second year in grammar school. In the Latin translation published in England and elsewhere for school use his is the first fable, hence used as an illustration by Brinsley, etc. We need no erudite source such as *Centum Fabulae* to account for him. He was in "Aesop" as Marlowe says he was.

The same thing is true of the Musaeus, for Marlowe has not used this Latin translation of F. Paulinus in *Centum Fabulae*, but the Greek itself and probably the parallel Latin translation of Marcus Musurus; these two being regularly published in the Greek Aesop, the Planudes collection, used in the upper forms of grammar school.[2] The boy got his Aesop in Latin not later than his second year in grammar school. When he came to Greek near the end of grammar school, he might repeat Aesop; and this Greek-Latin form of Aesop with additions was the ordinary one available for that purpose. It is the natural Latin translation to suspect, and our suspicions are verified.

Marlowe's opening passage in *Hero and Leander* will illustrate perhaps as well as any his use of Musaeus.

> In view and opposit two citties stood,
> Seaborderers, disioin'd by *Neptunes* might:
> The one *Abydos*, the other *Sestos* hight.[3]

[1] Martin, L. C., *Marlowe's Poems*, 1931, pp. 5–6. See also John Bakeless, *The Tragicall History of Christopher Marlowe*, 1942, II, 103–104.

[2] The Greek and this Latin translation had also been published elsewhere, for instance by Junta in 1519. This is also the Latin translation used by Ralph Winterton, 1635, for his grammar school text book, *Poetae Minores Graeci*. P. B. Bartlett, *Poems*, p. 438 says Chapman, who "completed" *Hero and Leander*, translated Musaeus (published 1616) from the Latin of Marcus Musurus. It was *the* Latin translation of Musaeus.

[3] Brooke, C. F. T., *The Works of Christopher Marlowe*, 1910, p. 492.

This is clearly Musaeus

Σηστὸς ἔην καὶ ἄβυδος ἐναντίον, ἐγγύθι πόντου,
Γείτονές εἰσι πόληες

"Sestos, and Abydos opposite, hard by the ocean, are neighbour cities."[4]

The parallel Latin translation of Musurus runs

Sestus erat & Abydus è regione, propè mare
Vicinae sunt vrbes.[5]

The Latin is a very literal translation, but Marlowe nevertheless was following the Greek. The key is in ἐναντίον, rendered into Latin by Musurus as *è regione*, which Cooper in his *Thesaurus* defines as "Streight ouer against: in sight." Marlowe has rendered the idea as "In view and opposit." The ordinary small Greek-Latin dictionary of Marlowe's day, that of Crispinus-Constantinus, defines the Greek word as *coram, contra*, following the complete Constantinus. Stephanus (1572) defines ἐναντίος as "Aduersus, Qui est in conspectu seu coràm, Qui est eregione, Oppositus," and the adverbial form as "itidē pro Ex aduerso, Aduersum, Coram." Scapula[6] repeats Stephanus. It will be seen that Musurus has used some early Greek dictionary with the definition *è regione*. It will be seen also that Marlowe is in the traditiu. of Stephanus and Scapula, "In view and opposit"; "in conspectu . . Oppositus." Marlowe has translated literally this definition eventually from some Greek-Latin dictionary. The various forms of Constantinus are in the general tradition, but Marlowe's specific rendering does not trace through them. The *è regione* of the Latin translation as defined by Cooper, with his eye on some form of this Greek-Latin definition, doubtless that in the Latin *Thesaurus* of Stephanus, reverses the ends of it. The Latin translation of F. Paulinus, which Professor Martin quotes not quite accurately, is completely out of this tradition.

Sestus erat pelagiq́; aduerso in litore Abydus,
Non longe diuisae vrbes.

[4] Blakeney, E. H., *Musaeus*, 1935, p. 25.

[5] Greek and Latin quotations are from the Plantin edition of Aesop, 1657 (Heber copy in my possession).

[6] I use my edition of 1589. Parker in 1574 provided the Constantinus, 1562, for the common use of his six Norwich scholars at Benet College (Strype, John, *Parker* [1711], p. 291). He also provided Cooper's *Thesaurus*, 1565, Curio's *Thesaurus*, 3 vols., 1561, and the Latin-Greek dictionary published at Paris in 1554. We do not know whether he duplicated this gift for Marlowe and his group at Corpus Christi, but at least Constantinus was a logical dictionary for Marlowe to use at Cambridge—and later when he could get access. Such dictionaries would also have been compulsorily available to him in grammar school.

This was most certainly not Marlowe's source. Here Marlowe has followed the Greek, with the ultimate aid of Stephanus or Scapula, or some other Greek-Latin dictionary containing their definition of the crucial Greek word. The Γείτονές ἐισι πόληες, *Vicinae sunt vrbes* (Musurus), has also helped round out the line

> In view and opposit two citties stood.

Similarly, ἐγγύθι πόντου , *propè mare*, has become the line

> Seaborderers, disioin'd by *Neptunes* might: . . .

Likewise, Σηστὸς ἔην καὶ ἄβυδος, *Sestus erat &Abydus* (Musurus) becomes

> The one *Abydos*, the other *Sestos* hight.

So in the opening passage Marlowe derives directly from the Greek of Musaeus and shows no certain sign of having used any translation as such, certainly not that of Paulinus. The knowledge displayed here, however, might readily go back to grammar school days.

Marlowe omits the two following lines of Musaeus, but he then expands enormously the next two lines in accord with contemporary ideas of composition.

> Ἱμερόεις τὲ λέανδρος ἔην, καὶ παρθένος ἡρώ,
> Η μὲν σηστὸν ἔναιεν, ὁ δὲ πτολίεθρον ἀβύδου

"and their names were lovely Leander and virgin Hero. She dwelt in Sestos and he in the town of Abydos."[7]

So Marlowe says "At *Sestos, Hero* dwelt," and then launches into an itemized description of her beauty according to the best precepts of the rhetoric of his time. After forty-five lines of this he turns to Leander

> Amorous *Leander*, beautifull and yoong,
> (Whose tragedie diuine *Musæus* soong)
> Dwelt at *Abidus*.

Again Marlowe has used his Greek-Latin dictionary on Ἱμερόεις. Stephanus defines the word as *Desiderabilis, Optabilis. Item Amabilis, Suauis, Gratus;* and again Scapula copies. Musurus prefers *suavis*, but

---

[7] Blakeney, p. 25.
> Suauisque Leander erat, & virgo Ero:
> Haec quidem Sestum habitabat, ille verò oppidum Abydi (M).
> Nomina erant, pueri Leander, virginis Hero,
> Haec tenuit Sestum, puer ipse colebat Abydum (P).

Marlowe *amabilis* Leander, which he shifts into "amorous Leander."
Marlowe continues

> since him dwelt there none,
> For whom succeeding times make greater mone.

This rephrases another statement of Musaeus in the same connection
six lines down

> Εἰσέτι που κλαίοντα μόρον, καὶ ἔρωτα λεάνδρου

"even to this day they mourn the fate and love of Leander."[8]

Having thus introduced Leander, Marlowe proceeds, of course, to a
companion description in thirty-six lines to match that of Hero. So
it will be seen that Marlowe's first ninety lines use Musaeus as a
springboard, as Marlowe himself by his reference to that author has
indicated. Of course, he has stretched the passage in Musaeus from an
inch narrow to an ell broad, but that was the essence of all these Renaissance treatments of classical subjects. These poets had not been
drilled upon their rhetorics for nothing. Some of the means Marlowe
has used for stuffing or farcing the slight framework from Musaeus the
reader may gather from the notes to this section by Professor Martin.
An intensive search would doubtless reveal the sources of all the
fragments from which Marlowe has built his mosaic.

Incidentally, on line 45,

> So louely faire was *Hero, Venus* Nun

"G. Lazarus notes also Marot's translation of Musaeus, l. 59, where
it is said that Hero 'Estait nonnain, à Venus dediée'." Musaeus says
Κύπριδις ἦν ἱέρεια, *Veneris erat sacerdos* (M). The *sacerdos* is the form
given for the feminine by Stephanus. Cooper defines the masculine
word as "A prieste: a minister of the churche." The feminine would
inevitably be a nun, even without benefit of Marot. Rider gives the
Latin for *nun* as *Coenibita, sacerdotissa, monacha.* Since one of the
regular words for a nun was *sacerdotissa*, as a feminine form of *sacerdos*,
the Greek feminine which was rendered in Stephanus by *sacerdos*
would as a feminine inevitably suggest the word "nun." So Marlowe
is again following Musaeus and shows no necessary use of any
translation.

---

[8] Blakeney, p. 25.
> Adhuc deflens mortem & amorem Leandri (M).
> Plorat adhuc sortē, & miseri qui fata Leandri (P).

Marlowe continues to follow the framework of Musaeus.

> The men of wealthie *Sestos*, euerie yeare,
> (For his sake whom their goddesse held so deare,
> Rose-cheekt *Adonis*) kept a solemne feast.
> Thither resorted many a wandring guest,
> To meet their loues, etc.

This is based directly on Musaeus

> Δή γὰρ κυπριδίη πανδήμιος ἦλθεν ἑορτή,
> Τὴν ἀνὰ σηστὸν ἄγουσιν ἀδώνιδι καὶ κυθερίη.
> Πασσυδίη δ' ἔσπευδον ἐς ἱερὸν ἦμαρ ἱκέσθαι,
> Οσσοι ναιετάεσκον ἀλιστρεφέων σφυρὰ νήσων

"Now it was so that there was held a public festival to Love, the which in Sestos men keep holy to Adonis and Aphrodite, and with all their company they would hasten to come on that sacred day, even as many as inhabited the uttermost parts of the sea-clad isles."[9]

Marlowe's first three lines are based on the first two of Musaeus, and the next line and a half of Marlowe sum up the next several lines of Musaeus. Here Marlowe shows more affinity with the Latin translation of Musurus, for he has translated as if it ran "Sesti Adonidi celebrant Venereum populare festum"; "The men of wealthy Sestos . . . For . . . Adonis kept a solemn feast." This is the sense but not the construction of the Greek.[10]

After some seven lines more upon the crowd, Marlowe comes with Musaeus to Hero.

> But far aboue the loueliest *Hero* shin'd,
> And stole away th'inchaunted gazers mind,
> For like Sea-nimphs inueigling harmony,
> So was her beautie to the standers by.
> Nor that night-wandring pale and watrie starre
> (When yawning dragons draw her thirling carre
> From *Latmus* mount vp to the glomie skie,
> Where crown'd with blazing light and maiestie,

[9] Blakeney, p. 26.
> Iámque Venereum populare venit festum,
> Quod Sesti celebrant Adonidi & Veneri.
> Cateruatimque festinabant ad sacrum diem ire,
> Quotquot habitabant mari circumdatarū extrema insularum (M).
> Nāq̃; aderāt magna celeberrima festa Cytherae,
> Quae Sesti celebrāt Veneri, Cynaraq̃; creato,
> Ad sacramq̃; omnes properabant vndique lucē,
> Qui pelago amplexi tractus extrema tenebāt (P).

[10] Blakeney has also inserted "men" as the subject of his verb.

> She proudly sits) more ouer-rules the flood,
> Than she the hearts of those that neere her stood.

This elaborates three lines of Musaeus

> Ἡ δὲ θεῆς ἀνὰ νηὸν ἐπῴχετο παρθένος ἡρώ,
> Μαρμαρυγὴν χαρίεσσαν ἀπαστράπτουσα τροσώπου,
> Οἷά τε λευκοπάρῃος ἐπαντέλλουσα σελήνη.

"Now maiden Hero drew near to the temple of the goddess, her lovely face aglow like a fair-cheeked moon when it rises."[11]

Marlowe uses the figure of Hero shining like the moon, but he metamorphoses it to his own uses. In the first line of the quoted passage, he appears to echo two lines of Musaeus.

> Ὡς ἡ μέν περὶ πολλὸν ἀριστεύσασα γυναικῶν,
> Κύπριδος ἀρήτειρα νέη διεφαίνετο κύπρις.

"Thus, far excelling other women, Hero, priestess of Cypris, shone forth, a new Cypris."[12]

> But far aboue the loueliest *Hero* shin'd . . .

Apparently Marlowe is here reflecting the Greek verb as neither Latin translation does; but the figure itself could be responsible. Marlowe develops even more freely the statement following that all the men fall madly in love with Hero.

Having described Hero and the crowd, as did Musaeus, Marlowe next inserts a description of the much ornamented temple, as a setting for Hero at the altar and for the besmiting of Leander. The dumb signs of love then follow in both Musaeus and Marlowe, though they are differently phrased. Night comes with its stars, though again phrased somewhat differently in the two authors, and Leander speaks. Marlowe had mentioned that among the love approaches made by signs

[11] Blakeney, p. 26.
> Verum deae per aedem incessit virgo Ero,
> Splendorem gratum emittens facie,
> Qualis alba genas oriens luna (M).
> Ast Hero incessit per Diuae templa Virago,
> Cui fulgens nitido scintillat gratia vultu,
> Qualis purpureo cum surgit Delia cornu,
> In niueis sed summa genis rubefacta nitebat,
> Vt rosa quae bicolor se trudit cortice (P).

[12] Blakeney, p. 27.
> Sic ea quidem plurimum antecellens foeminas
> Veneris sacerdos noua apparebat Venus (M).
> Foemineū namq̃; illa genus post terga relinquēs
> Sacra gerens Veneris poterat Venus ipsa videri (P).

before night fell, "He toucht her hand, in touching it she trembled."
In the present section after night, Musaeus spends three lines on
Leander's taking Hero's hand, which she withdraws. After she cuts
him off with words in both, Leander in both makes a lengthy speech
against virginity, of similar tenor in both, though not of exact phraseology. Marlowe does use, however, the chief argument of Musaeus
that it is not fit for a virgin to be a priestess of Venus.[13] In one speech,
Leander's text is the line

Παρθένον οὐκ ἐπέοικεν ὑποδρήσειν ἀφροδίτη,

"It is not fitting for Aphrodite to be served by a virgin."[14]
In the next, the preceding line is paraphrased.

Κύπριδος ὡς ἱέρεια μετέρχεο κύπριδος ἔργα

"As priestess of Cypris, accomplish her works."[15]

> Then shall you most resemble *Venus* Nun,
> When *Venus* sweet rites are perform'd and done.

Hero is persuaded, but as Leander attempts to embrace her she
says

> Gentle youth forbeare
> To touch the sacred garments which I weare

and makes an appointment at her tower. Martin thinks this is taken
from an earlier passage where Hero had said to the impetuous Leander

ἐμὸν δ' ἀπόλειπε χιτῶνα,

. . . .

Κύπριδος ὅυ σοι ἔοικε θεῆς ἱέρειαν ἀφάσσειν

"let go my garment . . . . It becomes not you to handle a priestess of
Cypris."[16]

---

[13] G. Lazarus has noticed the general parallels.
[14] Blakeney, p. 29.
> Virginem non decet administrare Veneri (M).
> Non decet intactam Veneri seruire puellam (P)
[15] Blakeney, p. 29.
> Veneris vt sacerdos exerce Veneris opera (M).
> miserereq́; saeui
> Ardoris, Venerisq́; subi illius ipsa sacerdos
> Munia, ades, legesq́; Deae, & connubia serua (P).
[16] Blakeney, p. 29.
> meamq́; dimitte vestem,
> . . . .
> Veneris non te decet deae sacerdotem solicitare (M).
> iā nostrā desere pallā,
> . . . .
> Nō tibi fas sacram Veneri attrectare puellam (P).

Hero finally describes her tower and only maid, and invites Leander there. The phraseology throughout is similar but not identical. Hero's confusion in Musaeus gives Marlowe an excuse for a long, inserted allegory of Cupid's beating down her plea to Venus and wounding the girl with love. Cupid makes a plea to the fates to be kind to the lovers but gets no encouragement, because they do not like Cupid on account of a courtship between Hermes and a maid, which is related at length, occupying the remainder of the sestiad, nearly one-fourth of it. Of course, such insertions were considered highly artistic.

In the second sestiad, I have found no specific use of Musaeus at all, though Marlowe does reflect a figure or so, etc.

So Marlowe's framework for the first sestiad is from Musaeus, but the details are very freely handled, and there are numerous highly embroidered insertions. Musaeus is almost lost under the encrusting ornamentation. But at the beginning Marlowe could even face the Greek with his dictionary, either directly or with retrospect to his days in grammar school. For some time he kept his eye upon the text, in at least one place in the conventional Latin translation of Musurus; but finally he simply followed the trend of Musaeus, presenting the details freely in his own way and making lengthy insertions of his own. These insertions themselves are for the most part classical embroidery, but little of which has been traced. Then eventually Marlowe ceases to use Musaeus specifically at all.

At least the groundwork of Marlowe's use of Musaeus had probably been laid in grammar school, and when he came to compose, he may have done no more than refresh his memory with the old texts. At most, the current text of Musaeus in conventional form is merely a springboard to get Marlowe's Pegasus into the air, where he soars on his own.

T. W. BALDWIN

HAWTHORNE AND THE PATHETIC FALLACY

EVERYONE knows what the pathetic fallacy is. Ruskin, in 1856, defined it with such precision that writers and critics have ever afterward been sensitive to its meaning and uses.[1] But Ruskin, like many later commentators, was interested more in description and analysis than in seeking the historical basis for the fallacy; he assumed that the fallacy was a way by which the natural world became a subjective extension of man's mind; nature would act out the interior drama of man: thus fog could weep, the sky be weary, the waves laugh, or the sunlight dance simply because a writer, or any artist, said so. The pathetic fallacy was based on the assumption that man and nature at every moment existed together in some kind of instant, mutual coherence: what man thought or did, nature at once reflected. Ruskin lodged his protest against the illusion that external reality could be an extension of the subjective consciousness of man.

Yet the pathetic fallacy is much older than the eighteenth- and nineteenth-century poetry or painting wherein Ruskin found his examples and demonstrations. There are "fallacies" in Shakespeare: Horatio tells us that "the Morn, in russet mantle clad, / Walks o'er the dew of yon high eastern hill," and we see not only the early morning light breaking over an Elizabethan stage but the inner condition of Horatio and the guards after their amazed terror in the presence of the Ghost. Donne, in the *Anniversaries*, made the whole earth shake and jar when the girl Elizabeth Drury died; in fact, those two poems are almost grotesques of the pathetic fallacy.

The point is, however, that these were not "fallacies" at all. They were not a set of artificial relations, apprehended by the mind of man; they were *"truth*, inscribed by God in the nature of things."[2] The correspondences between man and nature were facts which the mind discovered; man lived every moment of his life in a total reality which

---

[1] According to Ruskin, the pathetic fallacy " . . . is of two principal kinds. Either . . . it is the fallacy of wilful fancy, which involves no real expectation that it will be believed; or else it is a fallacy caused by an excited state of feelings, making us, for the time, more or less irrational" (*Modern Painters*, Vol. III, Chap. XII, sect. 5). An excellent treatment of the whole subject is Josephine Miles' "Pathetic Fallacy in the Nineteenth Century: A Study of Changing Relation Between Object and Emotion," *University of California Publications in English*, XII, No. 2 (1942), 183–304.

[2] Marjorie Nicolson, *The Breaking of the Circle* (Northwestern University Press, 1950), p. 108. For the period between the new science of the seventeenth century and the eventual collapse of the "correspondence," see Earl R. Wasserman, "Nature Moralized: The Divine Analogy in the Eighteenth Century," *ELH*, XX (March, 1953), 39–76.

was alive, and he was alive in it. When he said that life was like water, he did not mean to draw a mere comparison or a causative principle; he meant that life *was* water and that water *was* life because man and the universe existed together in a single, related, meaningful context. What Ruskin described as the pathetic fallacy was the still-continuing hold of the correspondence on the minds of men long after the rationale, the very reason for being, of the relation of man to the universe had ceased to exist.

The shift from the correspondence to the fallacy was long and slow. Under the impact of natural science and critical realism or eighteenth-century skepticism, the world steadily lost its ontological relationship to man, and man came to see that he and the universe were not units in a larger reality or mind of God. Yet habits die slowly; writers, in the eighteenth and nineteenth centuries, continued to employ the rhetoric of correspondences which once had meaning but which had become mere empty formalisms. Nevertheless, some writers, or even one writer, may revive or restore, for a brief moment in literary history, the sensibility of a past age and give that sensibility such an expression that critics might believe that a long-past age still survived into a much later time. Hawthorne was such a writer. He began his career as a conventional fallacist in the nineteenth-century manner and then, somewhere along the way, opened a new, or rather "old," communication with reality and looked at the world, not as mere convenient analogy and synecdoche, but as total harmony. In order to survey Hawthorne's employment of or departure from the pathetic fallacy, we might well begin with his first novel *Fanshawe* (1828) and then move through representative writings of his subsequent career.

Generally speaking, Hawthorne in the beginning of his career showed that natural phenomena are an ever-various kaleidoscope, at all times in harmony with the human mood and emotion. We read that "There was a little alternation of cloud across the brow of heaven . . . " (p. 86);[3] we learn of the "naked and desolate hills" and of a "little stream, peeping forth many times to the daylight, and then shrinking back into the shade" (p. 87); "a golden ray rested upon the spire of the little chapel" (p. 92), and "the vanished sun had made . . . the purple and golden clouds . . . the chief inheritors of his bright-

---

[3] All page references in parentheses refer to the respective volumes of *The Complete Works of Nathaniel Hawthorne*, Riverside edition, ed. G. P. Lathrop. 12 vols. Boston, 1883.

ness" (p. 103). These are a kind of instantly drawn fallacy; there are, however, a number of what might be considered "implied fallacies." These are hints that the human and natural realms are in sympathy and conformity, but the full resolution is never completed. One of these occurs when Ellen Langton, Walcott, and Fanshawe walk along that "little stream" wherein lives an especially large trout which has so far eluded capture; a stranger, in fishing for that very trout, induces Ellen to come near him. The whole scene is an anticipatory fallacy of how this dark stranger, Reuben Butler, will "catch" Ellen; the natural world exists as premonition for the eventual human struggle. Again, on the night Butler takes Ellen to the inn, there is a terrible storm, itself in complete harmony with the emotions of the pursued and the pursuers. Finally, the climactic scene of Butler's flight with Ellen and Fanshawe's chase is figured wholly in terms of how the natural order is precisely in keeping with the anguish and brutality of the human actors.

These examples suggest how readily Hawthorne adopted the then-prevailing pathetic fallacy. He tended to set his human dramas against a vast, inscrutable, yet sympathetic backdrop of nature; sometimes this scenic design is in a point-to-point relationship with man; yet he did not fall into the most obvious fallacies: trees do not sigh, rain does not laugh, nor does the sky mourn. His tendency, even so early as "The Hollow of the Three Hills" (1830), was to frame the natural order as having anticipated and as having long ago enacted the drama of man; the human mood and emotion become, as it were, a duplication of what nature has itself long known. The dark and moody opening of that short story fixes this strange similitude between the human and the natural orders of being:

Dwarf pines were numerous upon the hills and partly fringed the outer verge of the intermediate hollow, within which there was nothing but the brown grass of October, and here and there a tree trunk that had fallen long ago, and lay mouldering with no green successor from its roots. One of these masses of decaying wood, formerly a majestic oak, rested close beside a pool of green and sluggish water at the bottom of the basin. . . . The chill beauty of an autumnal sunset was now gilding the three hill-tops, whence a paler tint stole down their sides into the hollow (*Twice-Told Tales*, pp. 228, 229).

We are invited to understand, in this passage, that nature herself had long passed through and comprehended the human problem of evil and death. Man and nature do not exist in an immediate correspondence whereby the natural order is in convenient sympathy with man; nature has a kind of anterior awareness, as if nothing happens to man but what has occurred an infinite number of times in the phenomenal world. The pathetic fallacy is turned upside down: man becomes the "fallacy" to nature.[4]

This antecedent character of nature is more fully disclosed in "The Maypole of Merry Mount" (1836); from the very beginning we are brought into a sense of time backward: the celebrators at Merry Mount are a wearisome reduplication of what was once vivid and fresh in a far-past age—the clumsily garbed fauns and nymphs, the "Salvage Man," the Indian, and "the flower-decked priest" all participating in ancient rites. In that brilliant moment when Edith, queen of these revels, asks the question concerning "the mystery" in her heart, there is, "as if a spell had loosened them, . . . a little shower of withering rose leaves from the Maypole" (*Twice-Told Tales*, pp. 74–75). If this is a fallacy, then it is indeed a curious one, for "earth's doom of care and sorrow, and troubled joy" is revealed, not to Edith and Edgar, but to us, the readers; we and nature are, as it were, in the illusion and sympathy; we and "world" are understanding. Nature becomes, therefore, both inscrutability and moral commentary; for the moment the protagonists are permitted to come into some emotional and spiritual conformity with nature; then, as suddenly, they may lose that comprehension and slip back into the illusion of their separation from exterior reality. Nature is not the easy object and fallacy for man's interior drama; man exists, in any degree of understanding, by virtue of his known and expressed relationship to reality. He is, to repeat, the illusion, the fallacy; nature is the constant; it has long ago endured what he, for the moment, suffers.

[4] Nearly the whole of "The Hollow of the Three Hills" is an extension of this suggested similitude between nature and man: at every stage of the woman's confession there is established the concurrent and even antecedent tragedy of the natural world. True, this relationship is almost a one-to-one condition which bespeaks the pathetic fallacy; yet Hawthorne linked nature and the woman to a kind of third dimension which he termed "the Power of Evil"; that is, the woman and nature are but parts of an enlarging natural phenomenon which is "beyond nature." Thus the voices of the woman's broken-hearted parents "melt into the sound of the wind sweeping mournfully among the autumn leaves"; the wronged husband's damnations "rose up . . . till they changed into the hollow, fitful, and uneven sound of the wind, as it fought among the pine-trees"; finally, when the woman's child had died through her negligence, the "sweeping sound of the funeral train faded away like a thin vapor, and the wind . . . moaned sadly round the verge of the Hollow between the Three Hills" (pp. 231, 232, 233).

For a perceptive analysis of the pathetic fallacy in another early and significant tale, "Roger Malvin's Burial," see Seymour L. Gross, "The Technique of Hawthorne's Short Stories" (unpublished Ph.D. Thesis, University of Illinois, 1954), pp. 121 ff.

Hawthorne was not aware of a "movement" or a change of mind affecting him: that he should have at one time used the pathetic fallacy and at another time not used it is matter for only provisional speculation. He was, it is true, part of a literary sensibility which found the fallacy much to its taste and liking; nevertheless, he may be part of a tendency and then outside it. The best one can say is that Hawthorne's varying employment, early or late in his career, was somehow related to his response to reality: it was a means, one way or another, of making reality "real." What "reality" was and how it would be made "real" demand a set of distinctions which would be different every time they are made. Despite the obvious dangers of oversimplification, one might be able to make certain generalizations concerning the ways and reasons for Hawthorne's employment of or escape from the pathetic fallacy.

First, the pathetic fallacy occurs when man, or the writer, regards the natural world as completely subservient to his will and determination. Though nature is sometimes reluctant, it can be made to enact man's drama. In "The Hollow of the Three Hills" nature has her anguish too, just as does the sorrowing woman. This relationship is simply assumed to be "there" all the time; the writer, acting like a god, uncovers it and presents it for the instant acceptance and understanding of the reader. The fallacy dissolves, however, and becomes what I might term, for convenience, the "symbolic spectrum," when the forms of the natural world somehow pass into "psychology"; that is, a condition wherein nature animates man and when the two are linked in some total design beyond his world of ostensible reality.[5]

---

[5] Two notebook entries, chosen at random, might clarify this habit of Hawthorne's mind. The first is from the journal of 1842:

"One of my chief amusements is to see the boys sail their miniature vessels on the Frog Pond. . . . There is a full-rigged man of war. . . . All its motions—its tossing up and down on the mimic waves, and its sinking and rising in a calm swell, its heeling to the breeze,—the whole effect, in short, is that of a real ship at sea; while, moreover, there is something that kindles the imagination more than the reality would. If we see a real, great ship, the mind grasps and possesses, within its real clutch, all that there is of it; while here, the mimic ship is the representative of an ideal one, and so gives us a more imaginative pleasure" (*The American Notebooks*, ed. Randall Stewart. New Haven, 1932, p. 96).

The second is Hawthorne's memorable description of Sleepy Hollow in 1844 and concludes:

"And how strange is the gradual process with which we detect objects that are right before our eyes; here now are whortleberries, ripe and black, growing actually within reach of my hand, yet unseen till this moment. Were we to sit here all day, a week, a month, and doubtless a lifetime, *objects would thus still be presenting themselves as new, though there would seem to be no reason why we should not have detected them all at the first moment*" (p. 103; italics mine).

This penetrative and transforming power was one of the hallmarks of Hawthorne's method and achievement. Perhaps "The Custom House" chapter, prefatory to *The Scarlet Letter*, is one of the clearest expositions of that symbolizing process whereby the artistic mind does not simply *use* but succeeds in animating brute forms; it is a journey of the mind through the intervening veil of reality, or through what Coleridge termed "visionary deadness," and into some comprehension of the total phenomenal world.

Hawthorne states that his own family connections with Salem make for a "more sensuous sympathy with dust. . . . It is not love, but instinct." He goes on to speak of his imaginative torpor which rendered him incapable of creative action: "My imagination was a tarnished mirror." He feels the urgent necessity to open some fresh, renewed negotiation with the world, not only because of his long sabbatical from writing but because he cannot make Salem, the past, the imagined letter, or the theme of the suffering young woman in any way come alive. In a fallacy, the mind is an "I" and external reality an "It" which is instantly subservient to the mind's will; in the steadily emerging spectrum, as Hawthorne describes it, there must be an imaginative "neutral territory, somewhere between the real world and fairyland, where the Actual and the Imaginary may meet, and each imbue itself with the nature of the other" (p. 55). In some moment of the mind's searching, this event and meeting take place, a merging of inanimate fact and the provocative idea, self and reality, light and darkness: "we behold," Hawthorne continues in analyzing the process, "the gleam and shadow of the picture, with one remove further from the actual, and nearer to the imaginative. Then, at such an hour, and with this scene before him, if a man . . . cannot dream strange things, and make them look like truth, he need never try to write romances" (p. 56). At the end of his private journey of understanding, the world no longer remained a mere subjective "It," a willing concurrence to the inner determination of an arrogant "I," but had itself become living and sentient; its own sentience and response were part of the animation of the whole creative imagination. Hawthorne was able to animate the "visionary deadness" of the world because he saw that the vivification of his own mind was somehow related to his perception that the phenomenal world was not a mere brute thing but was capable of a concurrent animation too. The artistic mind and the exterior world existed in a total awareness beyond themselves and beyond even their own knowing. Thus, in their several ways, the characters of the novel all re-enact, either toward darkness and moral blindness or toward full comprehension, what Hawthorne himself negotiated before he could diffuse "thought and imagination through the opaque substance of to-day" and thereby "live throughout the whole range of his faculties and sensibilities" (pp. 57, 60).

The pathetic fallacy occurs, on the contrary, when the world is wholly disjunct from man but is somehow capable of being instantly subservient to his all-powerful will. Yet (to repeat our first condition for the symbolic spectrum) when "world" itself dissolves under the known conditions of its infinitely variable relationships to man and when the creative mind can see that it and "world" enact some indeterminate drama beyond even themselves, then reality ceases to remain passively convenient to the explication of man and becomes itself part of the variable quest for meaning. The symbolic spectrum is a means of viewing the world as animate and as having "mind."[6]

A second difference between the fallacy and some further range of speculation is implicit in the time-sense or time-world. The pathetic fallacy offers itself when the time-sense is only the present; that is, the relationship between man and nature can be simply drawn when nature is presumed to have had no pre-existence until man appeared. Then, and only then, it can do for him anything he wants. Nature's animate condition is "there" only now and thus can be made conformable to the dominating human mood. The world of reality passes out of the range of fallacy, however, when nature itself has an elaborate pastness and when man becomes himself almost a fallacy, a mere arbitrarily fixed moment in time. In a passage from *The Scarlet Letter*, this time-dimension of "world" is both set off against and yet made part of the human time-dimension. The event occurs when Hester and Pearl are in the forest awaiting the return of the Reverend Mr. Dimmesdale:

It was a little dell . . . with a leaf-strewn bank rising gently on either side, and a brook flowing through the midst, over a bed of fallen and drowned leaves. The trees impending over it had flung down great branches, from time to time, which choked up the current and compelled it to form eddies and black depths at some points; while, in its swifter and livelier passages, there appeared a channelway of pebbles, and brown sparkling sand. . . . All these giant trees and bowlders of granite seemed intent on making a mystery of the course of this small brook; fearing, perhaps, that, with its never-ceasing loquacity, it should whisper tales out of the heart of the old forest whence it flowed, or mirror its revelations on the smooth surface of a pool. Continually

---

[6] The above discussion owes much to Charles Feidelson, Jr., *Symbolism and American Literature* (University of Chicago Press, 1953), Chap. I.

... the streamlet kept up a babble, kind, quiet, soothing, but melancholy, like the voice of a young child that was spending its infancy without play-fulness, and knew not how to be merry among sad acquaintance and events of sombre hue (pp. 223, 224).

This is what Hawthorne, in another connection, termed the "moral scenery" or the "moral landscape." Here, the forest, the stream, and the sunshine project the past and the present conditions of Hester and Pearl: the human and natural orders exist in conjunction and parallel to each other. Yet, while the human characters are *in* time, the natural world is both with and beyond them—beyond them in time and be-yond their full comprehension; they exist in it, but it has long ante-dated them and thus can transcend the limits of their experience and knowledge.[7] Thus the reader, not the characters themselves, is re-quired to see the ever-continuing drama of these two orders, the nat-ural and the human; he is invited to add to the "moral scenery" a great deal which is not, at first view, there. The landscape is a symbolic abbreviation which is capable of an infinite extension beyond the mere spatiotemporal limitations of characters in a scene; they are in it, but it is never permissively subservient to them.

A third explanation for Hawthorne's shift from the pathetic fallacy to a wider range of speculation lies in the Puritan world-view; yet the "shift" could go the other way; that is, it could and did turn Hawthorne toward the immediate allegorizing of man and nature. A Puritan reading of "Earth" might easily establish the instant synec-doche: every act of nature becomes a moral lesson for man. Each event would be a direct exemplification of the universe of spirit; "every natural fact," to paraphrase Emerson, becomes symbol of "spiritual fact."

Yet the Puritan, at his most perceptive, went beyond the instantly

[7] Over and over Hawthorne's characters "feel" their tenuous relationships with the exterior world; sometimes the feeling is a profound one, as in the above-quoted scene of "The Forest Walk" in *The Scarlet Letter;* at other times it assumes the tone of irony or anticipation, as when, in *The Marble Faun,* Hilda says to Kenyon in the Colosseum, " 'How delightful this is!' " and Kenyon, though wiser than she, agrees (p. 185). The moment is significant, for it shortly precedes Donatello's murder of Miriam's model. The full knowledge of these "felt" situations is, however, denied the characters themselves, for they exist in the restricted locus of a place and time. But, almost as if he were presented with a Jamesian "test of intelligence," the reader is both permitted to know more than what the characters themselves can know and required to compre-hend those intangible relationships of the past to the present and back to the past again. The characters are, in short, denied a time-sense which the reader, like Haw-thorne himself, is presumed to have.

comprehended fallacy. He was forever reminded that fact and idea
do not exist in any easy association; the way of understanding is
always difficult, for—it must be stressed—nature is not the direct
handiwork and demonstration of God; no Puritan would entertain
the heresy of pantheism or anthropomorphism. Nature was, on the
contrary, only a means or instrument whereby God, at His mere
pleasure, might affect man; true reality was behind the veil, was
"there" in the realm of spirit; "world" was only an outward and
visible sign which testified to the invisible reality beyond. Man was
denied the capacity for full understanding; he lived in the world of
external reality which continually required that he know it but
which, nonetheless, withheld from him any final clue to understanding.
"Experience" was not the apprehension of man's relation to natural
forms but was the search for function and essence; by means of natural
phenomena God, from His side, could affect man, and man, despite
his primal corruption and the seeming chaos of the natural order,
sought to understand God.[8]

Hawthorne and the seventeenth-century New England Puritan
would well agree in a view that the activity of the world is not for
man's mere benefit and pleasure, as certain nineteenth-century fal-
licists might premise. The condition of man in the physical world is
one of perpetual interaction: man works in, acts on, and, simultane-
ously, receives effects from nature; the natural world is, however, not
a part of him nor is he a part of it; both are demonstrations of that
continual process which is forever in conformity to an anterior intelligence which the Puritan would call God but which Hawthorne preferred to leave as an undefined idea.[9]

Yet the Puritan of the seventeenth century was denied the full

---

[8] The literature on this "psychology" of religious experience is, of course, enormous.
It extends all the way from Bradford's *Of Plimoth Plantation* through Cotton Mather's
Magnalia to Jonathan Edwards' *Treatise Concerning Religious Affections* and the *Free-
dom of the Will*. The chief modern interpreter is Perry Miller, *The New England Mind:
The Seventeenth Century* (New York, 1939), Chap. VIII, "Nature"; and *Jonathan Ed-
wards* (New York, 1949), pp. 236 ff. and 254 ff.

[9] However Puritanly Hawthorne regarded the world, he was not concerned, as a
Puritan would have been, with the ways God affects the world; or, to put the matter
another way, he was not interested in the "God-end" of the mind's journey but only in
those clues to further reality which the world itself allows. The Puritan, one should
admit, tended to posit a static world of immutable and instantly apprehensible forms;
while Hawthorne employed the rather Puritan commonplaces of such forms, as the
leaf, bird, sunshine, or flower, all testified, however, not to a fixed but to an endlessly
variable reality, itself like the human mind engaged in the continual organic process
and change.

employment of a complex vision of reality because he was interested not in the "way" of understanding but primarily in the end or result of comprehension. He knew on the instant that the leaf, the falling rain, or the flashing meteor was a link between the infinite and the finite worlds: what concerned him was "meaning." The world was therefore a set of self-evident axioms to further reality; but he tended to be impatient with or abandon the outward manifestations if he could at once perceive the revelation, the meaning, behind the deceptive vesture of reality. He was, in short, both realist and allegorist because he regarded as presumptuous and suspect any view that the mind can ever understand itself or the world. Allegory, or a form of the pathetic fallacy, helped him make sense of a world which, he well knew, was sin and delusion anyway.[10]

Hawthorne was both Puritan and not Puritan. He could easily slip into allegory and readily equate "meaning" with its physical representation. A passage in the notebook for 1842 suggests how flatly he could make the identifying fallacy of man and world:

> The streak of sunshine journeying through the prisoner's cell; it may be considered as something sent from heaven to keep the soul alive and glad within him. And there is something equivalent to this sunbeam in the darkest circumstances; as flowers, which figuratively grew in Paradise, in the dusky room of a poor maiden in a great city; the child, with its sunny smile, is a cherub. God does not let us live anywhere or anyhow on earth, without placing something of Heaven close at hand, by rightly using and considering which, the earthly darkness or trouble will vanish, and all will be Heaven (*American Notebook*, pp. 97–98).

Such an easy connection between object and idea was the kind of imaginative lapse from which Hawthorne occasionally suffered; the allegorizing fallacy was the brake he tended to put on the riot of his imagination. He was, like a Puritan, impatient if the special insight and revelation were not already there, ready at hand for expression in word. When he had to pause and grope, as did Melville, he tended to thrust the irresolution behind the masquerade of an immediate allegorical identification.[11]

---

[10] Only when Puritanism produced a mind driven by some inner speculative need, as in Jonathan Edwards, do we come upon the Puritan world in its infinite complexity. Edwards attempted to restore the Puritan world-view of God's "affecting" man in natural forms and of man's capacity to come toward God through sensuous and aesthetic experience. But by Edwards' time the rational view of man's efficient knowledge through the twin avenues of sense and mind had gone too far ever to be questioned again until Hume and Kant.

[11] The following passage from *The Marble Faun* illustrates Hawthorne's veering

Hawthorne's view of the world and reality was, therefore, double. Man and nature, on the one hand, might inhabit only a single measurable context: they formed one allegorical dimension; they belonged together in a unit of understanding; one could not be separated from the other; in fact, man might be the monotonous reduplication of what had many times occurred in the realm of "world." On the other hand, Hawthorne's concept of the "moral scenery" connoted the subtle, unresolved variability which is man's relationship to reality. Man is lodged in an endlessly shifting prism of consciousness: everything that occurs in his life has reflections and implications beyond the known limits of the merely "actual." If leaves fall from trees or the sunlight goes behind clouds, these events take place (as they do so frequently in *The Scarlet Letter*) in some incomplete, yet infinite, complex relationship of things to ideas which man struggles to comprehend. The Puritan of the seventeenth century in New England called these events the signs of God's hand evident in the world; a writer of a later time may have lost the sense of an immediate God, and yet he had so to present the "scenery" that, in the very shift and variability of the design, there was some tentative comprehension toward which the understanding might move.

This double vision of reality may account for much of Hawthorne's symbolic treatment of "world" and, at other times, his flat identification of man and world in a consistent allegory. Yet, as much as any writer of the nineteenth century, he explored the infinitely variable relationship of appearance and reality. By bringing his characters and landscapes into suggestive co-ordination with some other, more total experience beyond what seems to be "reality," he anticipated, as much

---

away from the multiple suggestiveness of thing and idea and contenting himself with "fallacy"; he is trying to externalize the inner torment of Donatello after the crime, and he does it by describing "a certain little dell" very similar, in outline, to that in *The Scarlet Letter:* "A fountain had its birth here, and fell into a marble basin, which was all covered with moss and shaggy with water-weeds. Over the gush of the small stream, with an urn in her arms, stood a marble nymph, whose nakedness the moss had kindly clothed as with a garment; and the long trails and tresses of the maidenhair had done what they could in the poor thing's behalf, by hanging themselves about her waist. In former days . . . this lady of the fountain had first received the infant tide into her urn and poured it thence into the marble basin. But now the sculptured urn had a great crack from top to bottom; and the discontented nymph was compelled to see the basin fill itself through a channel which she could not control, although the water was long ago consecrated to her" (p. 281).

As contrasted with the dell in *The Scarlet Letter*, this passage allows only an immediate, finished, point-to-point identification with the broken condition of Donatello's mind.

as did Melville, what later writers would make the "moral scene"—
an unresolved expression of space and time. Hawthorne's truest
vision was Puritan, for he conceived that the drama of man was
merely an incomplete particle of the drama of the universe; man and
reality participate in the total, unresolved quest for understanding;
both are segments of the complete "mind" or the symbolic design
which forever eludes practical demonstration. At his best, therefore,
Hawthorne showed man as living in a meaningful reality; everything was alive and informative; nothing suffered from the resisting
"visionary deadness" which the fallacist seeks to bring alive. Yet at
other times, Hawthorne was content to bend reality into an instant
and easy conformity with man; it was in this comfortable logic and
pathetic fallacy that he lost his way in those last romances, *Grimshawe*
and *Septimius Felton*. Between those two measurements of his mind,
the pathetic fallacy and the symbolic spectrum, most of Hawthorne's
writing can be placed.

EDWARD H. DAVIDSON

THE "DERING MS" OF SHAKESPEARE'S *HENRY IV* AND SIR EDWARD DERING

OF THE THREE extant seventeenth-century transcripts of Shakespearean plays that of *I* and *II Henry IV*, known as the Dering MS, is the earliest and by far the most interesting.[1] The extent of its actual significance, however, depends in great part on two points: its date and its possible relation to the public stage. A recent study of the manuscript has led me to a conclusion which bears directly on both these points, for it appears that the first page not only bears revisions in the hand of Sir Edward Dering, but is copied as a whole by Sir Edward Dering. The remainder of this paper is concerned with the implications of this simple fact.[2]

Sir Edward Dering's interest in the drama and in private performances, performances in which he, members of his household, and friends all took part, is well known.[3] And it has long been accepted

---

[1] The Dering MS is now in the Folger Shakespeare Library (Folger MS 3.2). The other two MSS, also in the Folger Library, are of *Julius Caesar* and *The Merry Wives*. I am including a full study of all three MSS and collations of the last two in a study of seventeenth-century Shakespearean prompt-copy and related materials now nearing completion. I should like to record here my thanks to Dr. Louis B. Wright, Director of the Folger Shakespeare Library, for permission to make use of the Dering MS in the following study. A new critical edition is now being prepared by James G. McManaway and Giles Dawson, both of the Folger Library.

[2] In view of the forthcoming edition of the Dering MS referred to in Note 1, I am asking the reader to take my ascription of page one to Dering on faith and am not offering here facsimiles of Dering's hand in various parts of the manuscript. Something, however, may be done with the facsimiles already published by Halliwell-Phillipps: (1) examples of Dering's hand and of a section of page one in his Shakespeare Society edition of the manuscript (1845), p. xii (facing) and frontispiece; (2) facsimile of the whole of page one in *Works of William Shakespeare*, IX (1859), p. 274 (facing). Unfortunately, however, the most valuable evidence for establishing Dering's hand in page one lies scattered throughout the manuscript. The following clues (except for [2]) will be helpful only to someone with access to the MS: (1) compare "Enter" in first line of opening s.d. with the "Enter" in Dering's added s.d. on fol.6ʳ; (2) compare the "and" in Dering's correction of the original opening s.d. with "and" in line 15 of page one below; (3) compare catchword "Lanc:" at bottom of page one with "Lanc:" in Dering's addition to a s.d. on fol.6ʳ; (4) compare the capital A on page one in lines 3, 11, 13, 16, 22, 24 with the capital A in Dering's additions on fols. 8ʳ and 55ᵛ; and (5) compare the capital N on page one in lines 7, 8, 18 with the capital N in Dering's addition on fol.55ᵛ. Like so many of his contemporaries Dering seems to have written several distinctly formed hands.

[3] See S. B. Hemingway, *I Henry IV* (New Variorum ed.), 1936, pp. 495–97. Further evidence of Sir Edward's connection with play-acting may be found in the Padua First Folio prompt-copies of *Macbeth*, *Measure for Measure*, and *Winter's Tale* which, I believe, may be assigned to Dering's group of amateurs. This matter is discussed at length in the study referred to in Note 1.

that this manuscript, representing a telescoped version of the two parts of *Henry IV*, was at one time in the possession of Sir Edward and contains a good many corrections (against printed copy) and some original lines in his hand. The identification of Dering's hand in the corrections, etc. was made in the middle of the nineteenth century by Halliwell-Phillipps (then James Orchard Halliwell), who published a careful transcription for the Shakespeare Society in 1845, immediately after the discovery of the manuscript among the papers at Surrenden Hall, the Dering seat in Pluckley, Kent. Though he identified the hand of the corrector as Dering's, Halliwell-Phillipps failed to recognize that the manuscript itself was written in two different hands: page one (fol. 1^r) being in what we may call Hand I and the rest of the manuscript (fols. 1^v–55^v) in a different hand (Hand II).

More recently S. B. Hemingway included an account of the manuscript in his Variorum edition of *I Henry IV* (1936). He carefully distinguished what I have called Hand I from Hand II, but identified Hand I as that of another scribe.

> The first page of the manuscript is written in a clear flowing, and unprofessional hand; the remainder in a more cramped, but more professional hand.[4]

M. A. Shaaber in the Variorum *II Henry IV* (1940) added nothing to Hemingway's discussion of the handwriting.

The discovery that the first page of the manuscript was actually copied out by Dering himself (i.e., that Hand I is Dering's) ties the original composition of the manuscript much more directly to Dering than has hitherto been possible and makes it more than ever probable that what we have in the Dering MS represents Dering's own telescoping of the two-part play. Until now, it has been possible to argue that the manuscript was one procured in London by Dering and that it thus represented a form in which the play was being performed on the London stage any time after 1613 (the date of Q5 on which the text of the manuscript for Part I is based). Halliwell-Phillipps in his first account of the manuscript[5] suggests this view and Dover Wilson in his edition of *I Henry IV* (1946) writes:

> . . . the transcript itself is older than this [the private performance at Dering's seat], perhaps many years older, and Professor Hemingway believes it may actually have been used for performances at Court in May 1613 . . . .[6]

4 *New Variorum*, p. 495.
5 Shakespeare Society ed. (1845), pp. xii–xiii.
6 *New Cambridge Shakespeare*, p. 108. Wilson's reference is to Hemingway's Variorum ed., p. 496. Hemingway is cautious in his treatment of the antecedents of the

In a later account[7] Halliwell-Phillipps seems to have changed his mind and suggests that Dering himself may have been responsible for the combination of the two parts, causing the manuscript to be transcribed from his own personally marked copies of Q5 of *I Henry IV* and the quarto of *II Henry IV*. He does not, however, associate Sir Edward in any way with the actual transcription. His change of mind came about I suspect through an entry in Dering's household-book, which he notes here for the first time: in 1619 Dering records "for twenty-seven play-bookes, nine shillings." The connection is certainly not a necessary one, but it is tempting, and the new evidence which shows Dering as the transcriber of page one would seem to point in the same direction.

There is, of course, the possibility that Dering procured (perhaps among the "twenty-seven play-bookes") quarto copies of the two parts of *Henry IV* already marked for an earlier professional performance. This must I think always remain a possibility. But the balance of the evidence is against such a view. If it could be shown from other sources that a telescoped version of the two parts of *Henry IV* had been staged at Court or in the public theatre before say 1623, the case for the professional origins of the cutting behind the manuscripts would be more arguable. But no such evidence exists for *Henry IV*, nor, so far as I know, for any other two-part play before the Restoration.[8] Moreover the length of the Dering version (roughly 3,390 lines) is against a public theatre or Court provenience.

An examination of the first page and its relation to the rest of the manuscript suggests the following hypothesis: having decided to arrange *I* and *II Henry IV* as a single, rather overlong play for private performance,[9] Dering began to copy, intending to make his revisions as he went along. By the time he had finished the first page, however, it must have become clear to him that this method was going to produce a messy copy and only lead to a waste of time in the long

---

MS, but he nonetheless refers to it as being "acquired" perhaps in London at the time of Sir Edward's marriage in the early 1620's. J. Q. Adams (*The Folger Shakespeare Library*, 1933, p. 21) is less cautious, describing the MS as being "a version of *Henry IV* prepared about the year 1611, for use, it seems, at Court or at some private house."

[7] *Works of William Shakespeare*, ed. James O. Halliwell, IX (1859), 253. I must thank Dr. Dawson for calling this reference to my attention.

[8] Heywood's *The Escapes of Jupiter* (c. 1625) offers the closest analogy, but it is a telescoping of parts of *The Golden Age* and *The Silver Age*.

[9] I count roughly 3,390 lines in the Dering MS version. The two parts of *Henry IV* combined contain 6,148 lines, according to Alfred Hart's count (*RES*, VIII (1932), 21).

run. He therefore stopped transcribing and proceeded to make his alterations and changes in the copy of Q5 from which he had started copying.[10] Since now there was no longer a question of revision to be done as the copying progressed, he turned the business of transcription over to someone else, presumably a professional scribe.[11] After the copying was complete Dering read over the scribe's work and, as he read, naturally, made certain corrections, printed copy in hand,[12] and a number of new revisions.

Obviously Dering was dissatisfied with his revision of the opening lines, done we have suggested more or less *currente calamo,* and discovered that in making certain cuts he had failed to make a sufficiently explicit statement of the crusade and its intention.[13] He therefore fudged up on the spur of the moment (one can watch him in the throes of composition, uncertain about his choice of words)[14] eight additional

[10] The immediate derivation of the MS from printed rather than manuscript copy is evidenced (a) by the closeness of the punctuation on page one to that in Q5 (a correspondence which immediately ceases when the professional (?) scribe takes over on page 2) and (b) by two readings later in the MS. In III.iii.82 (Variorum numbering) an uncorrected state of Q5 omits the pronoun "I" in the phrase "I would cudgell him"; so likewise does the MS, but at the same time it leaves space for a short word. This implies that the scribe transcribing from a copy containing this uncorrected state of Q5 recognized that something was missing and so left space for a word (either "I" or "he") to be filled in. The other reading at v.ii.76 shows the MS reproducing the reading "fellow's [*unique to* Q5] souldiers," as "fellow's: souldiers:"

[11] The high-handed but fairly consistent treatment of the punctuation (as well as the hand itself) suggests a professional.

[12] That Dering had a printed copy ready to hand as he read over the MS is proved by his marginal note on a passage omitted in the MS at II.iv.286–289: "vide printed booke" and by the several other omitted passages which he copies in.

[13] Another way of looking at the eight new lines is to suppose that they belong not to Dering's revision of his revision, but to the time when he initially copied out page one and that the sudden need for an insertion which then presented itself discouraged his further transcription. However, this seems to me the less likely of the two.

[14] Both Halliwell-Phillipps' and Hemingway's transcriptions are misleading on this point. A glance at the facsimile of these eight lines offered by Halliwell-Phillipps in his Shakespeare Society edition (p. xii, facing) shows how Dering worked over the lines. In the first line, for "high" Dering first wrote "proud" and secondly "hault," "proud" being unsatisfactory because it repeated the "proude" of the preceding manuscript line. In line three the epithet "borrowed" is inserted above with a caret before "horned"; presumably "horned" was meant to be deleted (though it is not crossed out) and curiously enough both Halliwell-Phillipps and Hemingway omit the word but without any indication that it was ever there. Halliwell-Phillipps suggests that we should read "Englands royall" in line 6; the MS, however, indicates otherwise, inasmuch as Dering seems to have started to write "Englands" and then changed the initial "E" into an "r" and completed the word as "royall." One may notice that the tone and quality of the eight additional lines matches that of the preceding manuscript line, which on the hypothesis outlined above should also be attributed to Dering.

old-fashioned huffing lines which he jotted down on the first scrap of paper ready to hand.[15] That he chose this particular scrap is one of those lucky accidents upon which so much sometimes depends, for through the acting list for Fletcher's *Spanish Curate* which occupies the verso of the scrap it has been possible to establish a date before which Dering's additional lines could not have been written.[16]

There is no reason here to repeat Hemingway's arguments for dating *The Spanish Curate* acting list between 24 October 1622, the date on which Fletcher's play was licensed, and the summer of 1624, at which time one of the actors listed by Dering is presumed to have left the vicinity of Surrenden.[17] His argument remains unaffected by the new evidence. We may note, however, that his argument may now be applied to the dating, not of Dering's corrections and additions only, but to the manuscript as a whole. For though there is no means of proving the case, it is more logical to argue that Dering's work on the *Henry IV* plays was concentrated over a period of weeks or months than that he began copying the manuscript, turned it over to someone else for transcription, dropped the project, and then came back to it some years later to revise and add new lines. Against this "more logical" view, however, two points must be registered. First, if Dering still had the printed copy at hand, as he certainly had in a number of the corrections made in other parts of the play, why did he not restore some of the original lines in page one instead of laboring to invent his own? One answer, though certainly not the only one, might be that when he came to make this particular "correction" he no longer had access to a printed copy. Such an argument implies some probable lapse of time between the eight new lines and the bulk of the other corrections. Second, there is the obvious difference in the quality of the handwriting employed by Dering in the eight new lines and the general quality of Dering's hand in most of the other corrections.[18] Again a lapse of time may be the proper explanation. Quite clearly,

[15] This scrap of paper was presumably attached in some manner either to page one or to the verso of the flyleaf preceding page one. The point of insertion for the new lines is marked by Dering in the left margin of page one.

[16] The chronological priority of the acting list is clearly enough evidenced by the fact that the acting list is incomplete, having been torn across to reduce it to the size needed for the eight new lines.

[17] *New Variorum*, pp. 496–97.

[18] Evidences of this same undressed hand are to be found sporadically among a number of the other corrections. The lines added by Dering at the end of Part II are in a mixture of the more formal hand found in page one and in most of the "corrections" and the loosely formed hand of the inserted eight lines and the acting list.

then, considerable caution must be observed in assigning a date to
the manuscript as a whole and even to the greater part of the corrections. On one view, we would date the whole manuscript not earlier
than 1622; on the other view, we would have to say, except for the
eight new lines written on the verso of *The Spanish Curate* acting list
and possibly a few of the other corrections, that Dering may have
begun his transcription of the manuscript any time after the publication of Q5 in 1613. Everything considered, I would favor the first
view.[19]

G. BLAKEMORE EVANS

[19] After completing this article I discovered that a correspondent to *Notes and
Queries* (CXCIII [1948], 547), who signs himself "S.Y.E.," had already suggested that the
corrections and the hand on page one look to be by the same person. He makes nothing
of the suggestion, however, except to raise the point as possible evidence of a Collier
forgery.

DR. JOHNSON AND BENNET LANGTON

DESCRIBING, in his *Life of Johnson*, the first meeting between Dr. Johnson and one of his closest friends, Bennet Langton, James Boswell may have been guilty of suppressing, or at least omitting, certain pertinent facts which would have given this meeting a somewhat different character. Johnson's acquaintance with Langton began, Boswell wrote,

soon after the conclusion of his Rambler; which that gentleman, then a youth, had read with so much admiration, that he came to London chiefly with the view of endeavouring to be introduced to its authour. By a fortunate chance he happened to take lodgings in a house where Mr. Levet frequently visited; and having mentioned his wish to his landlady, she introduced him to Mr. Levet, who readily obtained Johnson's permission to bring Mr. Langton to him.[1]

This introduction must have taken place sometime between March 1752, the conclusion of *The Rambler*, and 6 May 1755, when Johnson wrote to the younger man in a manner which suggests that their friendship had not been of long standing.[2] Boswell's account certainly suggests that Langton not only had no previous acquaintance with Johnson, but also that Johnson had probably never heard of Langton and that the introduction was mainly the product of hero-worship and chance. That his facts are essentially correct seems to be corroborated by Johnson himself in a letter written to Langton, on 20 March 1782, shortly after Levett's death, in which he refers to Levett, "to whom as he used to tell me, I owe your acquaintance."[3] That Levett performed the actual introduction is highly likely; but it seems unlikely that he was introducing to Johnson, as Boswell implies, a youth the older man had never heard of.

What evidence there is suggests that Johnson probably knew a great deal about Bennet Langton when the two first met, and that Langton's father was at least indirectly responsible for the meeting. The elder Langton, also named Bennet, was an active country squire, who, according to the Lindsey Sessions Minutes, was a justice at the sessions of Louth, Spilsby, and Alford at least eighteen times between 1750 and 1767, and served as Sheriff of Lincolnshire in 1757.[4] In addi-

---

[1] *Boswell's Life of Johnson*, eds. George Birkbeck Hill and L. F. Powell (Oxford, 1934-1950), I, 247. Hereafter cited as *Life*.

[2] *Ibid.*, n. 1. See also, pp. 288–89.

[3] *Life*, IV, 145.

[4] *Lincolnshire Notes and Queries*, Supplement to vol. XXIV, p. 22.

tion to his county interests, however, the elder Langton also apparently had an extensive acquaintance among a number of literary figures of the time, including Joseph Spence. His friendship with Spence, author of the *Anecdotes*, probably came about as a result of Spence's friendship with William Burrell Massingberd (1719–1802), apparently a former student of his at New College, and a neighbor of the Langtons in Lincolnshire. Spence numbered among his acquaintances, in the early 1750's, the elder Langton; David Garrick; Robert Dodsley, the publisher; Edward Young, the author of *Night Thoughts;* and Joseph Warton.[5] It is possible that Langton's father knew all of these men and that Bennet met them fairly frequently, either in Lincolnshire or London, where his family had a house in Cavendish Square. In any case, the elder Langton seems to have been on very cordial terms with Spence; and before 14 September 1753, apparently offered the writer a living at his disposal, which Spence turned down.[6] Therefore, even if neither of the Langtons knew Garrick, Dodsley, or Warton, these men might very well have heard of the Langtons from Spence.

Since these particular friends of Spence were, for the most part, Johnson's friends,[7] it is not at all unlikely that Johnson had heard about the younger Bennet. At any rate, he must have known, even if only by hearsay, of the existence of Bennet's father, so that the name would not have been strange to him. The letter he wrote to Bennet, on 6 May 1755, suggests that he had met the young man's father as soon as, if not earlier than, he had met Bennet; and the conclusion of the letter intimates that he considered both of them his friends: "I assure you once more that to live in a House which contains such a

---

[5] Austin Wright, *Joseph Spence: A Critical Biography* (Chicago, 1950), pp. 119–20. Professor Wright assumes that Bennet Langton the younger was the Langton referred to by Spence in his papers, but he would have been much too young at this period. Later, however, Spence did maintain a friendship with Bennet; and there are two letters from him, and one from Young, to Langton in the Boswell Papers at Yale University. See Ralph Straus, *Robert Dodsley* (London, 1910), p. 144, and Wright, p. 236, for further evidence of the younger Langton's subsequent acquaintance with Spence and Dodsley.

[6] Wright, p. 140. Wright again assumes that Bennet the younger made the offer; but in 1753, Langton would have been a boy of sixteen and hardly in a position to offer a living to Spence. In later years, the elder Langton made the same offer to Johnson, who also turned it down (*Life*, I, 320).

[7] Johnson had known Garrick as a boy in Lichfield; had known Dodsley since at least 1738 (Straus, p. 45); and, in March 1753, knew Joseph Warton well enough to refer to him as a 'particular friend' and call on him to furnish essays for *The Adventurer* (*Life*, I, 253).

Father and such a Son [he had been invited to visit the Langtons] will be accounted a very uncommon degree of pleasure."[8]

It seems clear, then, that Levett did not bring to Johnson's quarters a complete stranger to introduce to him. If Johnson had not met Langton's father, he must at least have heard about him from Garrick or other friends. Boswell, either because of ignorance or because the version he printed seemed to him more dramatically effective, seems to have eliminated certain pertinent facts relating to the meeting between Johnson and Langton. Perhaps he wanted to stress Johnson's availability to strangers. But judging from Johnson's other actions, it seems likely that the introduction was brought off as easily as it was because Johnson knew about the young man and had undoubtedly been prepared beforehand for his coming.

C. N. FIFER

[8] *Life*, I, 289.

HEMINGWAY'S DEBT TO SHERWOOD ANDERSON

WHEN Sherwood Anderson died of peritonitis in 1941, he was the author of more than twenty-five volumes of verse, drama, fiction, and expository prose. This productive record seems rather extraordinary when one realizes that Anderson had been a businessman and an advertising writer until the age of forty, and that his first volume—*Windy McPherson's Son*—did not appear until 1916. Story-telling had always interested him, however, and oral narrative fascinated him long before his fiction found a public. His industry and prolixity are well attested to by the spate of volumes which poured from his pen during the last twenty-five years of his life.

More than most modern writers, nevertheless, Sherwood Anderson produced mingled critical reaction. His early novels had small sales, yet through the decade of the 1920's his name was increasingly familiar to readers. The stories collected in *Winesburg, Ohio* and *Horses and Men* attracted wide attention, and such novels as *Poor White* and *Dark Laughter* were admired despite their obvious flaws in structure. The "new looseness" which Anderson claimed he was striving for in *Winesburg, Ohio* was particularly appealing to a generation which was in revolt against both artistic and moral conventions, and his emphasis on situations was accepted as the proper substitute for a tight plot with a beginning, middle, and end. On the other hand, as Anderson's novels continued to appear, they seemed increasingly thin, chaotic, repetitious. He was not averse to using themes and situations more than once, and his lack of a sense of structure became painfully apparent when the substance—Henry James's "donnée"—of the later books became more and more tenuous. Even the stylistic qualities which in Anderson's early writing had seemed so attractive, the fluidity, the color, the simplicity, the tangibility of his diction, began to pale as his freshness vanished and his images grew fuzzy. Today no one denies Sherwood Anderson great gifts, but few are inclined to predict permanence for much of his work.

It is easy to grant him distinction as a writer of short stories, and "I'm a Fool," "A Meeting South," "I Want to Know Why," and "Death in the Woods" remain memorable.[1] *Poor White* is still readable and interesting; *Winesburg, Ohio* is impressive as a whole despite the unevenness of its sections; parts of an autobiographical volume like

---

[1] Cf. Henry Seidel Canby, "Fiction Sums Up a Century," in *Literary History of the United States*, ed. R. E. Spiller et al. (New York, 1948), II, 1229–33.

Tar are charming; and there are impressive passages in his notebooks and letters. But a well-structured, artistically sustained *book* Sherwood Anderson never wrote. Thus, in the studies of the literary 1920's that are now appearing, Anderson's personality and influence are not neglected, but his name is not equated with those of Sinclair Lewis, Theodore Dreiser, or Ernest Hemingway.[2]

One of the fascinating facts of literary history, however, is the impact that writers who themselves rarely reached the heights have had on other and greater figures. An artist who himself is limited can often guide, direct, aid, even if sometimes only half-consciously, the work of others, and can also provide a model or example which in the long run proves almost seminal. This role seems to have been Sherwood Anderson's at the very time that he was being most productive and most discussed.

In his Chicago years (from about 1910 to 1921) and even subsequently, Anderson was in close contact with most of the figures whose collective work made of the 1920's a great period in American literature. As a mature man but unpublished writer in Chicago before World War I he was patronized and aided by Theodore Dreiser and Floyd Dell. He was the friend of Sandburg and Masters and Ben Hecht. He encouraged young Ernest Hemingway and, somewhat later, served as a kind of mentor to James Farrell. In Paris he met Gertrude Stein and absorbed some of her theories of diction, and in New Orleans he was for a short time an intimate friend of William Faulkner. Many of these figures have paid warm tribute to Sherwood Anderson's inspiration and judgment, even though their own genius took them in contrary directions.[3]

James Farrell, for example, despite the fact that his urban naturalism seems far removed from Anderson's corn-fed mysticism, is outspoken in his feeling of obligation and guidance. It is commonly assumed that Farrell's chief teacher was Dreiser, but as late as 1954 Farrell asserted that "Sherwood Anderson influenced and inspired me, perhaps more profoundly than any other American writer" and even added that Anderson had introduced him to the work of Dreiser. Moreover, Farrell found Anderson's world, with its queer and gro-

[2] Anderson is omitted altogether from Joseph Warren Beach's *American Fiction 1920–1940*(New York, 1941). He is given a chapter in Maxwell Geismar's *The Last of the Provincials* (Boston, 1949), and a few pages in Frederick J. Hoffman's *The Modern Novel in America* (Chicago, 1951).

[3] Cf. the letters and tributes in the September-October, 1941, issue of *Story*, a Sherwood Anderson miscellany.

tesque characters, its intimacy and naïveté, close to his own.[4] It might be interpolated here that *Winesburg, Ohio* was written in a Chicago boarding house and utilized figures Anderson had known in the Windy City.

Ben Hecht, a Chicago newspaperman and literary editor of the early 1920's, likewise found his friend "Swatty" (his nickname for Anderson) stimulating even though he claimed that Anderson could not always convey his meaning clearly. Undisciplined and unrealistic, Anderson was yet both imaginative and perceptive, and was moreover most a poet when he was not writing poetry. And Hecht added:

He looked only into himself. Unlike most of his imitators or disciples, of whom Ernest Hemingway was the best, he did not hitch his poetry to ten-twenty-thirty melodrama. Nor did he ever weave his tales around gaudy escapist figures that are always the heroes of lucrative entertainment.[5]

In similar fashion William Faulkner was impressed by Anderson's genius and received personal help from him. In 1924 Faulkner was in New Orleans idling around the Vieux Carré and there he met Anderson, who had recently become a resident of the Crescent City. Anderson was then at the height of his fame, Faulkner unknown and unpublished. The two men talked and yarned together, concocting between them some fantastic tall tales about a fishherd named Al Jackson which Faulkner later incorporated in his second novel *Mosquitoes*.[6] Tradition has it that Faulkner brought to Anderson the manuscript of his first book of fiction, *Soldiers' Pay*, and that Anderson, although he didn't read it, persuaded Horace Liveright to publish it. At any rate Faulkner later dedicated his novel *Sartoris* to Sherwood Anderson, "through whose kindness I was first published," and also paid him the somewhat dubious compliment of modeling upon him his character of Dawson Fairchild in *Mosquitoes*. In a later pamphlet entitled *Sherwood Anderson and Other Famous Creoles* Faulkner burlesqued Anderson's literary style and offended the sensitive older writer, but Faulkner himself never forgot his obligations and handsomely acknowledged them as recently as 1953.[7] To Faulkner, Sherwood Anderson remained a giant among pygmies, even though he made only a few gestures commensurate with his gianthood.

    [4] James T. Farrell, "A Memoir of Sherwood Anderson," *Perspective* (Summer, 1954), VII, 83–88.

    [5] Ben Hecht, *A Child of the Century* (New York, 1954), p. 232.

    [6] William Faulkner, "Sherwood Anderson, An Appreciation," *Atlantic Monthly* (June, 1953), CXCI, 27–29.

    [7] *Ibid.*, p. 29.

At this point it is important to observe that the writers quoted, Farrell, Hecht, Faulkner, seem quite unlike Sherwood Anderson in their published work. Neither in style nor in substance does their fiction resemble Anderson's. The debt they all owed to the older man was one of stimulation, of perceptive interest, of encouragement. Because they never imitated him they had no need to repudiate him, and their feeling of obligation was consistent and sincere. The case with Ernest Hemingway is different.

In the late fall of 1921 Sherwood Anderson wrote letters to Lewis Galantière and Gertrude Stein in Paris introducing Ernest Hemingway, a "friend of mine and a very delightful man."[8] The two men had met in Chicago the previous year. Hemingway, already at twenty-one a war veteran and an accredited correspondent for the *Toronto Star*, had come to Chicago to do free-lancing. He saw a good deal of Anderson and treated him with deference although he rejected Anderson's concept of unconscious art and occasionally criticized his style.[9] According to James Schevill, "He saw in the older man a spirit that resembled his in many ways, the same turning away from organized education, the same revolt against bourgeois standards of security, the same interest in sports and the life of simple, unsophisticated people."[10] Hemingway was impressed by the fact that Anderson could write and could market the things he sincerely felt without regard to editorial criteria. Temperamental differences between the two men made any great personal intimacy impossible, yet as Hemingway's most reliable biographer contends, "His actual debt to Anderson was a large one."[11]

In later years Anderson followed the literary career of his friend "Hemmy" with considerable interest. He apparently wrote a blurb for the American edition (1925) of *In Our Time*, he praised highly the short story "The Undefeated," and he thought well of *A Farewell to Arms*.[12] But Anderson distinctly disliked *The Green Hills of Africa*. In a letter written January 13, 1936, he called it "a lousy book" and

---

[8] *Letters of Sherwood Anderson*, ed. Howard Mumford Jones (Boston, 1943), p. 82; *The Flowers of Friendship, Letters Written to Gertrude Stein*, ed. Donald Gallup (New York, 1953), pp. 142–43.

[9] Charles A. Fenton, *The Apprenticeship of Ernest Hemingway* (New York, 1954), p. 104.

[10] James Schevill, *Sherwood Anderson, His Life and Work* (Denver, 1951), p. 153.

[11] Fenton, *op. cit.*, p. 105.

[12] Cf. Anderson's letter to Gertrude Stein, April 25, 1926, *The Flowers of Friendship*, p. 191.

criticized Hemingway for "chucking the imaginative world." And then, he told his correspondent, "you see what he does. He romanticizes what he calls the real world, gets ecstatic about shooting and killing, guts and dung."[13] Anderson in other words criticized the very objective precision which Hemingway strove to reach, the specific and concrete details which were not made nebulous by the imagination. Certainly by the late 1930's Anderson had lost much of his admiration for the younger man's writing. Yet one remembers that he and Gertrude Stein once considered themselves as Hemingway's mentors. According to *The Autobiography of Alice B. Toklas* the two often discussed him. "Hemingway had been formed by the two of them and they were both a little proud and a little ashamed of the work of their minds." And then they agreed that Hemingway was "yellow," surely the most absurd charge ever leveled against him.[14]

Hemingway's enthusiasm for Anderson's work, on the other hand, had cooled early. According to Fenton, Sherwood Anderson was the first important writer whom Hemingway knew personally, and Hemingway "absorbed from the older man more than most commentators were subsequently willing to allow."[15] Not only had he been exposed to Anderson's theories of plot and diction but he had read carefully most of Anderson's early work. Despite his scorn for such a novel as *Many Marriages*, Hemingway retained his admiration as late as 1925, in which year he wrote a laudatory review of Anderson's *A Story-Teller's Story* for the Paris periodical *Ex Libris*. Beginning his notice with a comment that the book had already been compared to *The Education of Henry Adams*, Hemingway disdained the parallel since he thought that Anderson's book was well able to stand on its own feet.

There are very beautiful places in the book, as good writing as Sherwood Anderson has done and that means considerably better than any other American writer has done. It is a great mystery and an even greater tribute to Sherwood that so many people writing today think he cannot write. They believe that he has very strange and beautiful ideas and visions and that he expresses them very clumsily and unsuccessfully. While in reality he often takes a very banal idea of things and presents it with such craftsmanship that the person reading it believes it beautiful and does not see the craftsmanship at all. When he calls himself "a poor scribbler" don't believe him.

---

[13] *Letters of Sherwood Anderson*, p. 345.
[14] [Gertrude Stein], *The Autobiography of Alice B. Toklas* (New York, 1933), p. 265.
[15] Fenton, *op. cit.*, p. 148.

Hemingway concluded his review by asserting that Anderson was a very great writer and that he had made a wonderful comeback in *A Story-Teller's Story* after the failure of his novel *Many Marriages*.[16]

The publication of Anderson's *Dark Laughter* in 1925, however, put a definite end to Hemingway's admiration. The next year he wrote to Anderson from Madrid explaining that after reading that novel he had proceeded to write *The Torrents of Spring* as a joke, since his own literary standards compelled him to criticize work of which he strongly disapproved.[17] Subsequently Anderson recorded that he had received from Hemingway "the most self-conscious and probably the most completely patronizing letter ever written." Hemingway not only called attention to the speed with which he had composed his parody but denied that there was any value at all in Anderson's own work. According to Anderson's wry comment made much later, "It was a kind of funeral oration delivered over my grave."[18] Certainly to its chief victim (and one should remember that Hemingway was also ridiculing Gertrude Stein and H. L. Mencken in his book), *The Torrents of Spring* was anything but a joke.[19] The many-sided satire of his hilarious and often cruel burlesque requires some explanation.

Although *Dark Laughter* is the most insistently parodied novel in Hemingway's book, details from other Anderson novels are introduced to underscore the burlesque. *Windy McPherson's Son*, *Marching Men*, *Many Marriages*, *Poor White*, even *Winesburg, Ohio*, all contribute points to Hemingway's attack. Indeed one observes ridicule of Anderson's themes or subjects, his incidents and scenes, his philosophy and mysticism, and finally his style. In all, the book is a good deal more devastating than anything that a "joke" would imply.

Carlos Baker has cleverly defined *The Torrents of Spring* as "a satirical *jeu d'esprit* with a serious core, [which] got its title from Turgenev, its locale from the state of Michigan, and its *raison d'être* from the writings of Anderson and (to a lesser degree) Gertrude Stein."[20] Hemingway himself used a subtitle: "a romantic novel in honor of the passing of a great race." In *Dark Laughter* Anderson em-

---

[16] Review published in *Ex Libris* (March, 1925), II, 176–77. This periodical was published by the American Library in Paris.

[17] Schevill, *op. cit.*, p. 227.

[18] Sherwood Anderson, *Sherwood Anderson's Memoirs* (New York, 1942), p. 475.

[19] *The Torrents of Spring* was published by Charles Scribner's Sons on May 28, 1926, in an edition of 1,250 copies. It was reprinted in Paris in 1932. Cf. Carlos Baker, *Hemingway, the Writer as Artist* (Princeton, 1952), p. 300.

[20] Baker, *op. cit.*, p. 37.

ployed the Negro as a kind of chorus to comment on the stupidity and fumbling of his white characters. The laughter of the Negresses frequently rang out in the background and suggested that their primitive, earthy life was more real, more honest, than that of the white men and women who focused public attention. Hemingway used the country adjacent to Petoskey in Michigan's lower peninsula which he knew well from summer vacations spent there and substituted Indians for Negroes and warwhoops for laughter. The hero Yogi Johnson is introduced into an Indian club in Petoskey by his newly found friend Red Dog and there meets such other members as Sitting Bull, Poisoned Buffalo, and Running Skunk-Backwards. They order some Dog's Head Ale and the Negro bartender breaks out into a shrill haunting laugh. Thus one primitive race becomes a chorus for the other and both are lampooned. Earlier chapters are concluded with the sound of an Indian warwhoop borne distantly on the wind.

Hemingway also selected a theme which is central in much of Anderson's fiction just as it was once central in his own life, the decision of his protagonist as he approaches middle age to turn over a new leaf, give up his business or occupation, desert his family, and wander over the world seeking adventure and possibly the meaning of life.[21] Scripps O'Neil is just such a person. When a chinook wind stirs the torrents of spring in his breast, he leaves his wife, picks up a frozen dead bird which miraculously comes to life and remains with him, and meets a couple of literary waitresses (one reads *The Manchester Guardian* and various book reviews, and the other quotes anecdotes of Henry James). Like Anderson's protagonists again, Scripps complains about the wife he has deserted to anyone who will listen. Indeed, Anderson's reverent use of sex in his stories as something mystical and mysterious is a frequent butt for Hemingway's ridicule.

Moreover, Hemingway provided a southern father for Scripps O'Neil and made him into a Confederate soldier whose house was burned by Sherman on his raid through Georgia. Scripps' mother, like the mother of Anderson's Tar, was dark (probably Italian), strange, and mysterious. At Petoskey, Scripps looks for work and is engaged by a pump factory (like Anderson's carriage wheel factory in Old Harbor, Indiana) where most of the workers are Indians clad only in breech-clouts. Many of the Indians, substituting for Ander-

---

[21] Cf. Sam McPherson in *Windy McPherson's Son*; Bruce Dudley in *Dark Laughter*; John Webster in *Many Marriages*—and Sherwood Anderson himself escaping from his first marriage.

son's Negroes and poor whites, spend their time in breaking up misfit
pumps and rapidly recasting them into "axe heads, wagon springs,
trombone slides, bullet moulds, all the by-products of a big pump
factory." To be sure that nothing was wasted, Indian boys shaped the
fragments that remained into safety razor blades.[22] In another bit of
direct parody Hemingway has his figure Yogi Johnson, restless and dissatisfied, console himself with the realization that he still has his love
of horses (one remembers the narrator of "I Want to Know Why").
Horses are cleaner than men.

In his effort to ridicule the extraordinary behavior of many of
Anderson's characters, Hemingway multiplied absurdities. Indians
who received decorations for bravery in France are en route to Petoskey to join the Salvation Army. The Indian club in that town has
portraits of Chief Bender, Francis Parkman, Jim Thorpe, and Henry
Wadsworth Longfellow on the walls. In Chapter XIII Yogi Johnson
with a big Indian and a little Indian marches along the silent streets,
marching endlessly, aimlessly, but finding some kind of vague satisfaction in that very rhythmic movement just as Beaut McGregor
does in Anderson's *Marching Men*. In the last chapter a nude Indian
squaw, who has just been ejected from Brown's Beanery ("The Best
by Test"), joins Yogi and as the two walk up the railroad tracks on
this cold northern night Yogi strips off his garments one by one. The
reader of Anderson's *Many Marriages* will recognize a savage parody
of several scenes.

Throughout *The Torrents of Spring* Hemingway burlesqued the
specious profundity of Anderson's characters and the repetition of
senseless questions. Scripps O'Neil approaches a telegraph office and
sees a man operating the keys of the instrument. "Could he be a teleg-
rapher? Something told Scripps that he was." Scripps tries to find out.

> "Are you a telegrapher?" asked Scripps
> "Yes, sir," said the man. "I'm a telegrapher."
> "How wonderful!"[23]

Again, Scripps looks for something to eat and sees a sign "Brown's
Beanery." He goes through the door, sees a counter and tables, reads
other advertisements, and then addresses the elderly waitress. "I
wonder . . . if you could tell me if this is Brown's Beanery." When she
assures him that his suspicion is correct, he orders beans for himself

[22] *The Torrents of Spring*, chapter vi. Reprinted in *The Hemingway Reader*, ed.
Charles Poore (New York, 1953), p. 44.
[23] *The Hemingway Reader* p. 32.

and his bird.[24] On another occasion Scripps watches a Pullman train pass in the night and speculates on the occupants.

Who were in those cars? Were they Americans, piling up money while they slept? Were they mothers? Were they fathers? Were there lovers among them? Or were they Europeans, members of a worn-out civilization world-weary from the war? Scripps wondered.[25]

In just such fashion, of course, do Sherwood Anderson's characters meditate, ask themselves transparent questions, and convince themselves that they are philosophical.

Hemingway also burlesqued Sherwood Anderson's style in *The Torrents of Spring* by deliberately copying it. Repetition and simplicity become banal, sentences are fragmented, phrases are awkwardly detached and stand alone, and there is a loose association not so much of ideas as of names. Thus to Scripps O'Neil, the French people are a strange mixture, Eva Le Gallienne and Clemenceau, Joan of Arc and Sacha Guitry, Georges Carpentier and Grock—somewhat, one imagines, as the young Hemingway newly arrived in Paris might have associated names and as Anderson does in one of the flashbacks of *Dark Laughter*. But everything is overdone, emphasized to the point of senselessness. And Hemingway usually implies that much of the fiction he is ridiculing is bad because of its pretense and flatulence rather than because of its insincerity.

There is one final point. Anderson utilizing an older technique intruded in much of his fiction, interpolating his own views or comments, disrupting the very point of view he sought to establish. Hemingway as always goes him one better. Each of the four main parts of *The Torrents of Spring* has an epigraph from Fielding, by quoting which Hemingway suggests a philosophic basis for his comic art. And four times, too, Hemingway appends author's notes to the reader in which he alludes to personal friends (Ford Madox Ford, Harold Stearns, Sinclair Lewis, John Dos Passos, H. G. Wells), mocks himself (something of which Sherwood Anderson was incapable), and calls attention not only to his personal knowledge of Petoskey and the Michigan Indians but to the unimportance of the whole project. Nor should it be forgotten that there is one direct reference to Anderson's *Dark Laughter* or at least to one of its characters, "Fred Something" (actually Fred Gray, with whose wife Aline the protagonist Bruce Dudley elopes), and some brief account of Fred's role in the war, his

[24] *The Hemingway Reader,* pp. 35–36.
[25] *The Hemingway Reader,* p. 30.

killing of a German soldier, and his memory of the incident.[26] But "that fellow Anderson's book" is not singled out for further specific attention.

One might well ask what prompted Hemingway to make this attack. Gerturde Stein suggested to Anderson that Hemingway was jealous of him and particularly resentful of his invasion of the field of the sports story, a domain which Hemingway had apparently pre-empted for himself.[27] This interpretation seems untenable on two grounds: first, Hemingway could hardly have expected writers in general to shy away from the whole domain of sports; and secondly, although both Anderson and Hemingway did utilize a sports background for certain stories, there is a world of difference between the fishing scenes of "Big Two-Hearted River" and the horse-racing, county-fair atmosphere of "I'm a Fool" and "I Want to Know Why." Certainly Anderson was never capable of recording the precise details and technical processes of fly-fishing or stalking and shooting a kudu bull in which Hemingway excelled. Even "My Old Man," in which Hemingway used the racetrack background, has a brittleness and sophistication which are quite foreign to Anderson's work. One must look for other reasons.

In the middle 1920's Hemingway was a young man, a hard worker, a man fond of a physically active life. Although his early novel *The Sun Also Rises* now seems almost a classic picture of the frustrated, rootless, post-war group of neurotics and dilettantes who sought in sex and alcoholism an escape from their plight, Hemingway probably never sympathized with such people or took great pleasure in their company. Although he was on occasion a saunterer along the grand boulevards or a café-sitter on the Left Bank, he preferred to spend his leisure working out in a Paris gymnasium or boxing with Ezra Pound, and frequently he left the capital for fishing and hunting expeditions. The sensitive, indolent characters of Sherwood Anderson's tales, whom Anderson himself somewhat resembled, irritated him. When Hemingway first read Anderson in Chicago he was impressed by the older man's honesty and directness. Now, quite possibly, the supine-ness of Anderson's characters annoyed him, and the vagueness and fluidity of the background no longer seemed so impressive. Hemingway was more and more concerned with recording things as they were, the direct observation of an eye-witness. He was the man who was

[26] *The Hemingway Reader*, pp. 60–61.
[27] Cf. Baker's analysis, *op. cit.*, pp. 43–44. Also *The Autobiography of Alice B. Toklas*, pp. 265–70.

there. Anderson was interested in suggesting what might have been or in probing for motives. The grotesques of *Winesburg, Ohio* were all too human but they were also vague and soft. Hemingway could never draw such people and had little sympathy for them.

Perhaps there is another factor. Sherwood Anderson was an almost totally humorless author. It is not only that he had no genius for the comic but that he apparently seldom realized that scenes and events which were to him deeply poignant might to another temperament seem richly funny. As a consequence, he sometimes wrote stories which were unconsciously satiric. Hemingway himself remarked that Anderson told amusing anecdotes but could not himself be joked with as he took himself too seriously.[28] Because of this innate lack of humor and the unsure taste which was its result, Anderson is a very easy author to parody. A young writer, self-confident and uninhibited, could seize upon Anderson's eccentricities, his occasional banalities of style, his illogical repetitions, and his willingness to allow his characters to posture, and could produce a devastating satire. Obviously the temptation was too much for Hemingway: he fired his broadside and so we have *The Torrents of Spring*

But there was one aftermath. In an undated letter to Anderson (written probably in 1926) Hemingway expressed his concern over wounded feelings.

I still feel badly about having ever written to you in an ex cathedra or ex-catheter—they have catheters as well as cathedrals over here—manner but I think that is just that the young have to be very sure always, because the show is really very tough and it is winning all the time and unless you know everything when you're twenty-five you don't stand a chance of knowing anything at all when it's had time to shake down and you're thirty-five. And we've all got to know something. Maybe.[29]

Hemingway's literary debt to Sherwood Anderson is less tangible than his obligations to Mark Twain, yet it cannot be denied. Even a brief stylistic comparison can be revealing. In 1951 James Schevill printed two paragraphs from *In Our Time* side by side with two paragraphs from *Winesburg, Ohio*.[30] He added no comment, leaving the reader to draw the necessary conclusions, but the juxtaposition is striking. We see Nick Adams starting out on a fishing trip in the fall and George Willard leaving Winesburg for the big city in the spring. In

---

[28] Personal letter from Ernest Hemingway to John T. Flanagan, May 2, 1955.

[29] Letter from Ernest Hemingway to Sherwood Anderson in the Sherwood Anderson Papers, Newberry Library, Chicago, used here with the special permission of Mr. Hemingway.

[30] Schevill, *op. cit.*, p. 107.

each passage the protagonist acts without speaking, and the weather and background are carefully indicated. The sentences are short and staccato. Two of Anderson's sentences begin with adverbial clauses, none of Hemingway's. Each writer has several sentences introduced by the definite article and a common noun, and in both passages "and" is by far the most common conjunction. Adjectives are sparse and seldom cumulative, though Anderson in the penultimate sentence does write, "the silent deserted main street." Each sentence is a simple record of concrete action.

The closest analysis of Hemingway's style so far published is that by Harry Levin.[31] After some general comments on Hemingway's attitude toward writing and his reaction against the Wilsonian rhetoric of the first World War period, Professor Levin concentrates on Hemingway's language and syntax. The critic calls attention to Hemingway's fondness for short words and to his overuse of "nice" and "fine." Repetition is obvious, and a few familiar verbs replace more precise terms. Adjectives are eliminated as far as possible in favor of nouns, and on the whole literary diction is avoided. In general, as Professor Levin observes, in Hemingway's writing sequence supersedes structure. He scorns the complex sentence and normally writes simple sentences or simple sentences loosely compounded. Yet it is common knowledge that through concreteness, precision, and bluntness Hemingway achieves extraordinary effects.

At the beginning of his literary career, Ernest Hemingway obviously shared many of Anderson's literary principles and was encouraged by Anderson's successful advocacy of them. Both men revolted against what seemed to them a kind of conspiracy to avoid the facts of life. Sex is not such a predominant motive in Hemingway's fiction as in Anderson's but both men treated it honestly and directly. For the euphemisms and vagueness of a belated Victorianism they had only contempt. Both writers likewise objected to the elaborate descriptive passages of a more formal age, to the jewelled diction, the elaborate figures, the purple prose. Anderson strove to be suggestive and atmospheric; Hemingway preferred to be blunt and specific. But neither man relished formal exposition or elaborate stage setting.[32] It should

---

[31] Harry Levin, "Observations on the Style of Ernest Hemingway," *Kenyon Review* (Autumn, 1951), XIII, 581–609. Cf. John Atkins, *The Art of Ernest Hemingway* (London, 1952), chapter iv, "That Famous Style"; and Joseph Warren Beach, *op. cit.*, pp. 100–109.

[32] Maxwell Geismar contended in *The Last of the Provincials* (p. 256) that Hemingway actually missed fire since Anderson meant his *Dark Laughter* to be a debunking book. But the remark is not especially convincing.

be remarked here that the prolixity and repetition of Anderson's later work are not quite the same thing as the redundancy of the genteel tradition.

In their handling of plot, too, there are resemblances. Hemingway is the better storyteller largely because his narratives contain more action and therefore more drama, but also because he is more conscious of suspense, accelerated movement, and climax. Anderson's stories, on the other hand, depend more on nuances, on the right relationship of scene and character, on indirect revelation of crucial circumstances, on sympathetic insight into maladjusted or frustrated people. Yet both men rebelled against the story which was essentially a maneuvering of plot. Both men shunned the surprise ending and the purely narrative appeal. The impact of "Big Two-Hearted River" or "A Clean, Well-Lighted Place" basically derives no more from the action than "Death in the Woods" or "A Meeting South."

The preference of both men for simple, rather primitive characters must also be observed. One of the common charges made against Hemingway is that he is anti-intellectual, or at least that his characters rarely analyze or speculate. Men primarily concerned with action or emotion have little time for or interest in abstract ideas. But the same comment has been made about *Winesburg, Ohio*. Anderson's people too, real and poignant as they undoubtedly are, feel rather than think. Their whole contact with life is an emotional one, and their mental processes are either abeyant or absent. Both Hemingway and Anderson chose to present naïve, immature people, "primitives" in Hemingway's fiction, "grotesques" according to Anderson's own label. Indeed, Robert Penn Warren saw a striking resemblance between the figures of Hemingway and the rustic characters with whom William Wordsworth chose to deal. Novelist and poet repudiated the intellectual world of their own day, Wordsworth because it seemed unreal and limited, Hemingway because it had produced the mire and blood of a catastrophic war.[33] But whereas Wordsworth's people were simple and innocent (the farmer, the child, the leech gatherer), Hemingway's became violent (soldiers, pugilists, gangsters).

It is this very violence, indeed, which is not only deeply characteristic of Hemingway but which cuts him off from most of his contemporaries and predecessors. The battlefield, the bullfighting arena, the prize ring, the mountain valley or forest glade where big game lurk, the ocean—these scenes Anderson never touched and would not have

[33] Robert Penn Warren, "Hemingway," *Kenyon Review* (Winter, 1947), IX, 13–16.

known how to handle. Moreover, the foreign and exotic localities which the *aficionado* of Hemingway comes to expect, these are also antipodal to Anderson's middlewestern small towns and country fairs. Even the extreme masculinity of Hemingway's later work is far removed from the sensitive, almost feminine approach which marks Sherwood Anderson's most perceptive fiction.

But it is the similarities rather than the differences which linger. The honest revelation of the protagonist of the story is characteristic of the best work of Anderson and Hemingway. According to Maxwell Geismar, the calculated formlessness of Anderson became transformed into the plain flatness of Hemingway.[34] The brevity of the sentences, terse if not always crisp, the frequency of sentence parts joined by the conjunction "and," the scorn of conventional diction, the preference for and intelligent use of colloquial language, the careful and extraordinarily effective repetitions, the often poetic use of the familiar and the routine—these are characteristic of *both* Anderson and Hemingway and of no one else of their generation.[35] Moreover, these qualities appeared in Anderson's work *first*, and at a time when Hemingway was in the usual formative stage.

It is possible that Hemingway adopted some of these techniques subconsciously, that he accepted their value without realizing their provenience. It is possible that Hemingway observed their strong contribution to the success of Anderson's fiction and that he was so sympathetic with them from the start that Anderson's initial success was the compelling factor in his own use of them. It is not only possible but probable that Hemingway, once having adopted these techniques, proceeded to modify them or even improve them until in his best work they no longer suggest their source and have become Hemingway's own. But Anderson was the friend and the inspiration of much of Hemingway's early work, as he was of other young writers who later outdid their early mentor.[36] Of this select group Hemingway alone has failed to acknowledge his debt publicly.

JOHN T. FLANAGAN

[34] Geismar, *op. cit.*, p. 273.

[35] Fred B. Millett, *Contemporary American Authors* (New York, 1940), pp. 32, 35.

[36] Philip Young claimed in his *Ernest Hemingway* (New York & Toronto, 1952) that of the four writers who were generally credited with influencing Hemingway three have been written off by the novelist himself (Anderson, Fitzgerald, Miss Stein). With Ezra Pound, Hemingway remained on good terms until Pound became a fascist (p. 156).

A POSSIBLE ORIGIN OF MILTON'S "COUNTERPOINT" OR DOUBLE RHYTHM

IN TRYING to describe Milton's metrical patterns in his English poetry, various writers have resorted to many ingenious and often curious devices. A glance at Stevens's *Reference Guide* under the heading 'Metrics' will readily show the amount of attention that has been devoted to Milton's English metrics, although only a few of the writers there listed have contributed much to the solution of the problem.

One aspect of his metrics involving reversed stresses, observable especially in *Paradise Lost* although not restricted to that poem, has, perhaps, through neglect or misunderstanding, caused more trouble in trying to account for his rhythms than any other metrical feature of his poetry. Recently, Helen Darbishire in her edition of *Paradise Lost* (Oxford, 1952) made much of the various minor differences in the first and second editions of the poem, without, however, clearing up the real difficulties. Almost typical of attempts to deal with the metrical problems arising from trying to read the lines in which these changes occur is a perspicacious and highly suggestive paper by Robert Martin Adams (*Modern Philology*, LII [1954], 84–91), in which the author has tried to resolve the problem of emphatic and unemphatic spellings in the epic. Finding far less significance in the differences in spellings than Miss Darbishire, Adams almost dismissed them, yet was obviously puzzled by the strange cadences sometimes produced by the occurrence of these forms. Actually, Adams was perhaps as much disturbed by other hauntingly fleeting cadences as by those sometimes arising from Milton's two kinds of spelling, although he sensibly refrained from commenting on them. Miss Darbishire and Mr. Adams, like most writers on the subject, missed one of the more important ideas about Milton's English metrics that was first printed about 1918.

In that year, Gerard Manley Hopkins's *Poems* were first edited and published by Robert Bridges. (Subsequent editions were published in 1930 and 1948.) In Hopkins's discussion of his own metrics, he calls attention to an element in English verse which is

due either to a great want of ear or else is a calculated effect, the superinducing or mounting of a new rhythm upon the old; and since the new or mounted rhythm is actually heard and at the same time the mind naturally supplies the natural or standard foregoing rhythm, for we do not forget what the the rhythm is that by rights we should be hearing, two rhythms are in some

61

manner running at once and we have something answerable to counterpoint in music, which is two or more strains of tune going on together, and this is Counterpoint Rhythm. Of this kind of verse Milton is the great master and the choruses of *Samson Agonistes* are written throughout in it—but with the disadvantage that he does not let the reader clearly know what the ground-rhythm is meant to be and so they have struck most readers as merely irregular.

—Edition of 1948, p. 7. Ed. W. H. Gardner

In general, Hopkins thought that such rhythm arose almost entirely from inversions of normal accents within the feet of the lines, and pushed its origins no further. One scarcely needs the delicacy of Hopkins's ear, nor that of Bridges, to recognize and grant the general validity of what he said here about Milton's 'double' rhythms. It can be observed in the first line of the *Nativity Ode*, 'This is the month . . . ' and in *Paradise Regained*, III, 76, 'Peaceable Nations, neighbouring, or remote,' as well as in the *Samson* choruses mentioned by Hopkins. In short, throughout Milton's English poems, early or late, can be found the element that Hopkins called 'counterpoint' rhythm.

After makin gdue allowance for the common practice in English poetry of shifting accents within feet in any given line—a practice at least as early as Chaucer, and Hopkins found many examples in *Piers Plowman*—there remain many reversed accents in Milton's English verse that seem either too deliberately made or too remarkable to be accounted for entirely as imitative of earlier English poets. They are too dependent on Milton's remarkable ear to be allowed to have arisen by accident. The question that we shall try to answer here is, therefore, where did the practice come from in Milton?

Of course, there are many possibilities for the origins of Milton's use of such rhythms, but one great factor that operated on him throughout his productive life as a poet has never been invoked in this connection, although frequently mentioned without much analysis in other ways. This factor was the effect on him of his prolonged studies of the metrics of Greek, Hebrew, Italian, and Latin poetry, and perhaps of other languages, as well. For the ancient languages, it is a truism that today we are scarcely able to reconstruct the pronunciation by the ancients of the various languages native to their respective tongues. We scarcely know, except within narrow limits, how the Romans pronounced formal, classical Latin, or even their everyday speech. However, there is ample evidence before, during, and after Milton's time, of how the Renaissance thought that Latin should be pronounced, especially for the metrical values involved in writing verses in that language. By 1600, there were various ways of pronouncing Latin. Milton referred to three or possibly four of them, namely, the English manner, which he deplored, the Italian, the French, and 'Law Latin.' The Latin metrical patterns, on the other hand, were more or less immutable, although even they were modified by pronunciation.

For each language studied in the sixteenth, seventeenth, eighteenth, indeed, in the nineteenth and twentieth centuries, in so far as the ancient tongues were still studied metrically with the aim of writing verses in any of them, there were very early established certain principles of pronunciation. There was one set for Latin, a different set for Greek, and still a third set of even different principles of agreed on standards of pronunciation for Hebrew. These artificial standards were designed for writing verses in those languages, each set being applied to its own language. Milton wrote verses in Latin and in Greek, and we have preserved a good many examples of his Latin verses, and one or two of his Greek. Though we have no examples of his efforts in Hebrew verse, he undoubtedly wrote or worked at quite a few poems in that language, but saw fit to preserve none of them for posterity. We can be sure of the effort, since it was common practice in his day for boys to compose verses in Hebrew if, as, and when they studied it. Now if we take any language at all that is not native to the person who tries to use it, even assuming that the agreed on pronunciation of it is artificial and wholly arbitrary, and then try to write metrical pieces in that language, we shall always find certain metrical characteristics imbedded in those efforts. One of these characteristics will be that the agreed on metrical patterns which the student has learned to observe probably will be present in his finished verse to a more or less discernible degree, depending on the ability of the individual performer. That is, a person of marked poetic ability, such as Milton was, might succeed very well in attaining a high degree of metrical perfection in Latin, in Greek, or in Hebrew according to the agreed on metrical principles acquired from his textbooks and masters. Milton's Latin poems are notable examples of his success with the standard metrical prosody of his day. In addition to this element, there is in his best Latin verses a marked resemblance to the verses of such Latin writers as Ovid, Virgil, and others because he was taught deliberately to produce such marked imitation. One of the definite aims of all instruction in writing Latin in his day was to attain such a proficiency that the lines of verse could scarcely be distinguished from lines by Virgil, or Ovid, or Horace. That element must always be allowed for in the consideration of any Latin verse written in Milton's time. Thus, we have the beginnings of the process of creating rhythms that never before existed in any language. They will arise from the existence in his verses of what the would-be poet could attain through precept and imitation. But the verse was always read aloud, whether scanned or otherwise recited. Thus, there is always a metrical element that we can feel but not explain in reading aloud any neo-Latin verse of whatever period we may select. In Milton's case, we have the rhythms attained by following the rules of his day, but in addition we have what the language itself, regardless of how it is pronounced, imposed on the verse. This is a complex matter when first propounded, but simple enough in actual practice. Imagine if you please a language so completely dead that we have no idea at all of how it was pronounced when it was a living language in daily use. That is, if we exaggerate, the matter becomes clear. Take that imaginary, dead language, but leave our ability to read it and understand it. Now erect a set of wholly artificial rules for writing and pronouncing (*cantus*) metrically acceptable verse therein, the rules to be obtained by study of extant examples of verses in that language. Then read aloud the better results of such attempts to write such verse, and ask someone with a fairly sensitive ear to listen for the rhythm. He will almost invariably be aware of a double rhythm, the one built into the verse according to the rules, and the one imposed on the lines by the sound to his ear of the words themselves. And it will make not one particle of difference whether the pronunciation used is authentic or arbitrary. The words themselves will have their way, whether or not they are properly pronounced, or whether, as is actually the case with the ancient tongues, our pronunciations may be quite different from what those ancient people used. Milton wrote so much verse of this kind in languages other than English, that sooner or later—and certainly in his own surviving verse, not later than the *Nativity Ode* (1629)—he began to use a double set of rhythms in his English verses, whether consciously or, as at first well may have been, unconsciously. The first results were no doubt caught almost at once by his marvelously sensitive ear, and he liked them. Thus, he continued to use the device, perhaps attaining his most sustained success with it in the *Samson* choruses, although similar effects, but with different stresses and rhythms, appear in other verses and much earlier efforts than *Samson*. The unusual effects from what at first glance seem only regularly recurring irregular lines in the *Nativity Ode* and others of his early experiments as well as in *Lycidas* and to a limited extent in *Comus*, spring to mind. But to me the chief element that created such a metrical idea in him derived from his writing of verse in languages other than English, and then transferring the rhythms he so discovered to his English verse. The unusual rhythms are not consistently used, but are employed very adroitly as part of the entire metrical pattern of the particular piece. But they account for more of his unusual, not to say difficult rhythms than any other factor which I have ever encountered. It is for this reason, therefore, that I suggest that the most perplexing of Milton's rhythms, early or late, in his English verse are carry-overs from his study and metrical practice in languages other than English, especially the classical tongues and Hebrew. As Italian metrics are so much like those of Latin, it is scarcely necessary to invoke additionally Milton's studies of Italian poetry although throughout his Italian poems, when read aloud, Hopkins's 'counterpoint' rhythm can readily be found.

HARRIS FLETCHER

SIDNEY AND HARINGTON AS OPPONENTS OF SUPERSTITION

I

SIR PHILIP SIDNEY has never lacked admirers, but during the greater part of the last two hundred and fifty years it has been chiefly the romantic aspects of his life as soldier and poet that have received attention.[1] His contemporaries, however, saw in him not merely a tilter and a sonneteer but a statesman of great ability and of greater promise, and a powerful teacher of those arts, both private and public, by which men and nations alike attain eminence and power. They praised the fluent skill of the conventionally amatory *Astrophel and Stella* certainly; but it was the strenuous doctrine of the *Arcadia* which provoked their keenest interest and heartiest applause.

Perhaps it was some vague premonition of the misunderstanding that was later to arise concerning the nature and purpose of the *Arcadia* which prompted Fulke Greville to set them forth in such explicit terms in his *Life of the Renowned Sʳ Philip Sidney*, iterating and reiterating that the romance was a handbook in statesmanship and in self-discipline, that in recounting the adventures of Pyrocles and Musidorus Sidney's "end in them was not vanishing pleasure alone, but morall Images and Examples, (as directing threds) to guide every man through the confused Labyrinth of his own desires, and life."[2]

Though Greville's counsel has been unheeded and the *Arcadia* entirely misunderstood by many scholars in the past and even by some of the present day, there has been among serious students an ever increasing appreciation of its value since Edwin Greenlaw called atten-

<hr/>

[1] The complete history of Sidney's reputation would make a work of many volumes, and it still remains to be written. Brief treatments of the subject will be found in Principal Malcolm W. Wallace's agreeable essay, "The Reputation of Sir Philip Sidney," *The Johns Hopkins Alumni Magazine*, vol. XVII, No. 1, pp. 1–21, and in the present writer's *Sir Philip Sidney and the Arcadia* (Urbana, Ill., 1934), particularly pp. 17–51 and 122–43. Albert W. Osborn, in *Sir Philip Sidney en France* (Paris, 1932), has given an admirable account of Sidney's fame and influence in France. During the interval between the writing of this article and the preparation of a fair copy for the printer, there has appeared John Buxton's *Sir Philip Sidney and the Renaissance* (London, 1954), which studies in detail Sidney's reputation and influence among his contemporaries, making very effective use of the too-often-neglected rich Neo-Latin literature of the period. The present writer has not seen W. H. Bond's unpublished dissertation, "The Reputation and Influence of Sir Philip Sidney" (Harvard, 1941).

[2] Ed. Nowell Smith (Oxford, 1907), p. 223. Although David Lloyd was obviously indebted to Greville, his view reflects the consensus in Sidney's own generation and the one immediately following. See his short biographical essay on Sidney in *The Statesmen and Favourites of England since the Reformation* (London, 1665), especially pp. 314–16.

tion to it a little more than forty years ago;[3] and it seems probable that the time is not far off when the *Arcadia* will finally be recognized as a work of scarcely less serious and lofty purpose than *The Faerie Queene*.

The present writer has elsewhere discussed the larger aspects of the moral and political teaching of Sidney's romance.[4] Here, the intent is to treat, in somewhat greater detail than has been convenient previously, a single element in Sir Philip's philosophy of action, an element which is, as it were, the negative corollary to his belief that the true hero is master of his own destiny, his contempt for those who look to the occult arts for aid, and think to find by frequentation of astrologers and soothsayers a means to avoid dangers which they have not the courage to face.

Since it is very probable, to say the least, that Sidney's thrusts at soothsayers and diviners in the *Arcadia* were written with the hope of persuading his friends to be less credulous, it seems worth while to examine the manifestations of a similar zeal against superstition which are found in the writings of one who may justly be considered, with the single exception of Fulke Greville, Sidney's most fervent and steadfast admirer, Queen Elizabeth's merry godson, Sir John Harington of Kelston.[5] Sidney's family and friends were nearly all among Harington's friends,[6] and beliefs and practices that are condemned in

---

[3] "Sidney's *Arcadia* as an Example of Elizabethan Allegory," *Kittredge Anniversary Papers* (Boston, 1913), pp. 327–37. Greenlaw wrote a second paper dealing with another aspect of the same question, "The Captivity Episode in Sidney's *Arcadia*," *Manly Anniversary Studies in Languages and Literature* (Chicago, 1923), pp. 54–63.

[4] *Sir Philip Sidney and the Arcadia*, pp. 144–85 and 211–16.

[5] It is a pleasure to note that Dr. Townsend Rich shares this view. Cf. his *Harington and Ariosto: A Study in Elizabethan Translation* (New Haven, 1940), pp. 162–64. The most striking sentence in the discussion of the relationship between the two poets is: "The man whom Harington admired above all others was Sir Philip Sidney."

[6] It is to be remarked that despite his great admiration for Sir Philip, Mary, Countess of Pembroke, and other members of their family and circle, Harington thoroughly detested Robert Dudley, Earl of Leicester, whom he evidently considered both a hypocrite and a rascal. Although this feeling seems to have been matter of common knowledge at Court and evidences of it have been detected here and there in Sir John's writings, it is most repeatedly and freely expressed in the pamphlet in which he voiced his dissatisfaction with the state of England during the last years of Elizabeth's reign and his hope of better things under James. See *A Tract on the Succession to the Crown (1602) by Sir John Harington, Kt. of Kelston*: Printed for the First Time from a Manuscript in the Chapter Library at York, and edited with Notes and an Introduction by Clements R. Markham, C. B., for the Roxburghe Club (London, 1880), pp. 36–37, 44–45, 71. Harington did not dare to publish this work while Elizabeth was still alive but evidently intended to have it appear in support of the claim of the Scottish King should there be any strife over the succession. The manuscript Markham edited was at one time

the *Arcadia* inspired some of the younger poet's liveliest quips.[7] Certainly there is reason to suppose that Sidney glanced at Elizabeth I in the story of the credulous faith of Basilius in the oracle, for Mortlake seems to have been her Delphi, and we know that Harington, to whom much was permitted, admonished her in direct terms in this epigram which suggests a very imperfect sympathy for Dr. Dee:[8]

> *Of Soothsaying, to the Queene of England*
> Might Queenes shun future mischiefe by foretelling,
> Then among Soothsayers 'twere excellent dwelling:
> But if there be no means, such harms expelling,
> Knowledge makes the grief, the more excelling.
>   Well, yet deare Liege, my soul this comfort doth
>   That of theese Soothsayers very few say sooth.[9]

It was never, of course, Sidney's purpose to take the vicious or foolish directly to task in the manner of a Juvenal but to teach in fable, after the manner of the epic poets, that in wisdom and courage lie happiness and honor; in weakness and superstition, misery and shame.[10] It is probably the failure to look for a close and consistent

---

in the hands of Harington's friend, Toby Mathew, Archbishop of York, and bears short marginal annotations in his hand. Obviously the easy and unopposed succession of James to the English throne made publication of the tract both unnecessary and undesirable.

[7] The present writer intends to discuss in a later study quips which, though not germane to the subject of this article, throw interesting light on the nature and extent of Harington's indebtedness to Sidney.

[8] For mention of the Queen's interviews with Dr. Dee and her gifts to him, see his diary edited by J. O. Halliwell (London, Camden Society, 1842), pp. 4–5, 8–10, 19–21, 32, 35–37, 42–43, 49, 51–53. It would be rash to assume that Elizabeth was indifferent to Dee's practical services and favored him entirely on account of his skill and reputation in the occult sciences, but it is clear from his own account as well as from the testimony of others that she had faith in that skill. Interesting information concerning the scientific wizard's relations with Elizabeth I, Leicester, Albert Laski, and the Emperor Rudolph II is to be found in Charlotte Fell Smith's *John Dee* (London, 1909). The book is to be read with caution, however, for it not only contains errors of detail but views Dee with what must seem to many excessive sympathy. The author herself was aware of its faults and offered (p. 5) "a word of apology to serious historical readers for the incorrigibly romantic tendency of much of the narrative, which, in spite of the stern sentinel of a literary conscience, would continually assert itself."

[9] *The Letters and Epigrams of Sir John Harington,* ed. Norman Egbert McClure (Philadephia, 1930), p. 179.

[10] Although Sidney's kinship with the great writers of epic and romance was plainly discerned by the great majority of his contemporaries, the physician and entomologist Thomas Moffet (or Moufet), who wrote a Latin eulogy of him (which was apparently presented as a New Year's gift, in 1594, to his nephew William Herbert), chose to see in the *Arcadia* a greater indebtedness to Plautus than to Vergil or Malory. One is inclined to wonder whether, despite his long attendance on the Countess of Pembroke, Moffet had ever gone beyond the epistle dedicatory in the great romance when one

relationship between Sir Philip's imaginative work as a writer and his active life as soldier and statesman that has caused many scholars to miss the vigorous protest against the superstitions of sixteenth-century England which is to be found in the condemnation of the credulity of various personnages in an entirely fanciful ancient Greece. Even his most admired biographer was inclined to believe that Sidney shared the confidence in the occult arts which made so many of the chief figures of Elizabeth I's Court easy prey for astrologers and crystal gazers.[11] This belief rests upon Dr. Dee's record of two visits which Sidney paid him in the company of some of his most faithful and distinguished clients and upon Sonnet XXVI of *Astrophel and Stella*. But none of this evidence can be considered either very specific or conclusive.

Sidney first visited Dr. Dee in March 1577 in the company of his uncle, Robert, Earl of Leicester, and Sir Edward Dyer. Both Leicester and Dyer were considerably older than Sidney and were regular visitors at Mortlake. The young man could not have refused to accompany Leicester and probably would not have refused to ac-

---

reads this:" . . . he desired to smother the *Arcadia* (offspring of no ill pen) at the time of its birth. And in it he so cultivated the comic that he avoided the scurrilous; he so pursued the dramatic that he shunned the obscene; he so composed satires that he nicely ridiculed satyrs full of vices and their little grandsons full of wantonness. The blindness, vanity, and fickleness of Cupid, the harlots (allurements and banes of adolescents), parasites evilly gained, procurers evilly conditioned, the slippery ways of adolescence, the weak ways of youth, the wretched ways of age (upon which we cannot enter without peril, stand without irksomeness, or run without falling) how cleverly in that work, most illustrious Herbert, has he presented these for us, decked out and made odious! How, and with how sharp a sting, in a sort of dithyramb he has described, and censured these Demoenetuses with white hair, goatish beard, etc., etc." (*Nobilis or a View of the Life and Death of a Sidney and Lessus Lugubris*, with Introduction, Translation, and Notes by Virgil B. Heltzel and Hoyt H. Hudson [The Huntington Library, San Marino, Calif., 1940], pp. 73–74). It is difficult to understand why Moffet not only misrepresents Sidney's satiric manner but refers to incidental episodes as though they were the main theme of the *Arcadia*. The best guess would seem to be that the physician's Puritanism made him entirely unsympathetic toward the poetic merits of Sidney's work and that he was endeavoring to excuse the writing of a heroic romance by representing it as a rather bilious satire. It is instructive to reflect that if Sidney had actually written the sort of work which Moffet attributes to him he could not so easily have "avoided the scurrilous" and "shunned the obscene," and the *Arcadia* could never have become the favorite and permitted reading of many generations of carefully reared British maidens as it certainly did.

[11] Cf. Malcolm William Wallace, *The Life of Sir Philip Sidney* (Cambridge, 1915), pp. 173, 296. It should be pointed out that when Principal Wallace made his great contribution to Sidneian scholarship, Moffet's *Nobilis* with its categoric statement regarding Sir Philip's unwillingness to have anything to do with astrology had not yet been brought to light by Professor Heltzel.

company Dyer.[12] If either or both of these men asked Sidney to go to the wizard's house with them, as seems likely, his visit was no more than an act of courtesy, of courtesy not to Dee but to Leicester and Dyer.

But even if Sidney went to Mortlake to please himself rather than his friends, it is by no means certain that he went to consult Dee in his prophetic capacity.[13] The astrologer seems to have practiced at least one occult art which had nothing to do with the supernatural, the art of the political spy, and was, moreover, as Professor E. G. R. Taylor has pointed out, both a practical metallurgist and an authority on cartography and navigation.[14] An enterprising young man who was about to set out on an important embassy to Germany and who had risked some money on Frobisher's search for gold and the Northwest Passage might have wished to talk of English agents on the Continent, of the coasts of America, or of new methods of smelting, giving little thought to either planetary influences or elemental spirits.[15]

[12] Next to Fulke Greville, Dyer was probably Sidney's closest friend. On this point there seems to be little, if any, difference of opinion. He was also a friend of Mary, Countess of Pembroke, shared her interest in chemistry, and was a member of her circle at Wilton both before and after her brother's death. He stood godfather at the christening of Dee's eldest son, Arthur. Cf. Charlotte Fell Smith, *op. cit.*, p. 49.

[13] The idea that Sidney did on this occasion ask Dee to interrogate the future in his behalf has, of course, a certain romantic appeal. Professor Michel Poirier makes the most of it by beginning his very interesting book in this fashion:

"Le célèbre astrologue John Dee a consigné dans son journal la date de deux visites que lui rendit Sir Philip Sidney. On aimerait connaître les propos qu'échangea l'auteur d'un roman dont le point de départ est un oracle avec celui qui prétendait lire la destinée des hommes dans les constellations. Le gentilhomme croyait-il au pouvoir divinatoire de son hôte? Lui demanda-t-il de soulever le voile de son avenir? S'il avait pu obtenir satisfaction, quelle n'aurait pas été sa déception devant le tableau des brèves et vaines années qui lui restaient à vivre! Quel étonnement ne lui eussent pas causé la nature et la durée de sa célébrité posthume! Trois siècles et demi se sont écoulés. Cependant que l'histoire a presque oublié son nom, la critique littéraire scrute ses œuvres et interroge ses contemporains afin de préciser la nuance de sentiment qu'il éprouva pour la belle Lady Rich ou le dessein qu'il poursuivait lorsqu'il couvrait de son écriture régulière les nombreux feuillets de son *Arcadie*" (*Sir Philip Sidney, le chevalier poète elizabéthain* [Lille, 1948], p. 9).

[14] See *Tudor Geography* (London, 1930), pp. 37, 73, 75–139.

[15] It is possible, of course, that Dyer and Sidney came to Dee for a lesson in chemistry, for Moffet, in praising Sidney's scientific curiosity, says, after listing his earlier studies:

"Yet, not satisfied with the judgment and reach of common sense, with his eyes passing to and fro through all nature, he pressed into the innermost penetralia of causes; and by that token, led by God, with Dee as a teacher, and with Dyer as a companion, he learned Chemistry, that starry science, rival to nature. The variety of opinions, the tricks of the teachers, the high costs, the uncertainty of results, somewhat oppress the weakness of minds endeavoring to proceed so far, and have somewhat deterred (as well I know) me, myself. Yet so far did he have an unexhausted eagerness for complete (or

Before 1940, the view that Sidney's visits to Mortlake were prompted by motives of courtesy or by practical considerations having nothing to do with the supernatural, though supported by more evidence than could be mustered in behalf of a contrary opinion, lacked confirmation of the sort which could be supplied only by the testimony of some Elizabethan in a position to have direct knowledge regarding the matter. Professor Heltzel's discovery and publication of Thomas Moffet's *Nobilis* has provided exactly the sort of proof needed. However limited in his appreciation of poetry, and however swayed by Puritan prejudices the physician and pioneer entomologist may have been, he was admirably placed and equipped to learn about Sidney's attitude toward astrology. In the course of years of residence at or near Wilton, and frequent professional attendance upon members of Sidney's family and some of his most intimate friends, Moffet could not have failed to hear much talk of astrology; for whatever his own ideas regarding the subject were, there must have been among his patients some who, though taking pills or submitting to poultices or bleeding, kept an eye on the stars.

After a review of Sidney's literary activities in which he displays

---

rather for only the accepted) learning that he leaped over all the obstacles at one bound; nor, diverted by any baits of friends or by the tedium of the subject matter did he abandon the learning of a science so important and so pleasant. With the same alacrity be proceeded in other subjects of abstruse learning" (*Nobilis*, p. 75).

It seems strange that, if Sidney studied chemistry in the manner which Moffet's statement suggests, Dee did not make the fact known in one fashion or another. It is also a little difficult to see how Sidney could have found time and energy for very serious and sustained work in any one of the physical sciences when he had so many other irons in the fire. It is at least possible that Moffet, who obviously preferred science to literature, exaggerated his hero's chemical studies and attainments.

Perhaps the parenthetical phrase "or rather only for the accepted," in the Latin *"vel habitae,"* is intended to indicate a distinction between chemistry and alchemy, for by Moffet's references to the expense, uncertainty, and difficulty of the study one is reminded that in the days of Dee and Kelley, the Canon whose frauds were recounted by his yoeman for the delectation of the Canterbury Pilgrims would have been a small and amateurish operator indeed.

That some of the Countess of Pembroke's interest in chemistry was not motivated by love of science for its own sake is suggested by Aubrey, not a friendly gossip or an unbiased witness in matters concerning the House of Herbert, to be sure, but often offering a few grains of truth among much chaff or worse. "She was a great Chymist, and spent yearly a great deale in that study. She kept for her laborator in the house Adrien Gilbert, halfe brother to Sir Walter Ralegh, who was a great chymist in those days. . . . She also gave an honorable yearly pension to Dr. Mouffett, who hath writt a booke *De Insectis*. Also one Boston, a good chymist, a Salisbury man borne, who did undoe himselfe by studying the philosopher's stone, and she would have kept him, but he would have all the golde to himselfe, and so dyed, I thinke, in a geole" (*Scandal and Credulities of John Aubrey*, ed. John Collier [London, 1931], pp. 11–12).

scant approval of anything save certain letters, the translation of the Psalms, and the now lost translation of *Les Semaines* of Guillaume du Bartas, Moffet continues:

Having merely refreshed himself by these pursuits, Sidney devoted the greater share of his time and energy to philosophy and to the arts of observation, in which within a few years he so excelled that, having been crowned with the first and second laurels of the literati at Oxford, he both magnified and adorned the name of his ancestry. Astrology alone (which only chance and vanity have made an art)[16] he could never be so far misled as to taste, even with the tip of his tongue. Nay, he seemed purposely to slight it, among all accepted sciences, even with a certain innate loathing.[17] In fact as a young man precisely excellent and inspired with true religion, he feared lest, too receptive to the fables of soothsayers, he might in rashness diminish the Divine Majesty (always held in reverence, everywhere and always the disposer of all things) to particular modes and means.[18]

Whatever may have been the motive for the visit to Dr. Dee at Mortlake in 1577, the experience does not appear to have been of a sort which Sidney was eager to repeat, for six years passed before his name appeared again in the astrologer's diary. The second and last recorded visit Sidney made as one of the semi-official escort of "the Polonian Prince, Lord Albert Laski," who was to become the most credulous and the most generous of all Dee's patrons and dupes.[19]

---

[16] This parenthetical remark seems to indicate that Moffet took his stand squarely with Sidney in opposition to astrology. Evidently the good will toward Dee indicated by the opening lines of the quotation in note 15 above was of a strictly limited sort, directed toward the chemist but not toward the astrologer. Since, as Professors Heltzel and Hudson repeatedly point out, Moffet was an advocate of the new pharmacopoeia, he could not be indifferent to the possibility of its enrichment through the chemical and metallurgical activity of a man like Dee.

[17] Everything we know about Sidney's military and political life indicates that he was not only an energetic man but one sharply impatient regarding any delay in arriving at a decision or in carrying it out. Such a man must have found the consultation of astrologers and the postponement of action until a day when the auspices appeared favorable, a maddening waste of time. Sidney's opposition to superstition may well have been more a matter of temperament than of piety. Many writers, both early and late, seem to have slighted the practical motives behind Sidney's actions and over-emphasized the religious. This is not surprising, since it was the proper thing to do in the sixteenth and seventeenth centuries, especially among those whose religious fervor was at least partly of political inspiration; and in later times many persons, often quite unconsciously, would share the passions and prejudices of those among their predecessors for whom they felt the strongest instinctive affection and admiration.

[18] *Nobilis*, p. 75.

[19] One can not be sure that Dee consciously deceived Prince Laski, since he was probably quite as successful in deceiving himself as in deceiving others. For the relations of Dee with Laski, extending over a period of ten years, see Dee's *Diary*, pp. 19–23, 27–28, 43, 46. Charlotte Fell Smith, who gives, among other lively bits of narrative, an account of Dee's journey to Poland in Laski's service, was unwilling to believe the

On this occasion, we may be certain, Sidney did not go to Mortlake to see the Doctor but to oblige his guest.

The twenty-sixth sonnet of *Astrophel and Stella*, which contains the most favorable mention of one of the occult arts to be found in Sidney's writings, has probably done much to foster belief that its author fully shared the superstitions of his time. It runs thus:

> Though duskie wits doe scorne Astrologie,
> And fooles can thinke those lamps of purest light,
> Whose number waies greatnes eternitie.
> Promising wondrous wonders to invite,
>   To have for no cause birth-right in the skyes.
> But for to spangle the blacke weedes of Night,
> Or for some braue within that Chamber hie,
> They shold still daunce to please a gazers sight.
> For me I nature every deale doe know,
> And know great causes, great effects procure,
> And know those bodies high, raigne on the low.
> And if these rules did fall, proofe makes me sure,
>   Who oft bewraies my after following case,
>   By onely those two starres in *Stellas* face.[20]

Here Sidney's profession of faith in astrology seems more a matter of poetical expediency than of conviction. It is difficult to see how, in the sixteenth century, one could write a hundred and eight sonnets and a few miscellaneous pieces to a lady called *Stella* without being obliged to draw at least once upon astrology for a figure. The fact that Sidney found himself put to this shift but once and on that occasion made only the very slightest use of the technical jargon of the art, committing himself to nothing more specific than belief in a wise economy in the universe and a general influence of the heavenly bodies upon the earth, makes the sonnet very poor evidence to sup-

---

astrologer guilty of any intentional deception. She considers him a *seer* in the best sense of the word and concludes her book with these words:

"In all the vague hopes held out by him to Queen, Princes and Emperors, of enriching them through his alchemical skill, he was no conscious charlatan, playing a part to lure them on, but a devout believer in man's power and purpose to wrest scientific secrets from the womb of the future. Can we look back upon the discoveries of three hundred years and feel his certainty was vain?" (*op. cit.*, p. 305).

[20] *Complete Works*, ed. Albert Feuillerat (Cambridge, 1912–26), II, 253. The text of this sonnet is very uncertain, but by judicious selection from the variant readings offered by different early editions and by changes in punctuation, a number of editors have been able to construct fairly satisfactory, though not identical, versions for their respective editions of *Astrophel and Stella*. Among others those of Alfred W. Pollard (London, 1888) and Mona Wilson (London, 1931) may be cited. Here it has seemed most practical to use the text given by Feuillerat.

port an argument in favor of his credulity.[21] It is really better evidence for the other side, particularly if examined in proper relation to that found in the *Arcadia* and in the light of Moffet's categorical pronouncement.

Because of his ambitious nature and love of action Sidney had a decided preference for objective and didactic literature. For that reason he put far more of himself into the *Arcadia* than into *Astrophel and Stella*,[22] and it is in the romance rather than in the sonnet sequence that we shall find the fuller and clearer revelation of his attitude toward the occult arts. It is, accordingly, interesting to remark that though Sidney borrowed enormously from the *Æthiopica* of Heliodorus, *Le Morte Darthur* of Sir Thomas Malory, and the *Amadis of Gaul*, he made no use whatever of the enchantments and other supernatural prodigies with which these works abound. He did take over, as Samuel L. Wolff long ago pointed out,[23] the story of the oracle in the *Æthiopica* and made it the frame of his plot; but in so doing he subjected the whole practice of seeking to know the future by the aid of soothsayers, astrologers, or other diviners to the most searching and hostile criticism. In literature as in life Sidney aimed at practical results; and throughout the *Arcadia* he sought to dissuade his readers from frequentation of practitioners of the occult arts. Knowing that men may be roughly divided into two groups, the rational and the superstitious, he attempts to win over both at one stroke by arguing that the utterances of oracles, the predictions of diviners, and the horoscopes of astrologers are either pure fraud or the revelations of an inexorable destiny. If the first is true, the person who seeks to know the future is a gull; if the second is true, he busies and vexes himself to no purpose. For the rounding out of his plot, Sidney causes the predictions of the oracle of Delphi and the astrologer of the King of Phrygia to be fulfilled, but the characters who most clearly exemplify Sidney's general philosophy of life express in very forceful terms the suspicions of the skeptic.

When Philanax, the great minister of the superstitious Basilius, learns of the oracle which has caused his master to withdraw into a rustic seclusion, he writes a letter to him which begins:

Most redoubted & beloved prince, if aswel it had pleased you at your

---

[21] Principal Wallace, departing from his usual caution, does use it for this purpose. See *Life*, p. 296, n. 2.

[22] See Goldman, *op. cit.*, p. 47.

[23] *The Greek Romances in Elizabethan Prose Fiction* (New York, 1912), pp. 262–366.

going to Delphos as now, to have used my humble service, both I should in better season, and to better purpose have spoken: and you (if my speech had prevayled) should have beene at this time, as no more in danger, so much more in quietnes; I would then have said, that wisdome and vertue be the only destinies appointed to mā to follow, whēce we ought to seeke al knowledge, since they be such guydes as cannot faile; . . . I would then have said, the heavenly powers to be reverenced, and not searched into; & their mercies rather by prayers to be sought, then their hidden councels by curiositie. These kind of soothsayers (since they have left us in our selves sufficient guides) to be nothing but fansie, wherein there must be either vanitie, or infallibleness, & so, either not to be respected, or not to be prevented.[24]

Again, when Musidorus, who is one of the characters that represent Sidney's ideal of the young man, as Philanax represents his ideal of the seasoned warrior and statesman, tells Pamela the story of the prophecies concerning his own destiny, he gives evidence of a certain skepticism, even though the prophecies seem actually to have been fulfilled, and of a thoroughgoing contempt for astrologers and their clients.

Dorilaus . . . having maried his [*i.e.* Euarchus'] sister, had his mariage in short time blest . . . with a sonne, whom they named *Musidorus:* . . . scarcely was *Musidorus* made partaker of this oft-blinding light, when there were found numbers of Southsayers, who affirmed strange & incredible things should be performed by that childe; whether the heavens at that time listed to play with ignorant mankind, or that flatterie be so presumptuous, as even at times to borow the face of Divinitie. But certainly, so did the boldnes of their affirmation accompanie the greatnes of what they did affirme (even descending to particularities, what kingdomes he should overcome) that the King of *Phrygia* (who over-superstitiously thought him selfe touched in the matter) sought by force to destroy the infant, to prevent his after expectations: because a skilful man (having compared his nativity with the child) so told him.[25] Foolish mā, either vainly fearing what was not be feared, or not considering, that if it were a worke of the superiour powers, the heavens at length are never children. But so he did, & by the aid of the Kings of *Lydia* and *Crete* (joining together their armies) invaded *Thessalia.* . . .[26]

[24] *Works*, I, 24. The reasoning of Philanax, it should be noted, is exactly reproduced, though in more succinct terms, by Harington in the epigram *Of Soothsaying to the Queene of England* (page 528 above).

[25] This passage will immediately suggest to most readers the Scriptural story of Herod's interrogation of the Wise Men and slaughter of the Innocents (St. Matthew, Ch. 2). As the present writer has pointed out (*Sir Philip Sidney and the Arcadia*, pp. 206–07), it also has a closer parallel in the story of Merlin's propbecy that Arthur would be slain by a child born on May-day, found in the last chapter of the first book of *Le Morte Darthur*.

[26] *Works*, I, 188. As with other prophecies in the *Arcadia*, efforts made to prevent fulfillment of the astrologer's prediction merely hasten it.

Like almost everyone who has had contact with persons who put faith in astrologers or fortunetellers of any sort, Sidney must have observed how vague or ambiguously phrased warnings give rise to suspicions destructive of friendships and domestic peace. It may have been with such deplorable results of suspicion in mind that he devised the ironic story of Memnon.[27] In this and in several other episodes, as well as in the main plot of the *Arcadia*, the precautions taken to avoid the fate which has been foretold are quite useless, tending to bring about rather than to prevent fulfillment of the prophecy. This, of course, is not only a perennially effective device in fiction because it brings about the expected in an unexpected manner but had, during the Renaissance, the additional charm of reminding readers of such stories from Classical Antiquity as those of Croesus and of Pyrrhus.

In the *Arcadia* the credulity of the lower social orders is subjected to ridicule rather than to the serious criticism meted out to the superstitions of sovereigns and courtiers. It is by a story of a wishing tree that Musidorus gets rid of the most stupid and least experienced of Pamela's clownish guardians, "the prettie pigge," Mopsa. In the rebellion of the Arcadian commons, which Sidney treats in a manner to gratify the Elizabethan fondness for both buffoonery and bloodshed, Musidorus, "(leaving the miller to vomit his soul out in wine and bloud) with his two-hand sword strake of another quite by the waste, who the night before had dreamed he was growen a couple, and (interpreting it he should be married) had bragd of his dreame that morning among his neighbors."[28]

No man or woman, royal, noble, or simple, is able, in the *Arcadia*, to help himself in any way by the interpretation of dreams and prophecies or by having some "skilful man" draw up a horoscope, and all of the admirable characters who express an opinion protest against the folly of seeking to peer into the future. It is clear that Sidney in presenting "morall Images and Examples, (as directing threds) to guide every man through the confused *Labyrinth* of his desires, and life"[29]

---

[27] "Memnon ... had met with the same Prophet that olde *Æschylus* had, and having found many of his speeches true, beleeved this to, that he should never be killed, but by his owne companions: and therefore no man more valiant then he against an enemie, no man more suspicious of his friends: so he seemed to sleepe in securitie, when he went to a battell, and to enter into a battaile, when he began to sleepe, such guardes, he would set about his person; yet mistrusting the verie guardes that they would murther him. But now *Amphialus* helped to unriddle his doubts; for he overthrowing him from his horse, his owne companions coming with fresh supplie, pressed him to death" (*Works*, I, 389).

[28] *Works*, I, 313.

[29] See Note 2, above.

meant to lead his readers as far as possible from the consultation chambers of astrologers and diviners of every sort.[30]

II

Sir John Harington took full advantage of his special privileges as a queen's godson and celebrated wit. He spoke his mind with great freedom except when in a very tight place, or when very eager to prove a large point[31] for which he was willing to sacrifice smaller ones— on which occasions he could achieve miracles of trimming. It happens, curiously enough, that his earliest recorded pronouncement on the supernatural reveals him in the rôle of the special pleader who can do a little violence to his conscience in a good cause. In "A Brief Apologie of Poetrie, and of the Author and Translator" prefixed to his version of the *Orlando Furioso*, he was so eager to defend Ariosto against the objections of those who maintained that "nothing should be fayned vtterly incredible" that he wrote: "And sure *Ariosto* neither in his inchantments exceedeth credit (for who knowes not how strong the illusions of the deuill are?) neither in the miracles that *Altolfo* by the power of S. Iohn is fayned to do, since the Church holdeth that Prophetes both aliue and dead haue done mightie miracles."[32]

Later, on the occasions when fear of offending King James by too open a display of skepticism caused him to move warily, he always made use of this same shift which he had discovered in his youth, and referred piously to the witness of Scripture and the Fathers. It was a device which would work in a variety of ways for a variety of purposes, since display of deference for such authority provided an answer to almost any argument and protection against almost any charge. It was obviously foolish for a lover of light to get into trouble when he could quote Scripture for his purpose as easily as could the

[30] It is perhaps a minor point, yet still worth noticing, that although in his answer to Gosson and other Puritan enemies of the fine arts he drew upon the two antiquities, Hebraic and Classical, for arguments in behalf of poetry, emphasizing the poetic nature of the Psalms and the twofold meaning of the Latin *vates* (thus, in a manner, anticipating, and perhaps even influencing the claims Shelley was later to make for the poet as a sort of unrecognized Moses), Sidney is careful to denounce the superstitious use of verse. He declared that, despite stories of their accuracy, the *Sortes Vergilianae* "were a verie vaine and godlesse superstition, as also it was, to thinke spirits were commaunded by such verses, whereupon this word *Charmes*, derived of *Carmina*, commeth" (*Defence of Poesie, Works*, III, especially 6).

[31] The point might be a purely intellectual matter such as the legitimacy of Ariosto's narrative method, or a very practical and personal one such as his own suitability for appointment as Governor of the Prince of Wales or to high temporal and spiritual office in distracted Ireland.

[32] In G. Gregorie Smith's *Elizabethan Critical Essays* (Oxford, 1904), II, 216.

Prince of Darkness. Nobody could reasonably take serious issue with a skeptic who always, whatever the doubts he might express, left the last word to the Prophets and Apostles.

In a single instance, in his *Briefe notes upon the 6th booke of Virgils Æneads*,[33] a work which he wrote to instruct Prince Henry and to court the favor of his royal father, Harington appealed to the most appropriate and weighty modern authority, making "the less question" that "there be witches" because he had "credibly heard the Kings Ma^stie o^ur moste gratious Lord hath been maliciously attempted by them and even as miraculously preserved from them[34] and hath most justly sought to put them out of his Dominions"; but even here he throws the burden of proof upon Scripture and, despite declaration that a Christian must accept the story of the contest between Moses and Aaron and Pharaoh's magicians, not only fails to show real evidence of belief in the persistence of such mysterious phenomena but seems willing to suggest, so far as he can do so safely, that reputed witches do harm by natural rather than supernatural means.[35] It is

[33] The present writer deeply regrets the long delay in bringing out his promised critical edition of this work. He hopes, however, that more than five years of service in the United States Army since he first announced his discovery of what is apparently the sole surviving manuscript, and the difficulties arising from three deaths in his family will be considered by students of Harington as providing some measure of explanation and excuse.

[34] This passage echoes one in a political pamphlet that Harington wrote about a year and a half earlier, which runs as follows: " . . . my constant hope and heartie praier is, That that God that hitherto so graciouslie and (for I will not use that flattering tearme miracolouslie often usurped where there was far less reason) preserved that King [i.e. James] hitherto frome a pistoll bent at him in his mother's womb, as Sir Anthonie Standon can tell, who was present, from many mischievous practices and open attempts of seditious sectaries (least I should say Puritans), frome tempestes, from treasons, from sorceries, from so many evill men and evill Aungels, will still continue his holy protection over him, to the comforte of all honest heartes, and such in whome the feare of God hath any dwelling" (*A Tract on the Succession to the Crown (1602) by Sir John Harington, Kt., of Kelston:* Printed for the First Time from a Manuscript in the Chapter Library at York, and edited with Notes and an Introduction by Clements R. Markham, C.B., for the Roxburghe Club [London, 1880], p. 48). The date on the last page of the manuscript of *Breife notes upon the 6th booke of Virgils Æneads* is "June 19th 1604."

[35] In *Breife notes etc.*, after summarizing the scriptural evidence in support of a belief in witchcraft and alluding to the report of the danger to which King James had been exposed from practitioners of the black art, Harington observes: "The next question is what we should think of theire power & theire practices, to w^ch, for myne owne part I should answeare it were best not to think of y^m at all: but when occasion enforces to thinke of them, not rashly to beleeve all y^ts told of them, nor obstinatly to reject all y^ts objected against them, as some Judges have used to doe: for if on that steals one sheepe for want, may by lawe die except they can read, howe much more worthily should they suffer that of wicked mallice, either by poison or by any other sorcerie destroy horses and other cattall yea many times children? and yet by the lenity of the Judges too oft they escape. But concerning theire power wee are to thinke 'tis as

probable that if Harington had been born a century later he would have applauded Louis XIV's efforts to have the French courts concern themselves a bit less with sorcery and a bit more with murder.

Usually Harington did not make compromises with authority but spoke his mind. On one occasion, if we may trust his letter to the younger Sir Amias Paulett, he scarely concealed his impatience with King James' favorite studies. He says, in giving an account of a rather difficult interview:

His Majestie did much presse for my opinion touchinge the power of Satane in matter of witchcraft; and asked me, with much gravitie,—"If I did truelie understande, why the devil did worke more with anciente women than others? I did not refraine from a scurvey jeste, and even saide (notwithstandinge to whom it was said) that—'we were taught hereof in scripture, where it is tolde, that the devil walketh in dry places."

In the same letter Harington tells with evident weariness of the King's talk of second-sight and divination and reports with some pride the adroit reply he made when James warned him against the danger of an interest in books of magic.[36]

It may well have been with James in mind that Harington rewrote the epigram to Elizabeth given above, changing "Queenes" to "Kings,"[37] but it is scarely probable that he presented a copy to the learned monarch, who, after all, was not his godparent.

St. Augustin teacheth that noe power of witches can hurt a true Christian" (pp. 5–6 in the MS).

In this passage, as anyone acquainted with the history of social conditions in the sixteenth and seventeenth century will readily perceive, Sir John is presenting a sound formula for the preservation of one's mental balance and the advancement of justice. He was, in as clear and open terms as he dared employ, advising Prince Henry not to bother his head about witchcraft if he could avoid doing so, but to encourage careful examination of the possibility that in cases of alleged witchcraft, crimes had actually been committed, though by ordinary physical not supernatural means. As the late Professor George Lyman Kittredge never tired of pointing out, not all of those who were prosecuted for witchcraft were innocent of wrongdoing. There were many who would undertake to injure man or beast by magic for a consideration and earned their money by employment of means as well known to the apothecary as to the devil. Both before and after *La grande Affaire des Poisons* rocked the French Court, there were probably many little affairs in which witchcraft got the credit and some drug did the work. The careful judge needed to be on his guard against letting a criminal go free merely because he could not have committed the crime with which he was charged in the manner alleged. The phrase "either by poison or by any other sorcerie" is a real *trouvaille*. To those who shared his skepticism, it would make Harington's position quite clear, yet it would not scandalize those who shared the credulity of King James.

36 See *Nugae Antiquae*, ed. T. Park (London, 1804), I, 368–70 and *Letters and Epigrams*, pp. 109–11.

37 For the text of the rewritten verse, see *Letters and Epigrams*, p. 269.

Harington was provoked to write his *Supplie or Addicion to the Catalogue of Bishops to the Year 1608* by a rhymed prophecy,

> *Henry the* 8. pulld down abbeys and cells
> *But Henry the* 9. shall pull down Bishops and bells.

He calls the couplet "this most reasonless ryme" and declares that

... the guiddy puritan, that is most suspected of the making and meaning of it, is well pleased when he hears yt, hoping their presbitery would rise by the fall of Bishops. ... But the trew christian, that fears God and honors the King, doth neither dispise such lewd practices and preparatives to mischiefe, nor any whit deject his hart and his hope, either to beleeve or give way to them; but rather bestirrs himself the more couragiously, to discover the frawd and resist the mallice of the enemie. For this is no new practice of Sathan, nor the first of this kynde in theis latter times in which he sheweth this cunning; that mixing falshood with probabilities, and fore speaking some mischiefes he would effect, as well as foretelling some blessings he could not hinder; he getteth his disciples such credit as Agrippa atributes to astrologers,[38] who roving sometimes at some truthe, win fooles to give faith to much falsehood.[39]

This is certainly a statement which has both the patriotism and the common sense of Philanax's letter to Basilius, though it would be rash to assume that it shows any direct influence of that admirably contrived document. In the next paragraph Harington goes on to "show how stale this goodly prediction is of the rewin of Bishops, though some ill poet hath given it a new coate, the old vestiment made by Peirce Ploughman being belike worn out of fashion."[40]

After this he tells

... how Sr. Roger Manhood, a man nothing superstitious, and concerning all soothsayers and witches almost incredulous, yet out of some straunge speculation seemd to prognosticate two great matters, the one of which being

[38] This is evidently a reference to *De Vanitate et Inutilitate Scientiarum*, Chap. 31.
[39] *Nugae Antiquae*, II, 3–5.
[40] *Ibid*. It would be interesting to know what Harington thought of the reasonableness of the Puritan attempt to present the author of *Piers Plowman* as a sort of Protoprotestant. Perhaps he anticipated Jules Jusserand's view of Piers: "On le chargeait parfois de missions que Langland ne lui eut confiées. On avait de très bonne heure, chacun pour le besoin de sa cause, faussé le sens du poème. Tous les réclamants, les réformateurs, les protestataires tiraient de force le Laboureur par son manteau, ou s'en revêtaient eux-mêmes au besoin. Rien ne montre mieux que ces supercheries le renom et l'autorité des Visions" (*L'Épopée mystique de William Langland* [Paris, 1893], p. 200). Did Jusserand read Harington's remark sometime and later employ his metaphor in a somewhat different sense without realizing it? However that may be, the Elizabethan and the Frenchman of three centuries later were at one in their conviction that the manner in which Puritan polemists used Piers reflected no credit upon either their originality or their regard for truth. Yet the old garment, so well worn by Harington's time, was to be used for a good many years more.

allready falsified, makes me no less confident that the other shall prove as untrew.[41]

All of this shows clearly that Sir John was not only a penetrating observer of the various sorts of charlatans and sharpers "who roving sometimes at some truths, win fools to much falsehood," but had a very good understanding of those methods of influencing public opinion through the open or secret circulation of rumors, predictions, and easily remembered rhymes, which have been so effectively employed in our time both by great powers in what has come to be called psychological warfare and by partisan politicians eager to win elections and enjoy the spoils.

Harington endeavored to make use of rhymed predictions and old wives' tales, himself, in what he considered the best of causes, furtherance of the peaceful succession of James VI of Scotland to the English throne upon the death of Elizabeth, but "that damnable uncovered honestie," which his cousin, Robert Markham, had earlier predicted would mar his fortune,[42] made it impossible for him to pretend that he was convinced by that which he professed to think might carry conviction to others. It may be well to add that if "that damnable uncovered honestie" left anything unmarred in Harington's argument, his love of punning and other *jeux de mots* completed the work of destruction.

Yet it was, in its broad outlines, an excellent argument. There really were good reasons why Puritans, Protestants (the term by which Harington designated his fellow Anglicans but which he evidently disliked as much as some members of the Protestant Episcopal Church in the United States do today),[43] and Papists[44] should prefer the peace-

[41] *Nugae Antiquae*, II, 5–7.

[42] Quoted by C. R. Markham in his introduction to *A Tract etc.*, p. vi, and by the Rev. Mandell Creighton (later Bishop of London) in his article on Harington in the *DNB*, xxv, 388. The present writer cannot accept the view expressed by Jack Lindsay: "Despite his cousin's censure of his inopportune honesty we can wager that Harington would never go out of his way to be honest unless a very good jest or very good money was also part of the spoil" (*Metamorphosis of Aiax* [London, 1927, Introduction, p. xix). A man with so little regard for principle as Lindsay represents Harington as being would almost certainly have fared better at the Court of the first Elizabeth and the first James than Harington did. For a man in many ways so typical of the Renaissance, Sir John was a very indifferent exponent of the art of dissimulation. Bishop Creighton has remarked that Harington "certainly was not a hero to himself." This fact in itself provides the beginning of a claim to consideration as an honest man.

[43] In an eloquent personal profession of faith Harington formally rejected the designation *Protestant*, declaring "*Christian* is my name, *Catholique* is my surname" (*A Tract etc.*, pp. 108–09).

[44] Although Harington uses the term "Papist" in accordance with the general

ful, undisputed succession of James to anything else which could happen after the death of Elizabeth.

Harington's manner of beginning *A Tract on the Succession* promises well. He reviews the offer made by the Protector Somerset to the Scots when a marriage between Edward VI and Mary Stuart seemed to provide opportunity for the end of centuries of warfare through union of the two crowns, and points out that the objections made then are no longer valid. Since Somerset's proposal was closely reasoned and eloquently expressed, Sir John makes effective use of quotation and paraphrase. Unfortunately the Protector's tone of religious exhortation and emphasis upon the providential nature of the opportunity offered for the union, and upon the extraordinary, and possibly miraculous, concatenation of events which had led up to the situation in which two countries found themselves, proved a temptation to dangerous digression and lively play with two-edged words which Sir John could not resist. He must certainly have seen what his indulgence of temperament was going to do to whatever chance there may have been for him to exercise a real influence on public opinion, but he fully indulged it. Like most skeptical students of superstition, he had an excellent memory and a disposition to collect examples of the thinking and practices of which he disapproved. Also, he enjoyed paradoxes and was impressed and perhaps amused by the manner in which many persons are influenced by beliefs and practices which they are quite sure they reject.

The Duke of Somerset's readiness to discover miracles led Harington to reflect upon the ease with which one might, with the right sort of good will, discover the fulfillment of prophecies, and he carelessly permitted himself to write:

And though I knowe it is a note that Philip Commines observeth in disgrace of our nation to be fondly addicted to prophecies, and the wyser sort do for the most part scorn them, yet I fynde that they give a presage, and leave an impression in their myndes that seeme most to scorne them.

The offer is to chaunge the name of England and Scotland and call both by their old name of Brytaine.

---

usage of the time and place in which he wrote, he obviously disliked it and would have preferred to call Roman Catholics "those of the Old Religion" or to refer to them in some similarly inoffensive way. It seems to the present writer that an attentive reading of all of Harington's works should convince almost anyone that they display a spirit of tolerance very unusual among Englishmen of the late sixteenth and early seventeenth century. Sir John perceived that the religious zeal of extremists of all varieties of opinion often served very selfish and unchristian purposes. Much of the *Tract*, especially, is a plea for an end to persecutions and the beginning of mutual tolerance.

This makes me call to mynde a blynde prophesye that I heard when a child, namely

> After Hempe is sowen and growen
> Kings of England shall be none

This Hempe they understood to signify the five Princes that last reigned by the first lettres of their names, Henrie, Edward, Marie, Philip, Elizabeth. After which many, applying this fantasticke prophecie to their more fantastic humors, would have it—Some that the realm should be againe divided into a heptarchie or government of Seaven—Some, that like the Low Countries wee should be governed by States—Others feared some conquest of the King of Spaine, whereby wee should be governed by a Viceroy, as Naples, Sicily, and the Indies. Now I (for every one abounds in his own sence) imagine the likeliest and happiest way of performance of this prophecy wil be by the acceptance of this offer made so long ago by the Duke of Somerset, then Protector, and in the name of the King and Councell . . . . Lo then to you that attribute anything to such matters, a means how to performe without spoile or bloodshed this prodigious prophecy. Hempe thus gathered will imploy the fewest halters. Let England never have a King, so Britaine may be godlie and peacebly governed in a flourishing and durable Monarchie.[45]

Apparently reflecting that he had perhaps been doing more to vent his own skepticism than to advance the cause of King James, Harington started to hedge by a deferential reference to respectable and respected authority, but he could not stifle his sense of humor and love of anecdote and wrecked all at the end. The protective paragraph which does not protect reads:

Neither let any man reject as a thing to light in so important a cause that I make mention of prophecies, seeing one of the greatest and best learned prelates of this land in a sermon before the Queen at the beginning of a Parliament did ascribe so much to a prophecie of this kynde that he concluded, if it were an error, it was a learned error.[46]

One would suppose that one such flight in a work professing a most serious purpose would have been more than enough; but it was not. As he approached the end of his patriotic labor, having completed his appeal to Puritans and Anglicans and being at the point of rounding out the one addressed to Roman Catholics, Sir John remembered that these last are, at least among their religious opponents, "generallie charged to be more superstitious and credulous, and to attribute more to old prophecies and traditions of men then either Protestantes or Puritans,[47] especiallie the vulgar and unlearned sorte of them."[48]

---

[45] *Tract*, pp. 17–18.
[46] *Ibid.*, p. 18.
[47] It should be noted that Harington made war only on what would be clearly recognized as superstition by the more enlightened and reasonable members of all schools

Accordingly, he thought, or at least pretended to think, it appropriate to meet them generously on their own ground, and continued his discourse in this fashion:

> Now because in this matter I now handle I would be as St. Paul saith of himself in his Maister's cause, *Omnibus omnia sum ut omnes facerem salvos:* I became all to all, that I might save all, I will take on me in this one matter to be as credulous as the meanest. And here I present them with two prophecyes in a language that I understand not. . . . And I presume to translate it out of Welshe into Englishe, though I have been formerly tolde by one of that countrie, and I fynde it now to be true, that their language hath so peculiar a phrase by it selfe that *Her wilbe hard to make speak good English.*[49]

He then gives the main elements of the first prophecy in English, the original Welsh text, and finally his "English paraphrass to expound it as well as translate it," beginning:

> "Though plaine my muse, and never superstitious,
> In judgement cleer neglecte and not regardes,
> Most prophecies of those old Brittish Bardes

---

of religious thought. He did not share the disposition of Protestants in general and Puritans in particular to denounce either pious opinions or serious doctrines of the Roman Church as "mere superstition." Although he condemns, in a long chapter entitled "Of Hell & the state of the damned" in *Breife notes upon the 6ᵗʰ booke of Virgils Æneads*, abuses arising in relation to pardons and indulgences, he shows considerable sympathy for the doctrine of Purgatory. Also, he displays a decided fondness for the traditional conception of Christ's Harrowing of Hell, so popular in mediaeval literature and art. Perhaps his most significant and typical pronouncement on such matters is to be found—of all places!—in *The Metamorphosis of Aiax*, p. *66:* " . . . it is written by Authours, of some credite that [Trajan's] soule was delivered out of hell, at the prayer of great S. Gregorie, which though I am not bound to belueeue, yet as in loue, I had rather loue too manie then too fewe, so in charitie, I had rather beleeue too much then too little. As for that scripture *ex inferno nulla redemptio*, I haue heard it oft elledged by great Clarkes, but I think it is in the Epistle of S. Paul to the Laodiceans, or in Nicodemus Gospel, for I never yet could find it in the Bible." In a careful reading of his works it is difficult to avoid the conclusion that among the many things which made Harington dislike the Puritans their disposition to limit the mercy of God very sharply was not the least.

[48] *Tract*, p. 120.

[49] *Tract*, p. 120. When one compares Sir John's reckless manner with the tact and persuasiveness so often shown by St. Paul, one wonders how it was possible to hope that the *Tract* could have any useful effect on public opinion. It must be remembered, however, that the manuscript edited by Markham was not intended for a printer but for the private perusal of the author's intimate friend, Tobie Mathew, Archbishop of York. At the time of the writing, December 1602, publication was, as Harington well knew and frankly stated, not to be thought of, since Elizabeth was entirely averse to any discussion of the succession; but he obviously had in mind that after her death something might be done with it. Under the circumstances he doubtless felt free to indulge his sportive bent, leaving revision in the interest of practical purposes for another time. Since the manner of James' succession removed all occasion for argument in its favor, the *Tract* lost its *raison d'être*, and Sir John may have almost forgotten about it in his preoccupation with winning the King's attention and approval by literary efforts more

> That have been found, some false and some pernicious,
> Where errors meet mishappes their due rewardes.
> Yet far wee be from being so malicious,
> Where no just cause appeares to be suspitious,
> There to condemne, as doome of doting dizards,
> The safe old sawes of thier approved wizards;
> But rather here we'll shew ourselves officious
> To take from truthe their long mistaken vizardes.
> For earst in Wales this prophecie was found:
> A King of Brittish blood in Cradell crownd,
> With Lyon markt, shall join all Brutus ground,
> Restore the Crosse, and make this isle renown'd."[50]

After interpreting this to mean that James of Scotland is to rule all Britain for its good and for the advancement of true Christianity, Harington enters upon a peroration (not easily to be matched except in the more exuberant rhetorical flights of Thomas Nashe), in which respect for the vocabulary of religion is drowned by a ninth wave of punning:

> This is a gentle and easie exposicion, and will I am sure please the Papistes well: but prophecies ar ambiguous, and therefore I must give them a *Caveat*, that, if they shall by sedicious pampletes or by French or Spanish practices offer to crosse the King of Scots succession, he may *Restore them* so bitter a crosse as may make all his wellwillers crye *Crucifige* upon them, and so punish them as they shall have few crosses left in their purses.[51]

Whether or not it was wise to support the claims of a sovereign so credulous as James in regard to the occult sciences by casual and even hilarious though favorable exegesis of prophecies current among the people, expressions of skepticism regarding the power of witches could not be expected to recommend a courtier to the royal favor. Only "that damnable uncovered honestie" of which Robert Markham

---

closely adjusted to the developing situation—the *Briefe notes* and the *Short View of the State of Ireland* for example.

[50] *Tract*, p. 121.

[51] *Tract*, p. 122. Earlier in the *Tract* Harington had expressed his suspicion that "the nimble Ambassador of France" at the Court of Elizabeth I was involved in some intrigue which might be prejudicial to the claims of the Scottish King to the Succession. He had also at considerable length warned Roman Catholics against the folly of undertaking to put forward the Infanta Isabella as a candidate. It is possible, then, that he had conceived the idea that the old prophecies current among the folk might be employed by the opponents of James, and that he hoped by providing his own interpretation, after a frolicsome and rather contemptuous discussion of popular superstition in such matters, to render them useless for such a purpose. The direct warning against recourse to "sedicious pampletes" and "French or Spanish practices" would seem to give support to such a view. Harington evidently considered the Roman Catholics more powerful in Wales than in England itself, and he may have given special attention to Welsh prophecies for that reason.

complained can explain why Sir John, in speaking of his diocesan and great friend, John Still, Bishop of Bath and Wells, in the *Addicion to the Catalogue of Bishops,* found it desirable to remark:

... in one question this bishop, whom I count an oracle for learning, would never yet give me satisfaction, and that was, when I askt him his opinion of witches. He saith, "he knowes other mens opinions, both old and new wryters but could never so digest them, to make them an opinion of his own." All I can get is this, "that the devill is the old serpent, our enemy, that we pray to be deliverd from dailie; as willing to have us thinke he can do too much, as to have us perswaded he doth nothing."[52]

We may safely assume that Harington was pleased by the bishop's answer and hoped that Prince Henry would be influenced by it. If the devil "is as willing to have us thinke he can do too much, as to have us perswaded he doth nothing," he may not be behind his supposed agents after all. A monarch with this point of view would scarcely be either a client or a killer of diviners. He might even become the philosopher-king of the Platonic dream whom some had hoped to find in James and whom, like many others, Sir John, disappointed but not discouraged, believed could still be expected in the person of the thoughtful and attractive youth who, for a few brief years, seemed destined to the succession.

One might continue, if it seemed necessary, to quote passages from his writings which tend to show that Harington, though orthodox enough on the subject of God and Satan, was decidedly skeptical regarding the occult arts, whether black or white, distrusted modern prophecies, and was not greatly impressed by such modern miracles as were brought to his attention.[53] Even for discussion of the signs and wonders which are to attend the Last Day, always a pious sport among English-speaking peoples and particularly cultivated in the days of Elizabeth and James, he seems to have had little taste or aptitude. Though he evidently began his *Discowrse Shewing that Elyas Must Personally Come before the Day of Judgment* before he published the *Metamorphosis of Aiax,* he was never able to finish it.

Harington was almost the only Englishman of his time who had any real love for or understanding of the Irish; but even Ireland could not make him superstitious. While with Essex, he expressed his contempt for those who allowed "the idle faith which possessed the Irishry, concerning magic and witchcraft" to seize them and make

---

[52] *Nugae Antiquae,* II, 164–65.

[53] Harington did not, however, hold with those who maintained that all miracles ceased with the Apostles. He had a high regard for the Fathers and was respectful of pious opinions founded upon patristic tradition. In relation to this matter see Note 47, above.

them lose the victory,[54] and when, some six years later, he made the astonishing proposal that he be named at one stroke Archbishop of Dublin and Lord High Chancellor of Ireland—though he was still a layman and had no great experience in administration either temporal or spiritual—he put forward as one of his qualifications his ability to deal with Irish superstitions, boasting:

> Now for theyr visyons at Saint Patryk's Purgatory confyrmed by some, and theyr miracle of the water running backe 24 howrs at Athlone testyfyed by many, I discovered the naturall cawses of both. I confuted the Earl of Teroans preests in an argument before him, and made him say all was not so clear as they made it.[55]

It may be a mistake to bring this story forward in evidence. Even some of the most superstitious Englishmen scorn the superstitions of the Irish, but Harington's willingness to enter into discussion with the Hibernians and his ability to convince them are novelties. By his conduct on this and other occasions while a member of the ill-fated expedition led by Robert, Earl of Essex, Sir John showed himself superior to the greatest superstition of his own nation, the belief that the Irish were but beasts. Here for once he was superior to his master Sidney.

Perhaps it is a bit disappointing not to find any passage in which Harington specifically cites Sidney in vindication of his own skepticism regarding popular superstitions, particularly since there are so many passages in the *Arcadia* which might have been quoted or referred to for that purpose. What makes the omission the more surprising is that Sir John was accustomed to justify almost anything he did, or wanted to do, by appeal to Sidney's authority or example. He defended Ariosto's use of the tale within a tale by the simple declaration: "If S.Philip Sidney had countd this a fault, he would not haue done so Himselfe in his *Arcadia*."[56] In urging that a writer should not be criticized for occasionally employing a substantive as an adjective, he remarks: "Also the incomparable Poet of our age, to give a most artificiall reproofe of following the letter too much, cōmits the same fault of purpose.

> *You that do Dixionarie method bring,*
> *Into your rymes, running in ratling rowes.*"[57]

Then, to be quite sure that there is no mistake regarding the identity

---

[54] *Nugae Antiquae*, I, 267.
[55] *A Short View of the State of Ireland, Written in 1605 by Sir John Harington, Knt.*, ed. W. Dunn Macray, *Anecdota Bodleiana* (1879), I, 17–18.
[56] In "A Brief Apologie of Poetrie," ed. G. G. Smith, *op. cit.*, II, 217.
[57] *Metamorphosis of Aiax*, p. 120.

of "the incomparable Poet," he adds the marginal gloss, "Sir P. Sid."

He anticipated possible objection to his archiepiscopal and governmental ambitions by another remark of the same sort:

As for the name of a poet (of which I wold I wear worthy) I know not why that shold not bee a step rather than a stop to any preferment of learninge: for neyther did Sir Philip Sydney's poetry hinder him from being a great soldyer and wyse statesman, nor Dr. Eeds pleasant vayn in that kynde hinder him from being an excellent preacher and good Church-man.[58]

In praising the personality and talents of Sir Robert Stapleton, Harington says that he "in those dayes, for a man well spoken, properlie seen in languages, a comlie and goodly personage, had scant an equall and (except Sir Philip Sidney) no superior in England."[59]

But the most striking of all the evidences of devotion is found in an epigram in which Harington contrasts—a little ruefully, perhaps, but without any shadow of envy—the splendor of Sidney's reputation with the uncertainty of his own. The first five lines at least have the true lyric note of the Elizabethan age and suggest that Sir John was perhaps potentially a greater poet than his restless wit and incorrigible levity ever permitted him to become.

Of Sir Philip Sydney

If that be true the latten Prouerbe sayes
Laudari a laudatis is most praise;
Sydney, thy works in *Fames* books are enrold,
By Princes pennes, that haue thy works extold,
Whereby thy name shall dure to endlesse dayes.
But now, if rules of contrary should hold,
Then I, poore I, were drownd in deepe dispraise,
    Whose works base Writers haue so much debased,
    That *Lynus* dares pronounce them all defaced.[60]

From the beginning to the end of his career as a writer Harington spoke of Sidney as deserving of admiration and imitation in all things. It is therefore not unreasonable to suppose that his skepticism in regard to astrology, prophecies, witchcraft, and similar matters owed much to Sidney's, if it were not actually born of Sidney's influence. In any event, however inferior Harington may have been to Sidney in other respects, he deserves to be considered his equal as an enemy of superstition in an age when even the learned and the great were often childishly credulous.

MARCUS SELDEN GOLDMAN

[58] *A Short View of the State of Ireland*, p. 20.
[59] *Nugae Antiquae*, II, 235.
[60] *Letters and Epigrams*, p. 235.

HAWTHORNE'S "LADY ELEANORE'S MANTLE" AS HISTORY

HAWTHORNE'S "Lady Eleanore's Mantle" has customarily been accepted as one of the author's rather straightforward homilies on the sin of pride.[1] Two aspects of the tale, however, have been overlooked by the commentators. Although the primary emphasis is, to be sure, on the ruinous ramifications of pride as a Christian transgression, the tale can be read, or rather ought to be read, as an historical commentary on pre-Revolutionary America as well. Moreover, and this is even more crucial, critics have ignored the presence in the tale of an unmistakable counterstatement, in the form of the crazed Jervase Helwyse and the populace in general, by means of which a fairly pedestrian apologue is transformed into a drama of human weakness and fallability, and an unmodified tribute to pre-Revolutionary America is changed into a qualified statement about that historical epoch.

It seems clear to me that Hawthorne is deliberately attempting to root his treatment of the sin of pride in a readily definable historical context. First of all, "Lady Eleanore's Mantle" is part of the *Legends of the Province House*, a group of four tales which, from various points of view, illustrates the courage (and, as will be seen, at least in this tale, the guilt) of colonial America in its pre-Revolutionary struggle with the evils of monarchial persecution. Moreover, by setting the action in the year 1722, Hawthorne is choosing a crucial year in that struggle. Although Hawthorne says only that the action occurred "nearly a hundred and twenty years ago," his use of the smallpox epidemic sets the date as 1722, for in that year, as Hawthorne knew from his reading of Thomas Hutchinson's *History of Massachusetts*,[2] Massachusetts Bay suffered a terrible epidemic in which nearly six thousand people were struck by the "dread disease."[3] By setting his action during the tenure of Governor Shute, a period marked by severe conflict, which in 1722 reached almost rebellious proportions, Hawthorne underscores the historical tensions which lie behind the action. If it is true that the casual reader would be unaware of this

[1] Newton Arvin, *Hawthorne* (Boston, 1929), p. 64. Randall Stewart, *Nathaniel Hawthorne* (New Haven, 1948), p. 255. Mark Van Doren, *Hawthorne* (New York, 1949), p. 84.

[2] Hawthorne withdrew Hutchinson's *History of Massachusetts* from the Salem Athenaeum in 1826 and again in 1829 (Marion Kesselring, *Hawthorne's Reading: 1828–1850* [New York, 1949], p. 53).

[3] Thomas Hutchinson, *The History of the Colony and Province of Massachusetts Bay*, ed. Lawrence Shaw Mayo (Cambridge, Mass., 1936), II, 205–206.

historical context, it is also true that these historical facts are both an indication of Hawthorne's historical integrity and a key to his intentions in the tale.

What effect does this historicity have on our interpretation of the tale? Briefly it is this: by defining the historical context, pride takes the form of a monarchial (or aristocratic) violation of the equalitarian principles and rights of a democracy-to-be—a method of which the very liberal John O'Sullivan, in whose *Democratic Review* the *Province House* group first appeared, would have wholeheartedly approved. Mr. O'Sullivan, for whom democracy *was* Christianity,[4] would not, however, have approved the subtle counterstatement, had he been able to discern it.

The historical context is by no means kept solely in the background. By means of significant details, Hawthorne insists upon our recognizing the historical implications of Lady Eleanore's incredible pride. Eleanore, we are told, at the very outset, is a "lady of rank and fortune," and her pride is a monomaniacal consciousness "of her hereditary and personal advantages." Related to the royal governor, she comes to "the primitive society of New England" not with any positive sympathy for, or interest in, the New World, but rather to escape from the corruptions (of which she, ironically, is the most deadly carrier) of the Old. Her entrance into the humble domain of Massachusetts Bay is the very epitome of aristocratic arrogance: "Lady Eleanore was conveyed to Boston in the Governor's coach. . . . The ponderous equipage, with its four black horses [was] surrounded by the prancing steeds of half a dozen cavaliers, with swords dangling to their stirrups and pistols at their holsters." The horrifying intensity of the woman's preoccupation with her aristocratic position is pointed up in a scene reminiscent of the purple carpet episode in *Agamemnon*, in which Clytemnestra goads her husband into a symbolic display of *hubris*. As the lady is about to alight from her carriage, a wild-looking young man (Jervase Helwyse, "a youth of no birth or fortune," who had fallen in love with Eleanore when he was secretary to the colonial agent in London) prostrates his body for the woman to walk upon. For a moment she hesitates, not because of an insight into the intrinsic horror of the act, as Agamemnon had, but "as if doubting whether the young man were worthy of the weight of her footstep." Finally she does: with one foot on the cowering form, she imperiously

---

[4] See O'Sullivan's impassioned introduction to the first volume of the *Democratic Review* (October, 1837), pp. 1-15.

extends her hand to the royal governor. The tableau, as Hawthorne makes clear, defines the peculiarly historical nature of the spiritual sin: " . . . never, surely, was there an apter emblem of aristocracy and hereditary pride trampling on human sympathies and the kindred of nature, than these two figures presented at that moment."

Hawthorne, however, does not allow the scene to remain thematically unqualified. Although the obvious emphasis is on the horror of Eleanore's daring "to place herself above the sympathies of our common nature," there is, as well, an unmistakable intimation that pride on the human level is not, as it is in the higher Christian scheme, a wholly despicable thing; or, translating the action into historical terms, Britain's aristocratic excesses were only possible because of some fundamental shortcoming in the colonials who were being persecuted. First of all, Helwyse's self-imposed degradation, although implicitly condemnatory, has something reverential about it as well— a duality which Eleanore recognizes when she says, "When men seek only to be trampled upon, it were a pity to deny them a favor so easily granted—and so well deserved!" But even more telling is the reaction of the townspeople, that very "common nature" whose democratic integrity Eleanore is symbolically violating. Instead of being repelled by the loathsome act—as are the townspeople in the more mechanically democratic "Gray Champion"—they break out into "a simultaneous acclamation of applause," because "so essential did pride seem to the existence of such a creature." It seems to me to be no accident that the narrator of the tale, a Mr. Tiffany, is "one of that small, and now all but extinguished, class, whose attachment to royalty, and to the colonial institutions that were connected with it, had never yielded to the democratic heresies of after times." For by means of a point of view which is honest but essentially hostile to the colonials, Hawthorne is able to achieve that kind of objectivity which enables him to condemn the monarchial persecutions without having to deny the psychological and political inadequacies upon which the monarchial persecutions thrived.

The second scene, a ball given in Lady Eleanore's honor, carries the historical point and counterpoint even further, objectifying it, so to speak, in an ironically religious ritual. Although the extravaganza has been given for her, Eleanore stands aloof, viewing the festivities as nothing more than "a provincial mockery of a court festival," a vulgar display of common (or democratic) humanity playing at the sacrosanct rites of aristocratic England. By surrounding herself with a select group of appropriate consorts—an English captain, a royalist plantation owner, a Church of England priest whose grandfather was an earl, and Governor Shute's secretary—she is symbolically insulating herself from the "artisans and laboring classes" of what was later to become the essential America. This insulation, however, is suddenly disturbed by the emergence of Helwyse, who asks her to drink from a sacramental cup brimming with consecrated wine and then to pass it amongst the guests as "a symbol that you have not sought to withdraw yourself from the chain of human sympathies . . . " That is, Helwyse pleads with her to submerge her divine right of kings attitude (the episcopal chalice) in the democratic power of the people (by passing the cup amongst the "mob of guests"). But even as Helwyse (Hell-knowing?) offers her (and the monarchial attitude which she represents) the symbolic means of resurrecting herself from the spiritual death (and historical disaster) to which her pride must inevitably bring her, his ambivalent role as judge and victim is pointed up: "He bore his salver in his hand . . . which he offered as reverentially as to a crowned queen, or rather with the awful devotion of a priest doing sacrifice to his idol." There is unmistakable irony in the fact that Helwyse's plea for democratic humility is described in terms of the monarchy and of the church which sustains it. But the lady only laughs scornfully, drawing her mantle—the symbol of her aristocratic deadliness—more closely about her, "so as almost to shroud herself within it." When one of the royalist coterie jostles the wine from Helwyse's hand, the distracted young man makes his final plea: he begs her to cast the "accursed" mantle into the flames. But the lady rejects the offer of baptism by fire, and so seals her destiny.

The final scene, which revolves around the smallpox epidemic which has been traced back to Eleanore's mantle, is a prophetic forecast of what was to occur historically some fifty years later. The plague —the physical objectification of the spiritual arrogance of the Empire which ultimately destroyed itself—first strikes down the aristocracy, appropriately choosing for its first victims the four men who had surrounded Eleanore at the ball. Soon, however, it filters down to the common people as well, compelling "rich and poor to feel themselves brethren." Each sufferer laid low by the plague is the victim of the poison with which Eleanore filled her being, and which, ironically, fascinated the adoring crowds. In a real sense the "scourge and horror," and what it signifies allegorically, is not only the objectification of the ravages of aristocratic pride, but of the admiring toleration of it by those who suffered most from it as well. The people still applaud the Lady Eleanore, but now it is with grim irony. At the sign of a new victim, "they clapped their hands and shouted through the streets in bitter mockery: 'Behold a new triumph for the Lady Eleanore!'" But the "triumph" is theirs too. Still more paradoxical is the figure of Helwyse, who, even yet, is unable to rid himself of what Conrad later was to call "the fascination of the abomination." Rushing to the governor's mansion, he shrieks, "Let me behold her, in her awful beauty, clad in the regal garments of the pestilence! She and Death sit on the throne together. Let me kneel down before them!" Imagining that his "Queen" sits in her chamber with "her beauty heightened into superhuman splendor" by the destruction she has caused, he slips "reverentially" into her chamber, only to find a heap of diseased mortality. Trying to hide her blasted face, Eleanore pronounces her own damnation: "I wrapped myself in PRIDE as in a MANTLE . . . Nature is avenged." Snatching the fatal garment, Helwyse rushes from the mansion. That night a woman's figure is burned in effigy (as the figure of George III was later to be so frequently burned), and the plague ceases.

It was not until the 1850's and after that Hawthorne came to a rather uncritical acceptance of the extremely equalitarian and liberal principles of what was called the Young America movement. In 1838 he was still able to see what Professor Pearce has aptly described as "the guilt and righteousness" of our history.[5] As I have tried to indicate, "Lady Eleanore's Mantle" grew out of just such an awareness of the good and evil in man's history, both morally and politically. Although Hawthorne knew that pride was the death of the spirit, and that aristocratic monarchy was the manifestation of pride historically, his fundamentally democratic sensibilities did not blind him to the fact that the submissive "common nature" often tends to idolize what is destroying it—that, as he once jotted into his notebook, "Selfishness is one of the qualities apt to inspire love."[6] Although Helwyse represents the sacred humility of the democratic spirit, he also represents, paradoxically, the desire of that spirit to abase itself to aristocratic pride.

---

[5] Roy Harvey Pearce, "Hawthorne and the Sense of the Past, or the Immortality of Major Molineux," *A Journal of English Literary History*, XXI (December, 1954), 334.

[6] *The Complete Works of Nathaniel Hawthorne* (Boston, 1883), IX, 212.

Dr. Clarke, the tale's raissoneur, who is, significantly, described as a "famous champion of the popular party," and whose widsom is "a deep sense of human weakness," asks Helwyse rhetorically, "Wilt thou still worship the destroyer and surround her image with fantasies the more magnificent, the more evil she has wrought?" Only when pride has become a lump of diseased flesh can Helwyse burn the image of the Lady Eleanore from his mind; only when the streets are over-flowing with the bodies of the heaped-up dead does the populace's admiring acclamation turn to grim rejection. As Hawthorne says through his raissoneur, "Thus man doth ever to his tyrants." The history of the human race will bear him out.

SEYMOUR L. GROSS

THE NEW DRAMA OF THE SIXTEENTH CENTURY

IN BOTH the secular and sacred drama of the sixteenth century the term "new" often appeared on title pages and in prefaces and prologues. In comedy, the term certainly owed something to the New Comedy of Menander that was known to all educated men in the Latin imitations by Plautus and Terence. Donatus, for example, had recommended this *comoedia nova* of Menander and Terence as superior to the Old Comedy (*comoedia vetus*) of Aristophanes.[1] J. C. Scaliger, in his *Poetices*, 1.7, also recommended the *nova comoedia* as "stricter in its established laws for both plot and diction, and the new dramas are not so ridiculous that they find laughter in any kind of matter." Consequently many Renaissance playwrights thought of their comedies as new because they were imitations of Plautus and Terence and so better than the broader Aristophanic type. These comedies were also new because they were different from and presumably better than the medieval mysteries, farces, and moralities. The term was often extended to characterize new tragedy and, during the second half of the century, new tragicomedy as well. Thus that large and influential school drama made up of Latin plays, the Christian Terence, contained not only *comoediae novae et sacrae* but also *tragoediae novae et sacrae* and at least one *sacra et nova tragicomoedia*.[2] In the secular drama, there were many Italian *tragedie nuove*, and while neither the French nor English dramatists used the term "new" very often,[3] it was clearly understood in both France and England that the more sophisticated plays which were more or less patterned after ancient models were establishing a new fashion. Etienne Jodelle, whose *Cléopâtre captive* (1552) was the first "regular" French tragedy, remarked that his comedy *Eugène* (1552) was indebted neither to "an old Menander" nor to native farces and moralities.

Lintilhac has maintained that French comedy came of age with Corneille's *Mélite* (1629), when it was "freed from the tyranny of Italian models and disengaged from the [medieval] anarchy of genres."[4] A similar statement may be applied to Italian comedy of the

---

[1] See *De tragoedia et comoedia*.

[2] The *Baptistes* of Cornelius Schonaeus.

[3] At least one prominent French comedy was called new on the title page, namely Odet de Turnèbe's *Les Contens, comédie nouvelle en prose françoise* (1584). In England, William Gager published two Latin *tragoediae novae* at Oxford in 1592, *Meleager* and *Ulysses Redux*.

[4] *Histoire générale du théâtre en France* (Paris, 1904-10), II, 5.

sixteenth century, which became a truly new comedy when it freed itself from the tyranny of Roman comedy and its writers felt free to use modern arguments and prose as well as verse. Medieval drama exerted little or no influence upon the learned comedy (*commedia erudita*) of Ariosto and his followers. In England, to be sure, there was a somewhat different development, for there the medieval "anarchy of genres" continued to operate upon most playwrights throughout the sixteenth and, to a lesser extent, seventeenth centuries, although the English made good use of both ancient and Italian models.

Sixteenth-century drama was "new" because it was different from medieval drama in its use of classical patterns. It was also different from the ancient drama because it altered these classical patterns somewhat, adapting them to modern times, sometimes retaining some of the freer practices of the Middle Ages.

The *tragedie nuove* and the *commedie erudite* of Italy never strayed far from the Roman track, the practice of Seneca, Plautus, and Terence, and the theory of Horace, Donatus, and, later in the century, Aristotle. Nevertheless, certain changes were made that modified both ancient practice and theory. Thus Angelo Ingegneri, whose *Della poesia rappresentativa* appeared in 1598, could assert that the record of the ancients was not beyond equalling or even surpassing, that Terence, Plautus, Seneca, Aeschylus, Euripides, and even Sophocles, whom Aristotle praised so highly, did not know everything nor perfect every grace of the drama, leaving nothing for the modern poets to originate. "Various ages," he remarked, "carry with them their various customs, and manners change with the change of persons, and with the kinds of princes and governments. . . . Tragedy and comedy, according to Aristotle himself, take on not only additions but also changes in different times."[5]

There were many declarations of independence before 1598, and from both secular and sacred dramatists. Usually these dramatists tried to reconcile their changes with ancient theory and practice. Few men, for example, ventured to reject the Horatian dictum that the function of the poet was to teach as well as to delight, but many sixteenth-century writers believed that modern life required newer methods of teaching. Giraldi Cinthio always supported the didactic function of drama, but maintained that the fictitious plots of his new tragedies and their happy endings were better calculated to reward virtue and punish vice than were the historical arguments and un-

---

[5] Ingegneri's essay as reprinted in Guarini's *Opere* (Verona, 1737–38), III, 481.

happy endings of Seneca and Sophocles. The authors of the Christian Terence, most of whom were clergymen and schoolteachers, insisted that they had improved upon the teaching of Plautus and Terence, for they had rejected the allurements of Venus to be found in Roman comedy and moreover had avoided the bawdry and scurrility that attended such matters. One author, Andreas Diether, in the epilogue of his *Joseph* (1544), went so far as to boast that his play was so moral and so modestly presented that it never moved laughter. Such a position was extreme, however, and the leading authors of plays about the prodigal son, a favorite subject, found that they could not altogether dispense with lovers, courtesans, pimps, and parasites.

There were many declarations in the Christian Terence of this moral and religious reform of the ancient pagan drama. One of the clearest statements appeared in the prologue of the *Triumphus Christi* by Cornelius Schonaeus:

> Our age requires another life, other manners; not indeed plays that delight only or that insinuate the charms of sensual pleasure in the audience; but rather plays that teach and that make you better by means of wholesome admonitions and precepts.

Some years before Schonaeus, who flourished in the last quarter of the century, Johannes Sapidus (Johann Witz), a learned German poet, author of a "new and sacred comedy" *Lazarus Redivivus* (1539), complacently announced that he had improved upon his Roman models:

> But we were not able nor did we wish to follow the art and custom that antiquity observed; for in our age, and from early times, there is another fashion, order, and arrangement of experience, another way of life, another worship of God, another mutual communication among men, not only in public but in domestic life. Wherefore a work must be written according to another method.

In the secular drama, tragic poets like Cinthio, while ready to introduce certain changes, were anxious to keep the peace with classical theory and practice. The early authors of the learned Italian comedy also subscribed to classical methods, although Ariosto did say that modern comedy was necessarily somewhat different from the ancient.[6] Machiavelli paid tribute to the traditionally didactic function of comedy in the prologue to his *Clizia* (1506), an adaptation of Plautus' *Casina*, and even his masterpiece, *Mandragola* (c. 1523), for all its intimate revelation of Florentine life in realistic prose dialogue, fol-

---

[6] See his prologues to *I Suppositi* and *La Lena*.

lowed the Roman pattern. All of its principal characters, for example, save the incomparable Madonna Lucrezia, were descendants of Roman types: "A wretched lover, a stupid learned man, a dissolute friar, a crafty parasite will be your diversion today."[7]

Followers of Ariosto and Machiavelli, although they also made use of Plautus and Terence, sometimes openly rebelled at the classical yoke. Aretino, who often derided venerable institutions and authority, said in the prologue of his *Cortigiana* (1534): "Do not wonder if the comic style is not observed as it used to be, for we in [modern] Rome live in another manner than that of Athens." This remarkable play certainly departed in several ways from the ancient manner. Lodovico Dolce was more moderate than Aretino; his attitude, in fact, was like that of the English Ben Jonson. Dolce wished to improve Italian comedy and believed that many of these improvements could come from the ancients. In the prologue to his *Ruffiano* (1550), which was based on the *Rudens* of Plautus and therefore a "comedy dressed in the ancient habit and redesigned in modern form," he proclaimed: "Old things are better than new if, however, they have not become stale from too much age." His *Ragazzo* (1541), according to the prologue, was "new, neither stolen from the ancients nor founded upon a device of the moderns." The term "new" must be somewhat qualified in this instance, for the plot, which features the substitution of a boy for a young woman in order to hoodwink an old lover, points straight to Plautus' *Casina* or to Machiavelli's *Clizia*. Many details in the play were certainly new. While Dolce admired and imitated Plautus and Terence, he did not consider either of them truly inventive since they copied the Greeks, and he did not consider Roman models indispensable: "Do not believe, therefore, that it is impossible to make new comedies without drawing upon the ancients."[8] Furthermore, he rebelled against any inflexible application of ancient theory to the new comedy: "Nor should comedies be weighed with the balances of the rigorous and tiresome Aristotle, as do some petty philosophers today."[9]

Two Florentine comic dramatists, Anton Francesco Grazzini and Giovanni Maria Cecchi, went further in their protests against the tyranny of the ancients than did Dolce, further even than did Aretino, although their rather conservative practice, at least in the

---

[7] From the prologue, which is in verse.
[8] Prologue to *Fabritia* (1549).
[9] *Ibid.*

commedia erudita,[10] did not always square with their rebellious theory. Cecchi wrote many imitations of Plautus, as he admitted, but in the prologue to his masterpiece, *L'Assiuolo* (1550), he disclaimed the hackneyed arguments of Roman comedy. This "new" comedy, he said, was not drawn from Terence or Plautus:

> Let no one believe that this comedy begins with the sack of Rome or the siege of Florence or with the scattering of characters or the break-up of families or other accidents that end in marriages, as many comedies are wont to; nor will you hear any one in this our comedy grieving over boys or girls that have been stolen (because, as I said, no one here has lost any), nor giving wives or marrying anybody.

Grazzini also gibed at the ancient arguments and at the modern imitations with their inevitable discoveries of lost children:

> And worse yet are those that join the old with the new, the ancient with the modern, and create a hodgepodge, a mixture that has neither order nor method, neither head nor tail, and while making the scene a modern city and representing present times, introduce there ancient customs of the past, old and outmoded manners; and they then excuse themselves by saying that thus Plautus did and thus did Terence and Menander, not perceiving that one does not live in Florence, in Pisa, in Lucca as did the ancients in Rome and Athens.[11]

Grazzini even went so far as to renounce the almost inviolate prescription of didacticism. In an induction to *La Strega* he introduced two speakers: Prologo, who represents the traditional point of view, and Argomento, who seems to represent the author's. Part of this induction is worth quoting at some length since it not only represents the modern rebel but also offers a parallel—was it a source as well? —to Ben Jonson's induction to *Every Man Out of His Humor*. Of course Jonson did not agree with Grazzini's repudiation of the didactic function of comedy.

Prol. It will not observe decorum, art, and the comic precepts?

Arg. How do I know? It will be altogether joyful and merry.

Prol. Not enough. Don't you know that comedies are the images of truth, the example of customs, and the mirror of life?

Arg. You are an ancient and scorn the Italian. Today one does not go to see comedies performed in order to learn how to live, but for pleasure, for sport, for delight, to relieve oneself of melancholy, and to cheer oneself.

Prol. Could not one call on the clowns?

---

[10] Grazzini also wrote farces, and Cecchi used a variety of forms, including religious drama.

[11] First prologue to *La Gelosia* (1551).

Arg. Joyful and merry comedies would please more than do your wise and severe ones.

Prol. The poet ought to introduce good manners, to achieve seriousness, and to instruct by means of his main subject, as art demands.

Arg. Art or not art? Who is not weary of this art? The true art is to please and to delight.

Prol. Should there not be profit?

Arg. It is enough to please and to delight, but have I not said that comedies of today no more have such a purpose? Whoever wishes to teach a mannerly or Christian life does not teach by comedies, but by reading a thousand good and sacred books, and by going to sermons not only through Lent but all year long on the feast days enjoined, of which we have enough to render thanks to the Lord God.

Prol. I do not wish to enter now into the vestry, because neither the time nor place demands it, but I do say that observance of the ancient precepts as Aristotle and Horace teach is most necessary.

Arg. You miss the point, brother. Aristotle and Horace saw their own times, but ours are of another kind; we have other manners, another religion, and another way of living, and therefore comedies must be made in another fashion. One does not live in Florence as one formerly lived in Athens or Rome.

The new pastoral tragicomedy of Guarini also laid claim to a new form. The author of the famous *Pastor fido* boasted that while following both ancient tragedy and comedy, i.e. Sophocles and Euripides and Terence, and also the ancient theory of Aristotle and Horace, he had yet created a "modern poem," a drama that was neither tragedy nor comedy but a third new form:

He who composes tragicomedy takes from tragedy its great personages but not its action, its verisimilar plot but not one based on truth, its emotions aroused but their edge abated, its delight but not its sadness, its danger but not its death; from comedy laughter that is not riotous, modest merriment, feigned complication, happy reversal, and above all the comic order.[12]

The new drama of the sixteenth century, although primarily based on ancient practice and theory, modified and reformed this ancient heritage. Ancient tragedy presented great actions based on historical events (*res gestae*) that ended unhappily, and royal or noble characters speaking in a lofty style. Ancient comedy presented a commonplace action based on a fiction (*fictio*) that ended happily, and humble characters speaking in a plain style. The new dramatists made several changes, some of them radical, in these ancient prescriptions. Five of these changes were fundamental: (1) Either history or fiction could be used in either tragedy or comedy. (2) The happy ending

---

[12] *Compendio della poesia tragicomica*, in *Opere*, III, 403.

could be used in tragedy as well as in comedy. (3) Romantic love could be used in both tragedy and comedy. (4) Both exalted and humble characters could be used in both tragedy and comedy. (5) The classical hierarchy of styles was modified and sometimes discarded.

I

The ancient grammarians and critics left the prescription that tragedy should be based on the truth of history, comedy on a fiction. Donatus (or Evanthius) said, "All comedy is from feigned arguments; tragedy is often obtained from historical truth." Aristotle and Horace seemed to agree, and the extant examples of ancient Greek and Roman drama supported such a rule. Both secular and sacred dramatists of the sixteenth century were concerned with the rule but nevertheless often broke it.

Giraldi Cinthio led the way in introducing the fictitious plot into the new Italian tragedy. Trissino, in his *Sofonisba* (1515), had attempted a Grecian type of tragedy that was actually more Senecan than Euripidean. While Cinthio openly preferred Seneca to any of the Greeks, he nevertheless modified Senecan tragedy by introducing a structure borrowed from Terence. Only two of Cinthio's tragedies, namely *Cleopatra* and *Didone*, were based on ancient *res gestae*.[13] Seven others, *Orbecche, Altile, Antivalomeni* (Changelings), *Arrenopia, Euphimia, Epitia,* and *Selene*, were dramatizations of his own novels.

Cinthio was not without classical authority for his bold move, as he was careful to point out. Aristotle did mention at least one ancient Greek tragedy by Agathon that had a wholly fictitious plot.[14] But Cinthio went further than Aristotle, who recommended using the traditional myths as a general practice. Cinthio argued that the tragic poet may move his audience even better with a feigned plot than with *res gestae*, provided he stay within the limits of probability; for a new plot is better calculated to maintain suspense and to hold the attention of the audience to the very end. His own *Orbecche* (1541) was his principal demonstration of the validity of the fictitious plot. In an address to the reader appended to the published play, Tragedy explained:

[13] In the sixteenth century, history usually included ancient myth. The story of Dido could be interpreted as either historical or fictitious.

[14] *Poetics* 9.51ᵇ21–23. Cinthio referred to this passage early (pp. 12–13) in his *Discorso intorno al comporre di i romanzi, delle comedie, e delle tragedie, e di altre maniere di poesie*, Venice, 1554.

Nor should I be the less esteemed because I have sprung from new matter and not from ancient history, for he who looks at the truth with a straight eye will see that it is permissible for a new tragedy to spring without blame from new material and new names.[15]

Other Italian dramatists followed the practice of Cinthio. Dolce remarked in the *argomento* of his *Didone* (1547): "The subject is taken from the feigned story by Virgil and not from the truth of history." The Chorus speaking the prologue of Luigi Groto's *Dalida* (1572), a *tragedia nuova*, asserted that this play was "newly sprung from the head of the father, as formerly Pallas sprang from Jove." Another new tragedy by Groto, *Hadriana* (1578), was based on the story of Romeo and Juliet in contemporary Italian novels. Torquato Tasso's *Torrismondo* (1587), which imitated Sophocles' *Oedipus Rex* but used an argument drawn from a Gothic tale, combined ancient tragedy with fiction; in Bertana's words it was "una contaminazione dell' antico col nuovo."[16]

In France, Jodelle followed his *Cléopâtre* with *Didon se sacrifiant*, based on the fourth book of the *Aeneid*, which, according to Dolce, was fiction and not history. Robert Garnier's *Bradamante* (1582), a tragicomedy and not pure tragedy, to be sure, was based on an episode in Ariosto's *Orlando Furioso*, which became a favorite source for various plays, serious and comic, in the late sixteenth and early seventeenth centuries. In England, *Tancred and Gismund*, a tragedy by Robert Wilmot and others, first acted in 1567–68, published in 1591–92, was based on a famous tale by Boccaccio. Two early Elizabethan tragicomedies, Whetstone's *Promos and Cassandra* (1578) and Greene's *Scottish History of James the Fourth* (1598), borrowed plots from novels by Cinthio.

By the end of the century fiction was accepted in Italy, France, and England as a legitimate source of both comic and serious drama. Ingegneri apparently regarded a feigned argument as characteristic of the new Italian tragedies—*tragedie di nuovo et finto argomento*.[17]

The sacred Latin drama of the century offered some parallel to Cinthio's feigned plot in tragedy. Thomas Kirchmeyer, for example, admitted, in the prologue, that his *Pammachius* (1538), a *tragoedia nova*, had a fictitious argument: "It is fictitious matter, yet such that

---

[15] *Orbecche* (Venice, 1543), fol. 59v. Cf. Allan Gilbert, *Literary Criticism: Plato to Dryden*, (1940), p. 243.

[16] Emilio Bertana, *La Tragedie* (Milan, n.d.), p. 101.

[17] *Op. cit.*, III, 487.

the truth appears, which combination gives profit and delight." Generally, however, the authors of the Christian Terence upset the classical prescription in another way; they insisted that all plays, tragedies, comedies, tragical comedies, and comical tragedies, should be based on history, that is, on the sacred history of the Bible.

The medieval mysteries had been based on the Bible, and a few secular histories appeared early in the Renaissance. In 1493, Carolus Verardus dramatized an episode in recent Spanish history under the title of *Historia Baetica*.[18] As the prologue said, the author realized that his play did not follow ancient practice. He wrote it in prose, the language of familiar discourse, yet it was not like the comedies of Plautus. Although the leading characters were royal, he was not writing a tragedy. "Let no one," said the prologue, "demand that the laws of either comedy or tragedy be observed here; for a history and not a fable is to be acted."

Verardus apparently exerted no influence upon Italian playwrights, but did attract some attention in Germany,[19] where the Christian Terence flourished. The sacred dramatists not only rejected the prescription of a feigned plot for comedy, but made a virtue of their reform. Thus Cornelius Crocus, author of the popular *Joseph* (1535), said in his prologue: "I do not bring you Plautus or Terence, all of whose plays are fictions, untrue, profane, ludicrous, and deceitful; but I bring you one that is true, sacred, serious, chaste, and modest." William Gnaphaeus (Fullonius) remarked in the preface to his equally popular *Acolastus* (1529), the first of a series of plays about the prodigal son, that he had adapted an argument from Holy Writ to the form of comedy, and he acknowledged that his play went "beyond those laws of comedy that Horace gave us." Hieronymous Zielger's *Isaaci Immolatio* (1543) was called a comedy, but the prologue explained that it was an "old sacred history from the Bible" and "not the fictitious matter of Terence or Plautus." Furthermore, this same prologue asserted that the author had "provided a new form of comedy, which in another manner will be obedient to the laws of history."

This last statement by Ziegler indicates that the authors of the Christian Terence deliberately rejected the close-knit Terentian plot in favor of the looser chronological order of history. Perhaps the historical order was forced upon them by the nature of their material, the Biblical stories that were more or less familiar to their audience.

[18] Reprinted in *Revue Hispanique*, XLVII (1919), 319–82.
[19] See Wilhelm Creizenach, *Geschichte des neuren Dramas* (1901), II, 34.

Crocus knew that he was overstepping the classical bounds of comedy and he tried to mold his *Joseph* into some semblance of the Terentian pattern. He did not begin *ab ovo* but in *medias res*, that is, with Potiphar's wife trying to seduce Joseph. He was apparently worried about the lapse of time between his fourth and fifth acts (the interval of two years between the arrest of Joseph and his release from prison), but he could not bring himself to alter the account in *Genesis*. Georgius Macropedius, on the other hand, frankly accepted the less artistic chronological order as necessary for his argument and for his audience. As the prologue to his *Josephus* explained, the play was not a *fabula* but a sacred history and therefore not obliged to "answer to comic artifice."

The feigned plot opened rich new fields among romances and novels for the writers of secular tragedies, tragicomedies, and romantic comedies. On the other hand, "histories" flourished in England and also in France. The most popular type of play in Elizabethan England was the history, which could be tragical, comical, or tragicomical. French dramatists at the turn of the century did not call their plays "histories," but many before the time of Corneille were similar to the histories of the English drama and of the Christian Terence.

II

Giraldi Cinthio, who introduced the feigned plot into the new tragedy, also led the way in developing a new tragedy with a happy ending. There were some classical models for such a play, notably Euripides' *Iphigenia in Tauris*, *Ion*, *Orestes*, *Helen*, *Alcestis*, and Plautus' *Amphitryon*, which Cinthio classified as tragedy. Seneca, it is true, did not use the type, and Seneca was the principal model for virtually all Renaissance writers of tragedy. Aristotle did not commend the type, but at least recognized it:

After this [tragic plot with a single unhappy issue] comes the construction of Plot which some rank first, one with a double story (like the *Odyssey*) and an opposite issue for the good and bad personages. It is ranked as first only through the weakness of the audience; the poets merely follow their public, writing as its wishes dictate.[20]

Despite the formidable objections of Senecan practice and Aristotelian theory, Cinthio ventured to write tragedies with a happy ending.

Fundamentally this new "mixed tragedy" (*tragedia mista*) or "tragedy with a happy ending" (*tragedia di lieto fin*) was generated

[20] *Poetics* 13.53ᵃ30–35. Bywater's translation.

by combining the Terentian plot with tragic events, tragic characters, and tragic style. There was some debt to Euripides, and the Italians never deserted Seneca; but Cinthio's structure was Terentian. He borrowed the double action, for example, from the Roman comic poet, using two sets of lovers in the *Antivalomeni* and *Arrenopia*. Cinthio himself defined his method in the *Discorso* (pp. 214–15):

> While double tragedies are little praised by Aristotle (although some feel otherwise), this method is nevertheless very praiseworthy in comedy and has made the plays of Terence succeed marvelously. . . . I also believe that if it is well imitated in tragedy by a good poet, and the knot so made that the solution does not cause confusion, it will prove no less acceptable (always bearing in mind the reverence due to Aristotle) than it proves in comedy.

He admitted that his master Seneca never wrote such tragedies. "Nevertheless," he continued, "I have composed some in this form, such as *Altile*, *Selene*, the *Antivalomeni*, and others, only to serve the spectators and to secure a more pleasing effect on the stage and to conform more closely to the fashion of our time."[21]

Cinthio's *tragedia di lieto fin* attracted only a few imitators in Italy, but it aroused a lively critical controversy. His opponents based their objections on Aristotelian theory and ancient practice. His friends and disciples based their support on the same grounds, and emphasized one telling argument from the *Poetics*, namely Aristotle's high praise of the tragic situations in Euripides' *Cresphontes* and *Iphigenia in Tauris*, both plays with a happy ending. The passage runs as follows: "But the best of all is the last; what we have in *Cresphontes*, for example, where Merope, on the point of slaying her son, recognizes him in time; in *Iphigenia*, where sister and brother are in a like position."[22] The Cinthian tragedy with a happy ending certainly encouraged the development of pastoral tragicomedy. Guarini's *Pastor fido* was an extension of the *tragedia di lieto fin*, with more concessions to comedy. Cinthio merely borrowed the comic order from Terence; Guarini added ridiculous actions and humorous sentiments as well.

Since the authors of the didactic Christian Terence were primarily concerned with exhibiting the rewards of virtue and punishments of vice, many of their serious plays tended to become tragedies with a double issue. Bartholomaeus' *Christus Xylonicus* (1529) stopped at

---

[21] *Discorso*, pp. 220–21.

[22] *Poetics* 14.54ª4–7. For an account of the controversy over the *tragedia di lieto fin* and the Italian plays about Merope, see my *Tragicomedy* (Urbana, 1955), pp. 101–21.

the end of Act 4, with the burial of Christ, but with the implication
that a happy resurrection would follow, as indeed it did in a sequel,
the *Christus Redivivus* (1543) by Nicholas Grimald. Kirchmeyer's
Pammachius (1538), a *tragoedia nova*, also stopped at the end of Act 4;
the epilogue explained that the audience would have to wait a while
for the final fifth act. "That will be the catastrophe of the whole
play," and in it Christ "will raise up his own from the world, like gold
from filth, and consign the wicked to eternal fire."

III

The third change was corollary to the first and second; the new
freedom to use fiction in either comedy or tragedy led to the exploita-
tion of romantic sources, the Greek romances of Heliodorus and
Achilles Tatius, the Italian romances of Boiardo and Ariosto, the
Italian novels of Boccaccio, Cinthio, and Bandello, and the Spanish
novels of Cervantes. Italian dramatists, as usual, led the way. As mentioned earlier, seven of Cinthio's nine tragedies were dramatizations
of his own novels. All of these seven plays save *Orbecche* were tragedies
with a happy ending that emphasized love intrigues.

Cinthio was aware of the difference between his use of love and
that of the ancient poets. "[Ancient] comedy," he remarked, "does
not contain the loves of important women; tragedy nevertheless does,
though evil, as the love of Phaedra and that of Clytemnestra."[23] The
ancient tragic heroines were portrayed as evil in love because tragedy
should purge the audience, and women like Clytemnestra did not
arouse pity and fear for themselves but for their victims. In Cinthio's
new tragedy with a happy ending, it was permissible to "introduce
virtuous loves of virgins, of maidens, with that uprightness that
befits perfect decorum."[24] Moreover, it was proper in this new kind of
tragedy for the maiden to suffer the pangs of amorous passion on
stage—if she were alone. It was not decorous for her to discuss her
passion with a lover or with an intermediary. Cinthio remarked that
he had tried this innovation in his *Antivalomeni* (Changelings), a
romantic play in which two pairs of young lovers suffer many tribula-
tions before the happy outcome. In Scene 5 of Act 4, one of these
lovers, Elbania, expresses her despairing love for Emonio, who has
been condemned to death:

Unhappy Elbania, sad Elbania, more miserable than all and every other

[23] *Discorso*, p. 275.
[24] *Ibid.*, p. 276.

woman, why should you stay alive any longer if thy Emonio dies, Emonio who was thy life, thy soul, and thy heart? Unhappy love, bitter destiny, shall I be able to hear of the death of him who is the only life for my sad life, and remain alive?

The eroticism encouraged by Cinthio grew more prominent in plays by some of his followers; in fact, it became the principal theme of many Italian tragedies. Cupid spoke the prologue of Dolce's *Didone*, representing himself as the universal ruler in heaven, earth, and hell, "against whom neither force nor human counsel avails." Luigi Groto's *Dalida* was a horror play, but it was also erotic. The chorus remarked in the prologue that the author had departed from ancient practice in introducing the passion of a young woman. A better example of the tragedy of love was Groto's *Hadriana*, which recounted the pathetic story of Romeo and Juliet. The hero and heroine of Tasso' *Torrismondo* were victims of incestuous passion.

While the Italians led the way in introducing romance and eroticism into tragedy and tragicomedy, the French and English soon followed. Every student of Elizabethan drama is familiar with Shakespeare's use of novels and romances and with the similar practice of his fellow dramatists. In France, the romances of Heliodorus, Achilles Tatius, Ariosto, Montemayor, and D'Urfé, the novels of Boccaccio, Bandello, and Cervantes provided as many sources for Garnier, Alexandre Hardy, Mairet, Du Ryer, and Rotrou as did ancient history and ancient tragedy. By the middle of the seventeenth century romantic love had become the subject matter of most serious plays. Dryden in England, Corneille, Boileau, and Saint-Évremond in France recognized this emphasis upon love as the principal difference between modern and ancient tragedy.

The new secular comedy also made use of romantic love. It is true that there were romantic situations in Plautus and Terence, but these could not be well developed since respectable young women were denied prominent roles in comedy. The new dramatists of the Renaissance had no such inhibitions—even the authors of the Christian Terence often used young lovers—and consequently matter from romances and novels early appeared in the *commedia erudita* to add variety and a modern flavor to the ancient love intrigues between amorous citizens and pretty slave girls.

Ariosto followed the Roman pattern pretty closely, but gave the heroines much more prominence than they had enjoyed in Plautus or Terence. Machiavelli went further; he incorporated novelistic matter.

Lucrezia, the heroine of *Mandragola*, must have owed something to Boccaccio's Beatrice (*Decameron* 7.7) and probably something to his Marchesana di Monferrato (*Decameron* 1.5). The intricate romantic plot of Aretino's *Ipocrito* was indebted to the fantastic tale of Isoldo, Tisbina, and Prasildo in Boiardo's *Orlando Innamorata* (1.12) and probably to a similar tale in the *Decameron* (10.5). Grazzini's *Gelosia* was based on the romantic story of Ariodante and Ginevra in the fifth canto of Ariosto's *Orlando Furioso*. Cecchi's *L'Assiuolo* owed something to the amorous affair of Ricciardo and Catulla in the *Decameron* (3.6). Annibale Caro's *Straccioni* (Ragged Rascals), composed about 1544, first published in 1582, drew upon Achilles Tatius' Greek romance, the *Adventures of Leucippe and Clitophon*. *I morti vivi* (1576), by Sforza degli Oddi, was also based on Achilles Tatius. *La Donna Costante* (1578), by Raffaelo Borghini, was essentially the story of Romeo and Juliet further complicated by a parallel love affair between the sister of the hero and the brother of the heroine. Giovanni Battista della Porta's *Il Moro* used the same episode from the *Orlando Furioso* that Garnier used in the French tragicomedy of *Bradamante* and he went to Bandello for the plot of his *Due fratelli rivali*.

The Italians, then, enriched their comedy as well as tragedy by borrowing matter from novels and romances. The new French comedy of the century, largely the work of Jodelle, Grévin, de la Taille, and a few others, imitated the Roman and Italian drama. Both tragedy and comedy in France had to wait until the next century for full development. English comedy also offered little change from Roman comedy and native farce until near the end of the century, but from about 1590 until 1640 a new romantic comedy flourished under Shakespeare, Dekker, Middleton, Fletcher, and Massinger. The English comedy of these masters reflects the same fusion of ridiculous and romantic matter that the Italians worked out in earlier generations.

IV

In the first of his three discourses on dramatic poetry (1660), Corneille expressed dissatisfaction with Aristotle's statement that comedy deals with the worse sort of people. He argued that Aristotle's definition was not valid in modern times when even kings might be admitted into comedy if they were engaged in simple love intrigues that incurred no danger to their lives or to their kingdoms. Corneille was writing after French comedy had come of age, after the development of romantic comedy and tragicomedy.

Classical theory demanded a strict separation of tragic and comic characters. The ancient authorities, Aristotle, Horace, Diomedes, Donatus, all seemed to concur in assigning heroic characters to tragedy, ordinary folk to comedy. Scaliger expressed the traditional theory in his *Poetices* (1.6), where he remarked that the characters of comedy, the Chremes, Davuses, Thaises, come from rustic and humble life; those of tragedy, the kings and princes, from the city, fortress, or camp. Castelvetro was no less explicit when he asserted that royal and private station separate poetry into its species.[25]

Italians generally accepted this traditional division. Cinthio used "royal plots" (*reali favole*) involving the actions of kings and cavaliers.[26] He followed Aristotle in adopting tragic characters of middling virtue because these persons, part good and part bad, most effectively arouse compassion when something terrible happens to them, and he never questioned that tragic protagonists should be of the highest station. "Comedy and tragedy have one thing in common," he said, "to imitate an action; but they are different in that the one imitates the illustrious and royal [action], the other the vulgar and civil."[27] Cinthio followed this theory in his practice; the principal characters in his tragedies were royal and noble, those in his one comedy, the *Eudemoni*, middle-class people. All leading Italian writers of tragedy, Trissino, Aretino, Dolce, Groto, Tasso, followed the same practice.

Authors of the *commedia erudita* chose middle- and lower-class persons, citizens of Florence, Rome, Venice, or Pisa. The pathetic comedies of Della Porta, it is true, introduced some characters of higher rank, such as a governor in *Il Moro* and a Spanish viceroy in the "Two Rival Brothers." In other words, there was some tendency in Italian comedy of the late sixteenth century toward the mixture of high and low persons that was to characterize the romantic comedy and tragicomedy of France, Spain, and England.

In Italian tragicomedy, that is, in pastoral tragicomedy, there was more freedom in the use of characters. Guarini, for example, accepted the classical prescription but insisted upon mingling tragic and comic characters in the same play:

I confess, and moreover in accord with Aristotelian doctrine, that persons of high rank belong to tragedies and those of low rank to comedies, but I deny indeed that it is contrary to nature and to poetic art in general to introduce into one and the same plot persons of high rank and those not of high rank.[28]

[25] *Poetica d'Aristotele vulgarizzata et sposta* (Basle, 1576), p. 36.
[26] See prologue to *Arrenopia*.   [27] *Discorso*, pp. 202–203.
[28] *Compendio della poesia tragicomica*, in *Opere*, III, 397.

Therefore the author of the *Pastor fido* used both noble and ridiculous characters, a pious heroine (Amarilli) and a wanton nymph (Corisca), a pure-minded hero (Mirtillo) and a bestial satyr.

This mingling of great and humble characters in the same play did not mean exhibiting tragic and comic qualities in one and the same character, for Guarini, like virtually all Italians, was a devoted adherent to classical decorum, which meant keeping tragic characters tragic and comic characters comic. French and English playwrights, however, sometimes showed characters who could both rant and joke. Garnier introduced some levity among the cavaliers and ladies of his *Bradamante*. Tudor and Elizabethan dramatists never hesitated to mingle high and low characters in both tragedy and comedy and upon occasion to mingle high and low sentiments in the one character. Shakespeare's Henry V, both as prince and as king, was at once a royal hero and a humorous wag. Both French and English writers were influenced in some degree by medieval drama and also by the Christian Terence.

The authors of the Christian Terence knew what classical decorum was, but there was a still higher standard in the Bible, wherein saints freely mingled with sinners, angels with devils, kings with beggars, patriarchs with peasants. Consequently these writers combined Biblical and allegorical characters with types borrowed from Roman comedy and tragedy, royal villains, stately messengers, ghosts and furies from Seneca, citizens, braggart soldiers, cunning servants, parasites, and even courtesans from Plautus and Terence.

The degree of freedom with which the sacred dramatists treated characters was not uniform. Some writers, like the Portuguese Crucius, who wrote Latin plays for the undergraduates at Coimbra, were fairly conservative. In his *Sedecias*, which was "wholly tragic" (*tota tragica*), Crucius used only characters traditionally associated with tragedy, such as a guardian angel, a divine oracle, a prophet (Jeremiah), a king (Sedicias), an emperor (Nabuchodonosor), generals, officials of the court, criers, and a messenger. In his tragicomedies, however, he combined allegorical characters with middle-class citizens and with the humblest sort of people. Other sacred dramatists paid little heed to classical decorum of character.

Many sacred tragedies and tragicomedies, as did the *drame libre* of France and England, introduced low and ridiculous characters among royalty and nobility. Bartholomaeus' *Christus Xylonicus* employed such diverse characters as Christ, Mary, an angel, Herod, Pilate, Mary Magdalene, three drunken servants, and three rascally common soldiers. Nicholas Grimald's *Christus Redivivus* used about the same cast and added a fury (Alecto) and a devil. Petrus Philicinus went so far as to make a fallen woman the heroine of his serious play, *Magdalena Evangelica*. In view of such a humble heroine, however, he was doubtful that his play would be accepted as tragic and therefore called it a "tragic comedy." Kirchmeyer introduced a comic servant named Dromo into his tragedy *Pammachius*. Sixt Birck, who wrote several well-known tragicomedies, such as *Susanna, Judith, Sapienta Salomonis*, freely mingled emperors and judges with common citizens and soldiers.

This free mixture of high and low characters in the sacred tragedies and tragicomedies worked the opposite way as well; that is, the sacred comedies admitted characters traditionally assigned to tragedy. The cast of Hieronymus Ziegler's *Isaaci Immolatio* included Deus and three archangels, Gabriel, Raphael, and Michael. In the Joseph plays, which were called comedy or history or tragicomedy, the Egyptian Pharaoh might or might not appear. In Macropedius' *Josephus*, Pharaoh played an important part. In Birck's *Zorababel*, a "sacred comic drama" originally written in German but translated into Latin, Darius, King of the Persians, had as important a part as Zorababel. Birck's *Eva*, based on a prose fable by Melanchthon, depicted Jehovah's informal visit to Eve and her two children.

These illustrations might easily be extended, but they should demonstrate the manner in which the Neo-Latin dramatists modified the classical prescription on tragic and comic characters. A similar modification obtained in the vernacular drama of France and England. The neoclassical "rules" put at least a temporary stop to the *drame libre* in France by about 1640, but the new drama never surrendered all of its freedom; Corneille's objection to banning kings and princes from comedy was a representative protest. In England the new drama never came under the yoke of the rules, and most English playwrights continued to mingle high and low characters in tragedy, comedy, history, and tragicomedy.

V

The revival of classical literature in the Renaissance included the revival of the classical levels of style, especially the three Ciceronian levels of lofty, moderate, and plain.[29] The lofty style was recommended

[29] See the *Ad Herennium*, 4.8; Cicero's *De Oratore*, 3.45, 3.52, 3.55; *Orator*, 5.21, 23. Cf. Quintilian, 12.10; Dionysius of Halicarnassus, *On Literary Composition*, 21. Demetrius, known in the sixteenth century as Demetrius Phalereus, in his treatise *On Style* (36), defined four kinds of speaking, plain, lofty, ornate, and weighty.

for the heroic epic poem and for tragedy, the plain style for comedy, and the moderate style came to be accepted as proper for tragicomedy. It was generally understood among the neoclassicists that the lofty style should not be mixed with the plain. Horace had said, in the *Ars Poetica*, 89–92: "Comic matter refuses to be treated in tragic verse; also, the banquet of Thyestes disdains to be recited in familiar lines that are proper enough for the comic sock." Demetrius, who was often cited as good authority, had said in his treatise *On Style* (36): "The lofty and the plain do not mix because they are opposed to each other."

This classical hierarchy of styles was known in the Middle Ages, but was seldom observed in any vernacular literature before the time of Dante, and then only in Italy. Augustine, who was a good Ciceronian, had discussed the three styles in his *De Doctrina Christiana*, had illustrated them from the writings of St. Paul, and had advised the Christian preacher to master all three. Augustine, however, recommended a sparing use of ornament even when speaking of great matters, for the preacher ought to speak plainly:

Ought he who is teaching the unity of the Trinity to discuss it otherwise than plainly, so that his audience may comprehend, as much as is given them to comprehend, a subject that is difficult to understand? Should ornaments be sought here rather than proofs?[30]

There is plenty of evidence that the sacred dramatists of the sixteenth century, who inherited many medieval practices, were familiar with classical theories of style and at the same time determined to put the truth of Scripture before classical ornament. These playwrights took Terence for their principal model and often imitated Seneca as well, but they followed Augustine rather than Cicero or Demetrius.

Quintianus Stoa, who wrote several profane tragedies based on ancient Roman history, adopted a different style when he turned to sacred drama. In the dedicatory epistle of his *Theoandrathanatos* (1508), a "tragedy of the passion of our Lord Jesus Christ," he remarked that he had used "ordinary words and sentiments" rather than poetical images.[31] Bartholomaeus, in the preface to his *Christus Xylonicus*, stated that this tragedy of the crucifixion would be represented in "true and simple fashion, without any ornament at all." Théodore Beza, whose *Sacrifice d'Abraham* (1550) was one of the best

---

[30] *De Doctrina Christiana*, 4.19.38.
[31] Cf. the dedicatory epistle to his *Christiana opera*, Paris, 1514.

known sacred dramas of the century, announced in his preface that he had used a style partly tragic and partly comic, but mainly familiar:

And although the affections be very great, yet have I abstained from words and speeches too far estranged from the common ordinary, notwithstanding that I know it was the manner of the Greeks and Latins so to do, specially in their choruses, as they termed them.

Equally emphatic was the announcement in the prologue to Schonaeus' *Baptistes*:

It can be called neither tragedy nor comedy, since it is a tragic argument written in comic style (*comica oratio*). This is contrary to custom and seldom used before; for, as Horace declares, "The banquet of Thyestes disdains to be told in verses that are familiar and proper to comedy." Our poet, unconcerned about this admonition, has decided to exhibit a sacred history in a kind of language neither sublime nor ardent, but calm and sober, in speech truly fitted to the pious argument.

The Portuguese Crucius was more anxious, it may be, to uphold strictly classical standards than were most of his colleagues, but he also modified the levels of style. He boasted that his one tragedy, *Sedecias*, was "wholly tragic" (*tota tragica*), but admitted that his comedy of *Vita Humana* contained some tragic features:

Cadmus is not here changed into a snake, nor Procne into a bird, nor does Atreus cook human flesh, nor does Medea slaughter her boys before the spectators; but the greedy, because it sometimes happens, choke themselves, the envious perish from grief, robbers are punished by law, young men are carried off by gloomy death, which comes to everything in human life.[32]

In his three tragicomedies, *Prodigus*, *Josephus*, and *Manasses*, he used a mixture of tragic and comic styles:

For wheresoever we composed iambics (*senarii*) in tragicomedies they were commonly consistent with tragic law where the matter represented was more weighty and more serious; we changed to comic diction indeed where a more popular style was demanded.

The Englishman Nicholas Grimald offers a good parallel in his *Christus Redivivus*, which he called "comedy or tragedy or yet both," and in which he found it desirable to "mingle the great with the small, the joyful with the sad, the gloomy with the bright, the incredible with the probable." The accomplished rhetorician, as Grimald remarked, could always assign the right style to the matter at hand;

---

[32] *Praefatio ad lectorem*, in the posthumous *Tragicae, comicaeque actiones*, Lyon, 1605. Cf. Horace, *Ars Poetica*, 185–87.

for it is certain that one and the same kind of diction is not desirable for a rich and a poor estate, for a simple narration and a Thrasonical boast, for a soothing consolation and a quarrel, for a heavenly voice and hellish cries.[33]

Grimald's successor at Oxford, William Gager, wrote a "new tragedy" in Latin called *Ulysses Redux* which shows how the classical hierarchy of styles could be broken down even by a university scholar. Gager was careful to cite Horace's admission, that the tragic hero may "lament in everyday speech" when he falls into poverty or is exiled, before he pointed out that his own hero used familiar speech in the early scenes: "A tatterdemallion and made up like an old man (*senex*), he [Ulysses] does not march in the cothurnus, but, lamenting in everyday speech, he walks in the light sock [of comedy]."[34] In other words, Gager deliberately mingled the lofty and plain styles, and in the same character. He was somewhat worried, nevertheless, about the response of his learned readers, who might not accept the play as a tragedy. The author himself was not sure that it was a right tragedy and admitted that, in view of the mixed styles, the beggarly matter, and the introduction of some laughter, it might be called "tragedy or comedy or history or even something else."[35]

The secular Italian drama, as might be expected, was more devoted to the classical levels of style than was either secular or sacred drama of the other countries of western Europe. The theory and practice of Cinthio, the most influential Italian dramatist, may be taken as representative.

"There is a great difference," said Cinthio, "in the mode of speaking between a comedy and the other [tragedy]; because the speech of tragedy ought to be grand, royal, magnificent, and figurative, that of comedy simple, pure, familiar, and appropriate to common persons."[36] Only seldom should comedy make use of "those braveries of speech, those stately modes of speaking, those similitudes, those comparisons, those figures, those oppositions that the Greeks called antitheses." Tragedy, on the other hand, delights in all such lofty and figurative modes of speech, and very properly so long as decorum is always observed.

Although Cinthio insisted on the plain style for comedy, he did

---

[33] F. S. Boas, in *University Drama in the Tudor Age* (1914), p. 27, says that Grimald was repeating, in his dedication, the critical views of John Airy, his tutor at Oxford.

[34] Gager's remarks to the reader, *Ad Criticem*. See Horace, *Ars Poetica* 95–97, which Gager quoted.

[35] *Ad Criticem.*

[36] *Discorso*, pp. 263–64.

not favor using prose. He recommended unrhymed verse for both comedy and tragedy. Rhymes, he maintained, should never be used in comedy, for they are farther removed from everyday speech. He did allow, and so practiced in his own drama, some rhyme in tragedy, in dialogue that was highly emotional or sententious but chiefly in the choruses. He was dissatisfied with the unrhymed verse that Ariosto and his followers used in Italian comedy. This verse (*sdrucciolo*) seemed to him to be too labored, too literary for comic characters, whose speech should be like the talk between intimate friends and domestics, among whom a "sdrucciolo does not fall once a day."[37]

Cinthio recommended verse for all new drama, but prose appeared early in Italian comedy. Ariosto wrote two of his comedies, *Cassaria* and *Suppositi*, in prose. Later, it is true, he turned them into verse. Cecchi also turned some of his prose comedies into verse. Machiavelli used both prose and verse. So did Dolce. While the Italian dramatists could not, or did not, settle upon either prose or verse for comedy, they did agree on using the plain style. Thus Dolce maintained that the "pleasant and easy" verse of his *Marito* ought not to displease any one since it was so like prose that the spectator would not know which it was. Later in the century, Della Porta introduced a pathetic, sentimental type of comedy in which there were many highly emotional speeches, but he used prose. Sforza degli Oddi also wrote romantic comedies that mingled pathos with laughter, and he challenged the traditional separation of styles in the prologue to his *Prigione d'amore* (1590). This prologue is a dialogue between Tragedy and Comedy. When Tragedy complains that her rival has invaded tragic territory, Comedy admits that she shows the miseries of young lovers before bringing them to a happy conclusion. When Tragedy asks whether or not she still deals with the pleasant and the ridiculous, Comedy replies that she knows how to mingle a serious and moral story with wit and pleasant discourse so that both profit and delight ensue. Then Tragedy says, "But with what license do you usurp compassion and the emotions that are my own?" Comedy replies,

In the bitterness of tears there yet lies hidden the sweetness of delight; and so I, who wish to delight in every way, often make the most desirable mixture of tears and laughter, and the bitter tears make the laughter the sweeter.[38]

Oddi came late in the century, and his mixed style was hardly typical

[37] *Ibid.*, p. 229. *Sdruccioli versi* end with the accent on the antepenultimate syllable.
[38] Quoted by Sanesi, *La Commedia*, I, 349.

of the *commedia erudita* but rather shows the changes that began to appear as romantic comedy and tragicomedy developed.

Italian tragicomedy, that is, pastoral tragicomedy, exploited the mixture of styles. The romantic Cinthian tragedy with a happy ending tempered the weighty Senecan style somewhat, but Cinthio never admitted ridiculous sentiments or the plain speech of comedy. Guarini went further in his *Pastor fido*; he retained the lofty style for serious passages and also used a lighter diction in ridiculous scenes, e.g., in some of the scenes involving the wanton Corisca and the Satyr. He cited as authority Demetrius, who had defined four kinds of speaking, plain, lofty, ornate, and weighty:

> The proper and principal style [of tragicomedy] is the lofty, which, when accompanied by the weighty, becomes the Idea of tragedy, but, when mingled with the ornate, makes that norm which fits tragicomic poetry. Since it treats of great persons and heroes, humble diction is not fitting, and since it is not concerned with the terrible and the cruel, but rather avoids them, it foregoes the weighty and accepts the pleasant (*dolce*), which moderates the grandeur and sublimity that are proper to the purely tragic.[39]

The *Pastor fido* was admittedly a hybrid form and its author tried to devise a new style to fit it. Even so, he managed to find classical authority for the innovation. "This is not my doctrine," said Guarini, "but Hermogenes', the famous artificer of Forms."[40] In *De formis oratoriis* (1.2), Hermogenes had remarked that Demosthenes, Xenophon, and Plato used a style that was neither black nor white but a mixture, a third form that was "dusky." So Guarini contended that the proper style for tragicomedy was one that mingled the tragic and comic colors, and he believed that he had achieved such a style in the *Pastor fido*:

> Its diction is clear but not low, proper but not vulgar, figurative but not enigmatical, beautiful but not affected, sustained but not inflated, pleasant but not languishing; and, to conclude in a word, such as is not remote from common speech and yet not close to that of the common herd.[41]

In Ciceronian terms, Guarini's style was the moderate, and this moderate style became characteristic of tragicomedy in France and England as well as in Italy.

In sixteenth-century France and England, where native medieval plays and the Christian Terence were more influential than in Italy,

---

[39] *Compendio*, in *Opere*, III, 423.
[40] *Ibid.*, III, 425.
[41] *Ibid.*, III, 428.

and where the popular drama was a *drame libre*, the classical levels of style were not so readily accepted. Leading French critics like Du Bellay, Peletier, and Ronsard, who advocated rejection of medieval forms and emulation of the ancients, did separate tragedy from comedy in style as well as in subject matter and characters. Peletier, for example, stated, "Comedy speaks easily and, as we said, in a popular style. Tragedy is sublime."[42] Nevertheless, there was some concession to the new needs of modern drama. Ronsard, who supported the classical levels of style and spoke of the proper speech for tragedy as "lofty and weighty," recommended for the passions of love a lower level, a "Muse plus douce."[43] Conservative critics in England, like Sir Philip Sidney and Ben Jonson, were inclined to support the classical hierarchy of styles and to deplore their fellow countrymen's failure to do so. The tragedies, comedies, and histories of Greene, Marlowe, Shakespeare, Dekker, and Marston, however, continued to mingle various styles in the same play. French popular drama remained more or less a *drame libre* through the reign of Alexandre Hardy in the first quarter of the seventeenth century. With the establishment of the Academy the classical levels of style were as firmly re-established in France as they had been in Italy. The classical hierarchy of styles operated to some extent in English popular drama after the Restoration brought neoclassical French theory and practice to bear upon leading critics like Dryden, Rymer, and Dennis, and leading playwrights like Dryden, Otway, and Congreve; but the English never wholly surrendered their freedom.

MARVIN T. HERRICK

[42] *L'Art poetique* (1555), 2.7.
[43] In *Élégie à son livre* (1556). Quoted by W. F. Patterson, *Three Centuries of French Poetic Theory* (Ann Arbor, 1935), I, 560.

GILES FLETCHER AND THE PURITANS

ABSOLUTELY to define him," remarked Owen Feltham of the seventeenth-century Puritan, "is a worke, I thinke, of Difficulty. . . . "[1] Noting further that " 'tis for the most part held *a name of Infamie,*" Feltham supports John Ley and many others in regretting the habitual misapplication of the term by which malicious tongues "persecute many good men under the name of Puritans."[2] His point, so well taken then, retains its validity today. Although we no longer intend to slander our subjects, our tendency to categorize when we write of the past still occasions the defamation, as Feltham would have thought it, of some who escaped such calumny from their contemporaries. In applying the Puritan label to seventeenth-century figures, we might well practice the discretion implicit in John Jewel's observation that "Discention amongst those that professe the Gospell is no certaine note of Heresie."[3]

My interest at the moment centers in Giles Fletcher, whose religious affiliations might seem clear enough, since he lived and died a Church of England divine and member of a family notably prolific in Anglican clergymen. But had his prose been as generally available through the years as has his poetry, others might have joined a recent student of his works[4] in associating him with the Puritans. And since a clarification of Fletcher's position sheds light on the affiliations of numerous others who have been, for want of a better category, classified as Puritan, his paradoxical situation deserves a moment's notice.

What basis, then, underlies such an assumption about Fletcher? In an obscure tract called *The Reward of the Faithful,* written just before his death,[5] Fletcher pronounces unequivocally upon play-

---

[1] *Resolves, Divine, Morall, Politicall.* Second Century (London, 1628), p. 10.

[2] John Ley, *A Discourse Concerning Puritans* (London, 1641), p. 3.

[3] *The Apologie of the Church of England* (London, 1600), p. 92.

[4] David Clark Sheldon, "The Complete Poems of Giles Fletcher the Younger," a doctoral dissertation at the University of Wisconsin, 1938, only an abstract of which has been published in *Summaries of Doctoral Dissertations,* University of Wisconsin, II, 302–03. Presumably, since he exploits by no means all of the pertinent material, Sheldon reached his conclusion on the basis of rather lengthy excerpts from Fletcher's prose published in A. B. Grosart's *The Complete Poems of Giles Fletcher, B. D.* (London, 1876).

[5] *The Revvard of the Faithfull* (London, 1623). Although Grosart speaks of three copies, I know but two, one each in the British Museum and Cambridge University Library. Probably Fletcher's book represents a distillation of many sermons from his earlier years, but it clearly expresses also his final opinions. We know from Phineas

houses, tippling inns, and the like. Here follows a specimen of his opinion:

> . . . and such are all those curious & puppet-dressing trades that serue for nothing else but young Ladies, & Gallants to dresse and pride themselues vp in the superfluous vanity of ouer-rich and fashionable apparell, fit indeede for the corruption of the time, but vnfit for vncorrupted persons. . . . And among the crowde of this ranke, wee may thrust in our idle Pamphleters, & loose Poets, no better then the Priests of *Venus*, with the rabble of Stage-players and Balleters, and circumferaneous Fidlers and Brokers; all which, if they were cleane taken out of the world, there would bee little misse of them.
>
> Others bestow their time in Legall, and Callings vsefull to the Commonwealth, but as they abuse them, neyther honest, not iustifiable before God. Such are our Taphouses, & Gaming Innes, I meane not harbouring and viatory Innes, which questionless, in fit places, and where Iustice is neere at hand, if rightly vsed, are not onely lawfull and profitable, but necessarie and honest . . . but for our Tipling Innes in small & vntract Hamlets, without which our Country-Diuels of drunkennesse, Blasphemy, Gaming, Lying, and Queaning, could amongst vs finde no harbor (though perhaps in places of more resort they haue credit enough to be entertained in fairer lodgings) they are eyther the Diuels vncleane Ware-houses for his spirituall wickednesses to trade in; or in our plaine world hee hath no traffique at all. (*RF*, pp. 290 ff.)

Such comments, particularly when combined, as they are in Fletcher, with censure of Church abuses, might well suggest the Puritan. Yet in the same tract, Fletcher bares his theological position; and here he stands firmly in Anglican tradition. What makes the point particularly significant is our poet's temperament as well as his profession. A theologian by inclination and training, and the friend of men representing a wide range of opinion, he is in no sense doctrinally naïve. Subtle distinctions, theological complexities, and so forth, he handles with perception, patently aware of the implications behind his comments. In other words, with Fletcher, statements of doctrine rather than an opinion of players, tipplers, and the like indicate where his loyalty lies.

In order to establish his position, then, let us examine specimens of his opinions on controversial issues and compare these with the comments of accepted Anglican authorities. And as a starting point we can conveniently consider Fletcher's attitude toward natural theology, that increasingly debated proposition that the truth of Christianity, being perceivable through one's mind, must therefore become

---

Fletcher's lines in his "Upon my Brothers Book called, *The Grounds, Labour, and Reward of Faith*," that he finished it shortly before his death.

as apparent to a pagan, once he hears it described, as to a Christian. In general, three attitudes toward the issue existed. For some, accepting religious truth appeared to be entirely rational; others held its perception to result from the intellect, but insisted that men required a special insight through grace to experience complete union of soul and Deity (in other words, man came to Christianity through both reason and grace); and still others granted reason little function in the process, since man achieved a knowledge of Christianity, and hence acquired faith and ultimate salvation, entirely through the mysterious grace of God. The last attitude, of course, generally characterized Puritans.

Fletcher, however, holds firmly to the middle position. After discussing all creation as proof of God's presence and an inducement to faith, he continues: "This a naturall man [*i.e.*, one gifted with natural intellect] cannot deny in reason, because they of his owne tribe *Socrates, Plato, Aristotle* and all wise men euer confest it, not only to vse their owne words. . . . But proue it by necessary demonstration." (*RF*, p. 21) Then follows conventional, syllogistic evidence of the reasonableness of faith. And, a bit later, he insists that observation of the heavenly bodies in motion, of the rainbow, and other wonders of creation inevitably incites pious thoughts in a reasonable man, "whose eye lookes beyond the bright hilles of time, and there beholds eternity, or sees a spirituall world beyond this body. . . . " And these experiences, he continues, are by no means peculiar to Christians:

Which diuine thought wee shall not find in the hearts alone of the children of light, that haue the starres of heauen shining thicke in them (Hebr. ll. 16) but in the minds of heathen men, that lay shadowed in their owne naturall wisedome. . . .

Natural religion, however, must remain imperfect until rendered valid through God's grace. Here follows his statement:

For the natural righteousnes thogh it were in the kind of it perfect, yet it was of a short continuance . . . and therefore this life, which we could not acquire by our nature, because it is eternall; God is said in [t]he first Epistle of Sa. *Iohn* 5. 11. to haue giuen it to vs. . . . (*RF*, p. 41)

In other words, universal Christian truths, through their reasonableness, impress pagan and Christian alike. But salvation through Christ comes as God's gift.

Such was the Anglican position even before Fletcher's time. Note, for example, how closely our poet's opinions coincide with those of the renowned John Jewel, Bishop of Salisbury:

Is nature so blinde that shee can no way discerne what is likely or vnlikely in any part of Religion? Wherefore then doth S. Paul say, speaking only of naturall men, and of the light of nature, That thing that may be knowen of God, is opened vnto them. The inuisible things of God are knowen (naturally) by the Creatures of the world: euen the euerlasting power of God, and his Diuinitie?

Other examples from St. Ambrose, St. Jerome, and so forth follow. Then continues Jewel:

I say not that nature alone is able to lead vs into the perfection of faith, or to indue our hearts with the Spirit of God. But thus I say, Nature of her selfe is often times able to discerne betweene truth and falshood.

And again, a bit later: "All this notwithstanding, I say not, that nature is able to lead vs into all the secrecies and mysteries of Christs Gospell. . . . "[6]

Other authorities reinforce this principle. Donne, for example, in his Christmas Day sermon of 1621 thus addresses the Christian: "thy natural reason and even *humane arguments*, have brought thee to reade the Scriptures, and to that *love*, God hath set to the seale of faith."[7] And Richard Hooker makes the same point. Compare, for example, Fletcher's passage just quoted with these observations from *Ecclesiastical Polity:*

And because Nature can teach them but onely in part, neither so fully as is requisite for mans salvation; nor so easily, as to make the way plain and expedite enough, that many may come to the knowledge of it, and so be saved; therefore in Scripture hath God both collected the most necessary things, that the School of Nature teacheth unto that end; and revealeth also whatsoever we neither could with safety be ignorant of, nor at all be instructed in, but by Supernatural Revelation from him.[8]

Both Fletcher and Hooker emphasize identical corollary truths, insisting for example, that since only man is reasonable and only man

---

[6] *The Works of the Very Learned and Reuerend Father in God Iohn Iewell* (London, 1609), pp. 35 f. For a clear statement of the Anglican position on natural theology, see S. L. Bethell, *The Cultural Revolution of the Seventeenth Century* (London, 1951), pp. 13 ff., who also cites Jewel and to whose work on the Anglican attitude toward natural theology I am greatly indebted.

[7] Quoted by Bethell, p. 26.

[8] *The Works of Mr. Richard Hooker* (London, 1662), pp. 67 f. The quoted passage occurs in *Ecclesiastical Polity*, III, 3.

worships God, reason must therefore represent the common denominator between human and divine.[9] Fletcher further establishes through careful argument that "the soule and body haue their natural desires: so the whole person of man desires naturally as close an vnion with the Diuine being, as it is possibly capable of." (*RF*, p. 52.) And Hooker similarly observes that "all things in the vvorld are said in some sort, to seek the highest, and to covet more or less the participation of God himself. Yet this doth novvhere so much appear, as it doth in man. . . . "[10] At another point, Fletcher anticipates the frank appeal to self-interest expressed later by Archbishop Tillotson and many others. Observes Fletcher:

Wee are all naturally engrossers of goods for our selues . . . and therefore with more reason the religious man, who is the most ambitious creature vnder heauen, may whet and edge his flaming desires to goe through all the sweat and labour of righteousnesse with the same speech inuerted. . . . If a Kingdome be the reward of Piety, who would not be religious? (*RF*, pp. 97 f.)

And Tillotson quite baldly notes:

Upon the whole matter, all the Revelations of God, as well as the Laws of men, go upon this presumption, that men are not stark fools; but that they will consider their Interest. . . . Considering the Reasonableness and the Reward the Piety and Virtue, nothing can be wiser. . . . Nothing will give us that pleasure while we live; nothing can minister that true and solid comfort to us when we come to die: There is probably no such way for a man to be happy in this World. . . . [11]

Fletcher speaks with similar reasonableness about predestination. Though Laud's Arminianism, encouraged by Charles, was soon to gain wide acceptance, a modified version of the Calvinistic principles of predestination, election, and grace characterized Anglican thought under James.[12] Such, exactly, Fletcher gives us. Though he treats the problem at length, a passage here must serve:

Againe, if they shall be saued, let them liue how they will, they know God will saue them, but if he meanes not to haue them, all the meanes they can vse, they thinke but idle, and so they lie down in the secret decree of God which being imbrested in Gods owne bosome thoughts, they cannot possibly diue into; and neuer looke to the execution of Gods decree, which they may

[9] *RF*, pp. 26 f.; Hooker, p. 75.
[10] *Ibid.*, p. 8.
[11] *The Works of the Most Reverend Dr. John Tillotson, Late Lord Archbishop of Canterbury* (London, 1699), Sermon XXI, pp. 233, 235.
[12] Note, for example, Helen C. White, *English Devotional Literature (Prose) 1600–1640* (Madison, 1931), p. 187.

finde in the vse of the meanes & in themselues, if by them the meanes be wisely applyed, and faithfully practised. (*RF*, pp. 229 f.)

The untrained, "lewd" clergy of various Puritan sects often provoked Anglican ridicule. Upon the principle that God chose His elect without regard to birth or education, many Puritans hailed the inspired preaching of laborers and tradesmen. Observed Alexander Ross, "They permit all gifted men (as they call them) to preach and pray," believing "That Laymen and Mechanicks may preach and expound Scripture."[13] As a fair specimen of Anglican contempt for this practice, notice the following remark by Ephraim Pagit, who, like Fletcher, has been denouncing false prophets:

But whence come they now, from the Schooles of the Prophets? no, many of them from mechannicke Trades: as one from a stable from currying his horses: another from his stall from cobling his shooes . . . these take upon them to reveale the secrets of Almighty God. . . .[14]

Fletcher deprecates the use of untrained clergy in any church. But particularly in the following passage, his reference to "Trades-men" identifies his Puritan targets.

But as these blinde Guides are most insensible of their owne maladies, because ignorance is a disease (as the Greeke Tragedian calls it) that neuer paines a man . . . so it is no lesse then a myracle to a man of vnderstanding, to see the great zeale and little knowledge, some well, but weake minded people vse, to defend these Trades-men with. . . . (*RF*, p. 408)

He then proceeds to illustrate and refute conventional defenses of the untrained clergy of whatever sect.

Such examples sprinkle not only *The Reward of the Faithful;* they occur as well in his principal poem, *Christs Victory and Triumph.* Here as in his prose tract, Fletcher draws upon the Schoolmen, notably, of course, Aquinas, and also the early Fathers in approved Anglican fashion. Examples abound, though perhaps none serves our purpose better than his discussion of the "retruse, and hidden, but in truth a very diuine motion of the gracious and formal vnion, whereby God pleases to impart his Diuinity to his Creature."[15]

---

[13] *Pansebeia, or, A View of All Religions in the World* (London, 1653), II, 413, 403, 400. In these passages Ross treats specifically Independents, Brownists, and Anabaptists.

[14] *Heresiography: or, A Description of the Heretickes and Sectaries of These Latter Times* (London, 1645), preface "To the Reader."

[15] *RF*, pp. 69 ff. He relies here chiefly upon the *Summa*, particularly I, LVII, Article I, Reply to Objection 2; I, LXXXIV, Article 7; and II (Second Part), CLXXV, Article 4, in a conventionally Anglican passage. Scholastic philosophy, still emphasized in the Uni-

Obviously, then, Fletcher stands among the Anglicans; yet he leaves one the obligation of explaining those Puritan-like remarks. And, in this task, we ought to begin, I think, by noting that in these paradoxical attitudes, he is far from unique; in fact, as one examines the works of Fletcher's contemporary religionists, he understands how conventional such mixed opinions had become. The turmoil of conflicting ideas apparent in public and private discussions, in sermons and pamphlets, propagated a rich variety of thought on questions of theology, personal morality, church organization, and ritual. Men of open mind, impressed by arguments on various sides of an issue, often developed, like Scott's Davy Deans, eclectic systems peculiar to themselves and in perfect accord with no single sect as we now conceive it. The Anglican-royalist poet, Thomas Heywood, for example, in the opinion of his principal biographer, convicts himself of Puritanism.[16] Open to question also is the orthodoxy of Fulke-Greville, Lord Brooke. And, as a third example, note that scourge of heresy, Ephraim Pagit. Though an ardent royalist and defender of the prayer-book, who discovered his standard of doctrine in the articles of "our mother," the Anglican Church, he goes well beyond even King James' position in describing Calvin as "that admirable man of God, whose name is yet terrible in the Kingdome of Popery,"[17] and in refusing to recognize Calvinism as at all divergent from the principles of the Church of England. In presenting George Herbert as his model of Erastian piety, Barnabas Oley, in phrases that echo Fletcher, attacks the sins of the Anglican clergy in the days before the war, insisting that

If wee shall confesse, that wee neither understood nor valued our High and Holy Calling as Christians, much lesse as Ministers of Christ; That we did not thrive kindly, when Providence had planted and watered us in those Horns of Oyl, the two Universities; or removed us into Countrey Cures, we did not fructifie (as this Book will shew) in any proportion to his encouragements, & therefore are justly cashiered out of his service, and stript of his Rewards. . . .[18]

---

versities, underlay many a sermon. To the well-trained Anglican parson, the works of the Schoolmen provided a handy corpus ready for carving. George Herbert, for example, notes that the ideal country parson, having read "the Fathers also, and the Schoolmen, and the later Writers," he "hath compiled a book, and body of Divinity, which is the storehouse of his sermons and which he preacheth all his life." (*Works*, ed. F. E. Hutchinson [1941], pp. 229–30.)

[16] Arthur M. Clark, *Thomas Heywood, Playwright and Miscellanist* (Oxford, 1931), pp. 191 ff.

[17] *Heresiography*, preface "To The Reader."

[18] *Herbert's Remains* (London, 1652), Sig. a5r-v.

Sir Francis Nethersole, Fletcher's close friend and, except for Phineas Fletcher, the only contributor of commendatory verse to *Christs Victory and Triumph*, though always an Anglican, acquired Presbyterian leanings, on at least one occasion using his influence to aid a Puritan minister.[19] And Nicholas Ferrar who, in his monastic life at Little Gidding, epitomized for many the Anglo-Catholic spirit, left a deathbed statement reminiscent of Fletcher's Puritan-like passages. Here is a specimen.

In as much as all the Comedyes, Tragedyes, Pastoralls, &c: & all those they call Heroicall Poems, none excepted; & like wise all the Bookes of Tales, wch they call Novelles, & all feigned Historyes written in Prose, all love Hymns, & all the like Bookes are full of Idolatry, & especially tend to the Overthrow of Christian Religion, undermining the very Foundations thereof, & corrupt & pollute the minds of the Readers, with filthy lusts, as, woe is me, I have proved in my self.[20]

Such another was Fletcher. During his long career at Cambridge, among able exponents of many doctrines, Fletcher heard Puritan, Anglican, and Catholic issues vigorously debated. Here he found about him such intellectual turmoil as could change a Donne and a Benlowes from Catholic to Protestant. Here, in the midst of "swearing, drinking, rioting, and hatred of all piety and virtue under false and adulterate nicknames," which, according to Sir Simonds D'Ewes, in 1620 "did abound there and generally in all the University,"[21] someone of Fletcher's tastes must have found points of congeniality in Puritan morality, if not always in church government or doctrine. Such sympathies would naturally incline him to hear with open mind the reformers' point of view.[22] That some of his Puritan-like opinions had come from exactly this source long before he breathed the Separatist atmosphere of Suffolk, where he wrote his *Reward of the Faithful*, we have persuasive evidence. Possibly he felt the compelling influence, for example, of the Puritan divine Thomas Taylor while both were Cambridge youths. Or perhaps Taylor's sermons delivered later at the University caught our poet's ear. At any rate, on occasion Fletcher echoes Taylor. To save space I shall cite simply one selection

[19] *DNB.*

[20] *Ferrar Papers*, p. 63. The passage above appears in Joseph H. Summers, *George Herbert, His Religion and Art* (London, 1954), p. 50.

[21] *The Autobiography of Sir Simonds D'Ewes* (London, 1845), I, 141.

[22] For descriptions of the subjects discussed and informally debated see D'Ewes' *Autobiography* and J. H. Marsden's *College Life in the Time of James the First* (London, 1851), pp. 78 ff.

which I suggest as a likely source for the particular passage already quoted from Fletcher. Taylor insists that men often seek money through evil ways,

> as to make gaine by converting their houses into gaming houses, stage-play houses, or tipling houses, all which are the receptacles and roostes of filthy and vicious persons; and the gaine thereof cannot be but filthy: the last of which three, although there haue been and might be a necessarie vse of, yet such is the common disorder of them generally, that in stead of alehouses we may call them hell-houses: for a Christian man need no other hell then to be next neighbors vnto them: but if there be any better ordered, I speake not against them.[23]

At any rate, whatever the origin of such influences upon him, Fletcher offers proof that attempts to simplify men's religious opinions in the early seventeenth century through the application of such terms as *Puritan* and *Anglican*, as we usually understand them, is to increase misunderstanding and confusion.

ALLAN HOLADAY

---

[23] *A Commentarie upon the Epistle of Saint Paul Written to Titus* (Cambridge, 1619), p. 153.

THOREAU'S "THE LANDLORD": "SUBLIMELY TRIVIAL FOR THE GOOD OF MEN"

IN MAY 1843 Thoreau submitted a review of J. A. Etzler's *The Paradise within the Reach of all Men, without Labor, by Powers of Nature and Machinery* to the *Democratic Review*. But "Paradise (To Be) Regained," as he mockingly called his review, was not quite what John Louis O'Sullivan, the editor, expected of a friend of Hawthorne. O'Sullivan told Thoreau that the "collective we" could not "subscribe to all the opinions," and asked Thoreau for "purely literary" matter.[1] Balked in his first attempt to write for the New York market, Thoreau immediately turned out "The Landlord," a "short piece," he said, "that I wrote to sell. . . . "[2] The hackwork of genius, however, is not necessarily insignificant; and "The Landlord" shows us how Thoreau, who was never a popular writer, faced the major problem of audience. Later on, in the excursions, he managed through his subject matter to find an audience—he wrote a species of travel literature. In "The Landlord," however, he experimented with tone and humor, refusing to foresake his serious themes or make them subserve narrative. He was moderately successful in this first essay at finding the proper, genial tone; but later on, in *Walden*, the edge of his humor was discomfiting. In fact, in his lifetime he was known by his tone, by a humor sharpened at the expense of the foibles of mankind, a humor that etched his truths all the more sharply.

"The Landlord," therefore, had a muffled seriousness, or a distortion of theme and image—as if Thoreau had rehearsed his serious routines before the mirrors of a Coney Island fun-house. His theme, of course, is serious, that the landlord is the spheral man, the good man, the whole man; but this assertion in itself is paradoxical, challenging the common estimate of tavern- and inn-keepers. In projecting a "man of more open and general sympathies, who possesses a spirit of hospitality . . . and feeds and shelters men from pure love of creatures,"[3] Thoreau was presenting a compensatory image for his own retired life. The landlord was his equivalent of Emerson's Osman, his alter-ego, who "had a humanity so broad and deep," and a great heart "so sunny and hospitable in the centre of the country,—that it seemed

---

[1] *The Writings of Henry David Thoreau, Familiar Letters*, ed. F. B. Sanborn (Boston and New York, 1906), VI, 102.

[2] *Ibid.*, p. 111.

[3] All quotations, unless specified, are from "The Landlord," *Writings*, V, 151–162.

as if the instinct of all sufferers drew them to his side."[4] Here, balancing the solitude and chill of purity and idea in transcendentalism, was the heat of the heart, the desire for warmth and sociality: the landlord was the "public and inviting" man. His inn, too, was the nearest to the "entire and perfect house"; for Thoreau—with Nature for his reference—claimed that the perfect house should shelter most of humanity, especially "all pilgrims without distinction. . . . " The landlord, then, was a stationary Whitman, minding the open road, greeting the seeker, making him "feel *in* and at home," a host who "is indeed a *host*, and a *lord* of the *land*, a self-appointed brother of his race. . . . " (In this essay Thoreau first began the wholesale use of puns—but the puns drive to the radical meanings of things. Take, for example, "he only can be called proprietor of the house . . . who behaves with most propriety in it" and "there can be no *profanity* where there is no fane behind. . . . ")[5] This landlord who "loves all men equally" and "treats his nearest neighbor as a stranger" (both Emerson and Thoreau preferred to discover their friends anew) was indeed a Whitman: "a man of such universal sympathies, and so broad and genial nature, that he would fain sacrifice the tender but narrow ties of friendship, to a broad, sunshiny, fair-weather-and-foul friendship for his race; who loves men, not as a philosopher, with philanthropy, nor as an overseer of the poor, with charity, but by a necessity of his nature, as he loves dogs and horses; and standing at his open door from morning till night, would fain see more and more of them come along the highway, and is never satiated." Thirteen years before he met the universal democrat, Thoreau was prepared for his appreciation of Whitman—although in that curious shock of recognition, Thoreau took a darker view of democracy than did his host. "We ought to rejoice greatly in him," he nevertheless told his friend Blake. "By his heartiness and broad genialities he puts me into a liberal frame of mind. . . . " "He is very broad, but . . . not fine," Thoreau explained. "He is apparently the greatest democrat the world has seen."[6]

Neither philosopher nor overseer, the landlord was closer to Thoreau at Walden than one at first suspects. "All the neighborhood is in his interest," Thoreau said; and his tavern, set in a retired place, offered "a primitive hospitality." In fact, the tavern he had in mind

---

[4] *The Complete Works of Ralph Waldo Emerson* (Boston and New York, 1903), III, 154.

[5] He had already shown his proclivity for puns in his college essays.

[6] *Writings*, VI, 291, 296.

was very much like the hut he later built. "In these retired places the tavern is first of all a house," he wrote, "and warms and shelters its inhabitants. It is as simple and sincere in its essentials as the caves in which the first men dwelt, but it is also as open and public." Furthermore, the landlord was a man-in-nature, a pioneer with axe and spade, making nature supply the wants of many. "To my imagination," Thoreau said, "the Landlord stands clear back in nature. . . . Surely, he has solved some of the problems of life." And as surely, the landlord of Walden was not a hermit, even if his girth was not quite that of the portly, "spheral" man. He was not a genius but a man of "health above the common aspects of life," with a vast "relish or appetite" rather than "taste," and with a "certain out-of-door obviousness" in his freely delivered and original sentiments. "He is not one of your peaked and inhospitable men of genius with particular tastes," Thoreau wrote. "The man of genius, like a dog with a bone, or the slave who has swallowed a diamond, or a patient with the gravel, sits afar and retired, off the road, hangs out no sign of refreshment for man and beast, but says, by all possible hints and signs, I wish to be alone—good-by—farewell." Not so the landlord, who "can afford to live without privacy," who "sleeps, wakes, eats, drinks, sociably, still remembering his race," who "walks abroad through the thoughts of men, and the Iliad and Shakespeare are tame to him," and whose life "is sublimely trivial for the good of men." The landlord, as Thoreau quoted from Chaucer, "of manhood him lacked righte naught." Living an exposed life, standing in "broad and catholic relation" to all men, he was for Thoreau the representative of human nature, and of the sympathy all men want. And knowing the needs of men—their "needs and destiny" —he was "the farthest travelled, though he has never stirred from his door." Finally, he was the "man of infinite experience, who unites hands with wit," and who, because of his public character, deserved, as Menu said of the Brahmin householder, to be "exempted from taxation and military duty."

The house of the landlord was also as open as himself. Like both Thoreau's hut and the ideal house he described in *Walden*, its privacies were exposed. "All the secrets of housekeeping," Thoreau said, "are exhibited to the eyes of men, above and below, before and behind." Even the kitchen, which in the analogy of man and house suggested the alimentary functions, did not excite disgust. Kitchens, Thoreau wrote, "are the holiest recess of the house. There is the hearth, after all. . . . " Indeed, the hearth was the center of the house, the heart of warmth and social life. With Hawthorne in "Peter Goldthwaite's Treasure" and "Fire Worship," and with Melville in "I and My Chimney," Thoreau used the hearth to represent the real self. Kitchens "are the heart, the left ventricle, the very vital part of the house," Thoreau explained. "Here the real and sincere life which we meet in the streets was actually fed and sheltered. Here burns the taper that cheers the lonely traveller by night, and from this hearth ascend the smokes ["Go thou my incense upward from this hearth, / And ask the gods to pardon this clear flame."][7] that populate the valley to his eyes by day. On the whole, a man may not be so little ashamed of any other part of his house, for here is his sincerity and earnest. . . . " The hut at Walden was dominated by its hearth. Though the hut itself was raised by his friends, Thoreau built the fireplace and chimney himself, and kept its fires burning, ready to share his vital heat with anyone who would take the road to seek it.

But he was a traveler as well as an innkeeper. The landlord was not only a projection of his own willingness to offer "himself to the public," but a projection of his own need for robust sympathy. By giving his essay the larger significance of religious pilgrimage, Thoreau made the innkeeper a symbol of his vision of life. The road itself was the way. And when Thoreau spoke humorously of the landlord's religion, he said that he was "a firm believer in the perseverence of the saints"—of the saunterers, the *saint-terrers*. The tavern, he concluded compared favorably with the church; for the landlord "gives the wayfarer as good and honest advice to direct him on his road as the priest." His quotation from Chaucer's Prologue to *The Canterbury Tales* helped him establish this metaphor; but his remark that "the great poets have not been ungrateful to their landlords" spoke for the traveler that he had become.

SHERMAN PAUL

[7] "Smoke," *The Dial*, III (April 1843), 505.

ALEXANDER POPE'S *UNIVERSAL PRAYER*

ALEXANDER POPE first published his *Universal Prayer* in June, 1738, at a time when the orthodoxy of his *Essay on Man* was being seriously challenged in France and had been questioned, somewhat more hesitantly, in England. William Warburton, in his commentary upon the *Universal Prayer*, argued that Pope had published the poem in order to "shew that his system was founded in *free-will*, and terminated in piety."[1] Warburton also implied that Pope had composed the lines after the *Essay* had been "unjustly suspected of a tendency towards Fate and *Naturalism*." We now know, however, that the *Universal Prayer* was first written many years before the *Essay on Man* was conceived. The heading of one interesting transcript of it declares that it had been "Written by Mr. Pope at 15 Years Old." A more credible statement concerning the origin of the poem occurs in a letter which Pope sent Ralph Allen in September [1736].

> I've sent you the Hymn, a little alterd, & enlargd in one necessary point of doctrine, viz.: y⁰ third stanza, which I think reconciles Freedom & Necessity; & is at least a Comment on some Verses in my Essay on Man, which have been mis-construed. Mʳ Hooke transcribed this Copy, without having one himself; as I believe no man has, since I gave it twenty years ago, in its first State, to the Duke of Shrewsbury.[2]

Pope's statement that the poem was in existence in 1716 carries some weight, particularly since he was giving expression to sentiments in letters written between 1711 and 1717 which share the tolerant free-thinking that produced the *Universal Prayer*.[3]

I do not know of any manuscripts of the *Universal Prayer* in Pope's autograph; but there are four transcripts which purport to be based on authoritative manuscripts. Taken together these give us a reasonably reliable picture of the way in which the poem developed before Pope published it and of the way in which Pope sought to justify himself in

---

[1] *The Works of Alexander Pope* (London, 1751), III, 155.

[2] The original of the letter is in the University of Chicago Library. Attention was first called to its existence by George Sherburn, "Two Notes on the *Essay on Man*," *PQ*, XII (1933), 403.

[3] Pope wrote Bishop Atterbury, November 20, 1717: "I verily believe your Lordship and I are both of the same religion, if we were thoroughly understood by one another; and that all honest and reasonable Christians would be so, if they did but talk together every day, and had nothing to do together, but to serve God, and live in peace with their neighbour" (*The Works of Alexander Pope*, ed. Whitwell Elwin and W. J. Courthope [London, 1871–89], IX, 11). See also Pope to Lady Mary Wortley Montagu, August 20, 1716, (E-C, IX, 346–47); and Pope to John Caryll, July 19, 1711, (E-C, VI, 150).

the light of criticism of his *Essay on Man*. One transcript, made in 1740 by Lady Mary Wortley Montagu and now among the Harrowby MSS at Sandon Hall, suggests an early state. There are two important transcripts in the University of Chicago Library. One of these was made by Nathaniel Hooke and enclosed by Pope in the letter to Ralph Allen of September, 1736, already referred to; it can be definitely traced to Pope, and it reflects the state which the poem had achieved at a specific time. The second transcript in the University of Chicago Library is perhaps the most interesting of all, especially since its existence has not previously been remarked. The note at the head of it reads: "A Hymn to God Written by Mr. Pope at 15 Years Old." The transcript was, however, made in the nineteenth century—the watermark is "I & E S 1811"—but because it includes corrections which are indicated as Pope customarily indicated corrections in his own manuscripts, and because the whole fits into the pattern set up by the other transcripts, it seems to have genuine authority. There is still a fourth transcript, or rather a report of one, by Mrs. Hester Lynch Thrale who described a transcript of the poem sent to her by the Rev. Michael Lort and based on "the first Copy of Pope's Universal Prayer."[4]

I am printing below the text of Lady Mary's transcript (designated *A*). The transcript reported by Mrs. Thrale (*B*) and that drawn up in the nineteenth century (*C*) follow it. The fourth text (*D*) is that found in Nathaniel Hooke's transcript; and the last (*E*) is the text of the poem in the first printed version (the folio edition of 1738, Griffith 492). They are presented in what I believe to be the order in which the manuscripts upon which they are based were written.

Lady Mary's transcript (*A*) is probably derived from the earliest manuscript, though not necessarily the one which Pope may have given the Duke of Shrewsbury about 1716.[5] It contains the stanzas

---

[4] Katherine C. Balderston (ed.), *Thraliana* (Oxford, 1951), I, 405–407.

[5] The circumstantial evidence supporting the thesis that Lady Mary's transcript represents an early text has been summarized by Norman Ault and John Butt, *Alexander Pope: Minor Poems* (New Haven, 1954), pp. 149–50: " . . . (i) it does not follow any of the printed texts, although it was copied out by her [Lady Mary] *after* the poem had become easily accessible in three or four different editions; (ii) it is entitled simply *A Hymn*, which is what . . . Pope calls the poem in 'its first state'; whereas (iii) the 'alterd' version which he sent Allen was entitled *A Prayer to God*, and the published version was always called by its title *The Universal Prayer*; (iv) Pope and Lady Mary were intimate friends at or about the time the Hymn was originally written, and were also in the habit of exchanging poems with each other in manuscript; whereas (v) they had long been completely estranged when the poem came to be rewritten and published . . . "

later suppressed; and it lacks the stanza on free will that Pope composed about 1736—as well as all three of the concluding stanzas appearing in the published version of the poem. Moreover, several lines in it (for example, ll. 9, 13, 15) lack the finish of comparable lines in the other transcripts. *B, C,* and *D* are closely related to one another; and, despite the head-notes of the transcribers of *B* and *C,* both of these probably reflect efforts by Pope to refurbish his poem in 1735–36. *D,* we know, represents the state of the poem when Pope sent it to Ralph Allen in September, 1736. *B* and *C* represent states of the poem prior to *D;* but the number of different readings in them rules out the possibility that they may be derived from the same manuscript. To determine which one represents the earlier manuscript is, nevertheless, difficult. In important ways *C* is similar to *A:* it has the suppressed stanzas, it lacks the stanza on free will; it has two of the three concluding stanzas (but a note in the margin declares that these were added to the original text).

B is a puzzling text. Twice the phrasing in *B* is closer to *A* than is the phrasing in *C* (ll. 40, 41); but it is more often closer to *D* than *C* is to *D* (for example, ll. 18, 27, 36)—if we disregard the corrections to be found in *C. B* has the important stanza on free will, which *C* does not; and it also has, Mrs. Thrale says, all the concluding stanzas, which means that it has the last stanza of the printed version, which does not appear in *A, C,* or *D.* The presence of these stanzas would seem to lead unquestionably to the conclusion that *B* reflects a later state in the development of the poem than *C;* but examination proves that this seemingly compelling evidence is suspect. In stanza four the reading of l. 13 ("Yet gave me in this dark Estate") does not agree with that of the comparable line in *D;* it does agree with the line appearing in *E* and in all later printed editions. The reading of l. 16 ("Left free the human Will") occurs in neither *D* nor *E;* it does occur in the text of the poem printed in 1740, two years after first publication. Such evidence suggests that this stanza was introduced into the transcript, not from a manuscript, but from a printed text. One may also assume that the last stanza, which Mrs. Thrale says was in the transcript presented to her, came from a printed text rather than from a manuscript, since it appears otherwise only in printed texts. Thus the materials that seem to link *B* with *D* and *E* most closely show strong marks of being sophistications by a transcriber working with a printed text. *C,* on the other hand, is closely linked with *D* by the corrections occurring in it; many of them point directly to *D.*

Because of the presence of these corrections, it seems juster to place the nineteenth-century transcript after *B* and immediately before *D*, though the reasons for doing so are admittedly open to argument.

Unless otherwise indicated in notes to the following texts, the material between brackets has been crossed out in the manuscript. Material between caret marks has been substituted for what has been crossed out or appears as an alternative reading to what precedes.

A. Transcript by Lady Mary Wortley Montagu.[6]

A Hymn

Father of All! in ev'ry Age
In ev'ry Clime ador'd
by Christian Saint, by Heathen sage,
Jehovah, Jove, or Lord.

O First of things! least understood!   [5]
Who hast my Sense confin'd
To know but this, that thou art good,
And that my selfe am blind.

Who all dost see & all dost know
And all dost Love the best   [10]
bidst Fortune [guide] ⟨rule⟩ y° World below
And Conscience guide y° Breast

W'ever Conscience thinks not well
W'ere it bids me do
That let me shun ev'n more than Hell   [15]
This more than Heaven persu.

W' pleasures thy free bounty gives
Let me not cast away
For Heav'n is paid w'' Man receives
To enjoy is to Obey.   [20]

Can Sins of Moments claim y° Rod
Of Everlasting Fires?
Can those be Sins w'' Natures God
W'' Natures selfe inspires?

But if to Earths contracted span   [25]
Omnipotence I bound
Or think thee Lord alone of Man
W'' thousand Worlds are round.

If 'ere this weak [yet] unknowing Hand
presume thy Bolts to throw   [30]

And deal Damnation round yᵉ Land
On each I judge my foe

If I condemn one Sect or part
of all yᵗ seek thy face
If Charity wᵗʰin this Heart   [35]
Hold not yᵉ highest place

If 'ere my foolish breast knew Pride
for ought that thou hast given
If 'ere the Wretched I deny'd
Do thou deny me Heaven   [40]

As from my little I bestow
Wⁿ I the needy see
That Mércy I to others show
That Mercy show to me

If I am right, thy Grace impart   [45]
still in yᵉ right to stay
If I am wrong, Oh teach my Heart
to know yᵉ better way

B. Transcript by Mrs. Thrale.[7]

"The first Copy of Pope's *Universal Prayer*"

Father of all, in every Age,
    In ev'ry Clime ador'd;
My Christian Saint, or heathen Sage
    Jehovah! Jove! or Lord!

Thou great first Cause least understood,   [5]
    Who last my Sense confin'd;
To know but this, that thou art good,
    And that myself am blind.

(Who all dost see, who all dost know,
    And all dost love the best;   [10]
Bidst Fortune rule the World below,
    And Conscience guide the breast.)

Yet gave me in this dark Estate,
    To know the good from ill;
And binding Nature fast in Fate,   [15]
    Left free the human Will.

---

[7] The parentheses are those of Mrs. Thrale, who has used them to distinguish suppressed stanzas. The text provided here is drawn from *Thraliana: The Diary of Mrs. Hester Lynch Thrale*, ed. Katharine C. Balderston (Oxford, 1951), I, 405–407. Professor Balderston has been more than gracious in replying to my minute queries about the text which Mrs. Thrale gives.

What Conscience dictates to be done,
 Or warns me not to do;
This teach me more than Hell to shun,
 That—more than Heaven pursue.   [20]

(Can Sins of Moments claim the Rod
 Of everlasting Fires?
Can those be Crimes to Natures God
 Which Nature's Self inspires?)

What Pleasures thy free Bounty gives   [25]
 Let me not cast away!
For God is paid when Man receives.
 T'enjoy is to obey.

But if to Earth's contracted Span
 Omnipotence we bound;   [30]
Or think thee Lord alone of Man
 Whole Systems flaming round:

If e'er this weak unknowing hand
 Presumes thy Bolts to throw;
And deal Destruction round the Land   [35]
 Of each I judge thy foe.

(If I condemn one Sect or part
 Of those that scck thy Face;
If Charity within this Heart
 Holds not the highest Place!   [40]

If e'er my foolish breast knew Pride
 For ought that thou hast given;
Or other's wants with Scorn deride
 Do thou deny me heaven.)

But if I feel another's Woe   [45]
 Or hide the Fault I see,
That Mercy I to others show,
 That Mercy shew to me.

"The rest of the Poem is as we read it in the common Editions of Pope [Mrs. Thrale's concluding note]."

C. Transcript made in the nineteenth century.[8]

  A Hymn to God Written by Mr. Pope
  at 15 Years Old, from his own M. S.

Father of All in ev'ry Age
 In ev'ry Clime ador'd,

[8] Printed here with the permission of the trustees of the University of Chicago

By Christian Saint & Heathen, Sage,
Jehovah, Jove, or Lord.

Thou great first Cause, least Understood;   [5]
Who hast my Sense Confin'd
To know but this that Thou art God,
And that myself am Blind.

Who all dost see who all dost know
And all dost Love the best,   [10]
Bidst, Fortune rule the World below
And Conscience guide the Breast

What Conscience dictates to ⟨tells me shou'd⟩ be done
Or Whispers not to do;
This, teach me more than Hell to shun   [15]
That, more than Heav'n pursue

[Those] pleasures ⟨What Blessings⟩ thy free Bounty gives
Let me not cast away,
For Heav'n is paid when Man receives
T'Enjoy is to Obey—   [20]

[Can Sins of moment claim the Rod
Of everlasting Fire?
Can those be Crimes to Natures God,
Which Nature's self Inspires?]

But if to Earths contracted Span   [25]
[Omnipotence I] ⟨Thy Glory let me⟩ bound
Or think thee Lord alone of Man
When thousand Worlds are round ⟨whole systems flaming round⟩

If eer' ⟨let not⟩ this weak unknowing Hand
Presume thy Bolts to throw   [30]
And deal damnation round the Land
On each I judge my ⟨thy⟩ Foe

[If I condemn] ⟨Let me not name⟩ one Sect or part[9]
Of all who seek thy Face
3   [If] ⟨let⟩ Charity within this Heart   [35]
Still hold the highest Place

Library. In the manuscript stanzas two, nine, ten, and eleven are distinguished, in the left-hand margin, by a bracket. The notes alongside stanzas eight, nine, and ten point to a contemplated rearrangement in the order of these three quatrains. The two dots between stanzas twelve and thirteen are explained in a marginal note: "By this Mark which is in the Orig: it should seem, the two last Stanzas are added to what was at first design'd."

    [9] The following words appear in the right-hand margin, next to this line: "Let not my!"

If e'er my foolish Breast knows Pride
This first   For aught that thou hast given
            Or others wants with scorn [deny'd] ⟨deride⟩
            [Do thou] ⟨If so⟩ deny me Heav'n   [40]

            But if I feel anothers Woe
            Or hide [the Faults] ⟨a Fault⟩ I see
2   That Mercy I to others shew
            That Mercy shew to me[10]

            If I am right thy Grace Impart   [45]
            Still in the right to stay
            If I am wrong O Teach my Heart
            To know that better way

                        ∴

            Mean tho' I am not wholly so
            Since quicken'd by thy Breath   [50]
            O Lead me wheresoe'er I go
            Thro' this days Life or Death

            This day, be Bread & Peace my Lot
            All else beneath the Sun
            Thou knowst if best bestow'd or not,   [55]
            And let Thy will be done

            This day
            Whether tomorrows Sun
            Shall Glitter in my eyes or not
            O may thy

D. Transcript by Nathaniel Hooke.[11]

A
PRAYER TO GOD.
1715.

Father of All, in ev'ry Age,
   In ev'ry Clime ador'd,
By saint, by savage, and by Sage
   Jehovah, Jove, or Lord!

Thou Great First Cause, least understood,   [5]
   Who hast my sense confin'd,
To know but this, that Thou art Good,
   And that myself am blind.

---

[10] The following words appear in the right-hand margin, next to this line: "Let me not Blame."

[11] Printed here with the permission of the trustees of the University of Chicago Library. Crosses (x) appear in the left-hand margins opposite lines twenty-eight and thirty-seven.

Yet gav'st us in this dark Estate
   To know the Good from Ill;   [10]
And, binding Nature fast in Fate,
   Left'st Conscience free, and Will.

What Conscience dictates to be done,
   Or warns me not to do,
This, teach me more than Hell to shun,   [15]
   That, more than Heav'n pursue.

What Blessings thy free Bounty gives,
   Let me not cast away,
For God is paid when man receives,
   T'enjoy, is to obey.   [20]

But not to Earth's contracted span
   Thy Goodness let me bound,
Not think Thee Lord alone of Man,
   When thousand Worlds are round.

Let not this weak unknowing hand   [25]
   Presume Thy Bolts to throw,
Or deal Damnation round the land,
   On each I judge Thy Foe.

Save me alike from foolish Pride,
   Or impious Discontent,   [30]
At ought thy Wisdom has deny'd
   Or ought thy Goodness lent.

Teach me to feel another's woe,
   To hide the fault I see;
As I to others mercy show,   [35]
   That mercy show to me.

If I am right, Thy Grace impart
   Still in the right to stay,
If I am wrong, oh teach my heart
   To find that better way.   [40]

Mean as I am, not wholly so,
   Since quicken'd by Thy Breath,
O lead me wheresoe're I go
   Thro' this day's Life or Death.

This day, be bread and peace my Lot,   [45]
   All else beneath the Sun,
Thou knowst if best bestow'd or not,
   And let Thy Will be done.

E. Text of the poem as first printed.

THE
UNIVERSAL PRAYER
DEO. OPT. MAX.

Father of All! in every Age,
  In every Clime ador'd,
By Saint, by Savage, and by Sage,
  Jehovah, Jove, or Lord!

Thou Great First Cause, least understood!   [5]
  Who all my Sense confin'd
To know but this,—that Thou art Good,
  And I my self am blind:

Yet gave me, in this dark Estate,
  To see the Good from Ill;   [10]
And binding Nature fast in Fate,
  Left Conscience free, and Will.

What Conscience dictates to be done,
  Or warns me not to doe,
This, teach me more than Hell to shun,   [15]
  That, more than Heav'n pursue.

What Blessings thy free Bounty gives,
  Let me not cast away;
For God is pay'd when Man receives,
  T'enjoy, is to obey.   [20]

Yet not to Earth's contracted Span,
  Thy Goodness let me bound;
Or think thee Lord alone of Man,
  When thousand Worlds are round.

Let not this weak, unknowing hand   [25]
  Presume Thy Bolts to throw,
And deal Damnation round the land,
  On each I judge thy Foe.

If I am right, thy Grace impart
  Still in the right to stay;   [30]
If I am wrong, oh teach my heart
  To find that better Way.

Save me alike from foolish Pride,
  Or impious Discontent,
At ought thy Wisdom has deny'd,   [35]
  Or ought thy Goodness lent.

Teach me to feel another's Woe:
  To hide the Fault I see:

> That Mercy I to others show,
>   That Mercy show to me. [40]
>
> Mean tho' I am, not wholly so
>   Since quicken'd by thy Breath,
> Oh lead me wheresoe'er I go,
>   Thro' this day's Life, or Death:
>
> This day, be Bread and Peace my Lot; [45]
>   All else beneath the Sun,
> Thou know'st if best bestow'd, or not;
>   And let Thy Will be done.
>
> To Thee, whose Temple is all Space,
>   Whose Altar, Earth, Sea, Skies; [50]
> One Chorus let all Being raise!
>   All Nature's Incence rise!![12]

In comparing these texts, one will be struck by the fact that major features of the poem remain constant. All versions are addressed to a deity whom all rational minds may worship. Discreet references are made to man's depravity; and the concept of grace is mentioned in each transcript (Warburton, after Pope's death, gave it more emphasis by printing "grace" in capitals).[13] Acquiescence in one's

---

[12] I have collated this first printed text with the texts appearing in the following later editions (copies in the University of Illinois Library):

The Universal Prayer, 8vo (London, 1738; Griffith 493). Ref. *38a*.

The Works of Alexander Pope, 8vo (London, 1738; Griffith 507), vol. II, pt. ii. Ref. *38b*.

The Works of Alexander Pope, sm. 8vo (London, 1740; Griffith 523), vol. II, pt. i. Ref. *40*.

The Works of Alexander Pope, sm. 8vo (London, 1743; Griffith 583), vol. II, pt. i. Ref. *43*.

An Essay on Man, 8vo (London, 1745; Griffith 607). Ref. *45*.

An Essay on Man, sm. 8vo (London, 1748; Griffith 631). Ref. *48*.

The Works of Alexander Pope, 8vo (London, 1751; Griffith 645), vol. III. Ref. *51*.

This collation reveals some effort to improve punctuation as well as the following verbal variants:

l. 8. 1] that *38b, 40, 43, 45, 48, 51*.

l. 12. Left . . . Will.] Left free the Human Will. *40, 43, 45, 48, 51*

l. 29. thy Grace impart] oh teach my heart *40, 43, 45, 48*.

l. 31. oh teach my heart] thy grace impart *40, 43;* thy GRACE impart *45, 48*.

[13] Pope evidently experienced some doubts about the most effective way in which to introduce the concept of grace. As first published the stanza read:

> If I am right, thy Grace impart
>   Still in the right to stay;
> If I am wrong, oh teach my heart
>   To find that better Way.

When the text was revised for publication in the octavo edition of the *Works* (1740),

appointed role and the cultivation of those attitudes of mind associated with charity are portrayed as the primary obligation of man; and in all four of the transcripts conscience rather than the promise of a future life of rewards and punishments is explicitly made the principal guide to virtue.

But while these major aspects of the poem remain virtually unchanged, interesting alterations were undertaken. The poem, originally a hymn, was recast as a prayer—Pope was still thinking of it as a hymn in his letter to Allen, although the accompanying transcript is definitely labelled a prayer. Other changes in the poem give it a more definitely Christian coloring. In *A* the "Father of All" is conceived as an omnipotent and stern judge denying heaven to one who fails in his moral and spiritual obligations. In *D* and *E* the character ascribed to the deity has been altered: He is a god of goodness and mercy who must provide the support, the aid necessary for the individual man to live up to his ideals. If Pope does not explicitly speak of supernatural revelation, these changes in his poem make him admit to something very like it. Verbal changes often involve the substitution of words and phrases more directly Christian in connotation than those they supplant. Pope altered the line, "Thy Omnipotence I bound" by substituting the word "Glory" (*C*), and then "Goodness" (*D*) for "Omnipotence." In the line, "What pleasures thy free Bounty gives" Pope substituted "Blessings" for "pleasures"; and he added two concluding stanzas in which occur direct echoes of the Lord's Prayer (ll. 43, 45, 48 of *D*).

Other changes were accomplished through the rewriting or elimi-

---

Pope, evidently believing that grace should more properly be associated with the sinner than the righteous man, altered the stanza to read:

> If I am right, oh teach my heart
> Still in the right to stay;
> If I am wrong, thy grace impart
> To find that better Way.

The stanza was allowed to remain in this form until after Pope's death and until the official edition of Pope's *Works* was published by Warburton in 1751. At this time Pope's editor reverted to the earlier reading, possibly because the change offered him another opportunity to display his dialectic skill: "As the *imparting grace* on the christian system is a stronger exertion of the divine power, than the natural illumination of the heart, one would expect that the request should have been expressed reversely; more aid being required to restore men to the *right* than to keep them in it. But as it was the poet's purpose to insinuate that Revelation was the *right*, nothing could better express his purpose than the making the *right* secured by the guards of *grace*" (*Works* [1751], III, 157). Warburton did not state that Pope had altered the reading.

nation of stanzas. One of these (ll. 33–36 of *A*) pointed directly at factionalism among Christian sects:

> If I condemn one Sect or part
> of all y^t seek thy face
> If Charity wthin this Heart
> Hold not ye highest place.

Pope, perhaps remembering difficulties which a similar statement in the *Essay on Criticism* had occasioned, wrote a new and less pointed stanza:

> Save me alike from foolish Pride
> Or impious Discontent,
> At ought they Wisdom has deny'd
> Or ought thy Goodness lent.

Two other stanzas were dropped—the third of *A* (ll. 9–12), in which the deity is portrayed as having bid "Fortune rule ye World below, and Conscience guide ye breast," and the sixth of *A* (ll. 21–24), in which Pope declared that Nature, not the abuse of free will inspires "Sins of Moments." Both of these stanzas were fatalistic in tone; and to prevent misunderstanding Pope not only eliminated them but also introduced a new stanza, expressly asserting the will to be free.

In recasting the *Universal Prayer* Pope obviously tried to secure more precise and effective phrasing, to improve the lyric tone of the poem. He also attempted to make his position regarding free will very clear and to outline a relationship between God and man generally consistent with basic points of Christian doctrine. In clarifying his views, the poet did not, however, alter main tendencies of the argument in the earlier version—a point that is often overlooked. The changes do eliminate important contradictions. The stanzas which imply necessity or fatalism appeared alongside other stanzas in which freedom of the human will is implicitly assumed. The stanzas in which Pope solicited damnation if he failed to perform his duties, were hardly consistent with the stanza in which he declared that conscience rather than the threat of hell should be the principal agent of virtue. Moreover, the stanza in which Pope condemned factional disputes in religious matters merely reiterated what had been said in the previous stanza. Its suppression may readily be explained in terms of an effort at greater conciseness. One can assert that the *Universal Prayer* would have been much less satisfactory than it is—a much more confused undertaking—if Pope had ventured to publish it before 1736.

ROBERT W. ROGERS

THE FAILURE OF SOLITUDE: WORDSWORTH'S
IMMORTALITY ODE

CRITICS and biographers of Wordsworth are practically unanimous in their agreement that in his best work poetry and philosophy are so interdependent as to be virtually inseparable; consequently, most studies of his poetry include careful examination of his beliefs about man and the universe, and studies of his thought are based, for the most part, on the evidence of his poetry. Without exception, these studies emphasize the well-known and important fact that he forsook his worship of nature to adopt substantially orthodox religious beliefs about 1807, the year usually chosen to mark also the end of his "great decade" of poetic production. Critical recognition that his spiritual condition influenced both the meaning and the quality of his work is indicated by the significance assigned to that date; but another, and equally important fact is either overlooked or implicitly denied by most critics of his poetry: that any discussion of his philosophy, if it is to be accurate, must confine itself to a particular time of his life.[1] His thought was neither static nor consistent during the ten years preceding his return to Christianity, and the poems he wrote during those years do not reflect an unchanging view of nature. The emotional and intellectual forces which were to cause his acceptance of Christian dogma were already exerting a strong influence on him by 1802, when the Immortality Ode was begun; and all the poems completed between that year and 1806 reveal convictions about man and the visible world which are markedly different from those expressed in 1798 in *Lyrical Ballads*. This four-year period was one of difficult transition for Wordsworth. Because his worship of nature had been a private substitute for the doctrines of theology, his eventual espousal of those doctrines was to necessitate renunciation or radical modification of his former beliefs; and the painful inner conflict that he endured before he was able to make the change is evident in the poetry he wrote at the time, most clearly and vividly in the Ode. What is recorded at length in *The Prelude* is expressed with powerful brevity in the Ode: his desperate effort to reconcile old convictions with new experience,

---

[1] Two important exceptions to this generalization are Joseph Warren Beach, in *The Concept of Nature in Nineteenth-Century English Poetry* (New York, 1936), and Basil Willey, in *The Eighteenth Century Background* (London, 1949). The former, how-ever, is concerned with the history of ideas, rather than with literary criticism. To the latter book, and others by Professor Willey, I am much indebted throughout this essay.

or, more specifically, to derive spiritual strength from memories of a kind of mystical rapture that he could no longer experience directly.

Much of the wide disagreement about the meaning of the Ode can be traced to the assumption, mentioned above, that Wordsworth's world view was constant in all his early work, and to consequent efforts to make the "uncharacteristic" import of the poem conform with his normal or "real" beliefs. Sometimes these efforts lead the critic to confuse Wordsworth's desires with his convictions or his intentions with his accomplishment. Such confusion can be found in a recent essay, generally thoughtful and often illuminating, by Thomas M. Raysor, who deals with the Ode only as a product of Wordsworth's "poetic maturity," with almost no attention to its transitional importance in his spiritual biography. As a consequence, Raysor uses earlier and later poems to explicate parts of the Ode, especially to clarify philosophical problems which did not even occur to Wordsworth until his religion of nature began to prove unsatisfying.[2] Other critics have contended, as an indirect result of the same erroneous assumption, that the poem is inconsistent within itself. Nearly all the so-called inconsistencies, however, are changes in tone rather than logical flaws; the quasi-Platonic concepts of pre-existence and reminiscent knowledge are quite in accord with the dualistic view of the universe which the rest of the poem reveals. Of course, Platonic dualism would have been violently incongruous in Books I and II of *The Prelude* or in "Tintern Abbey," both of which had been inspired primarily by Wordsworth's mystical sense of oneness with what he felt to be a monistic universe. But by 1802 his beliefs had already undergone fundamental changes, and he was to give more and more unreserved assent to a dualistic concept of nature in the four years that followed.

Several contemporary critics have insisted that because the mature Wordsworth always thought of the deity as not merely immanent in the universe but also transcendent to it, he was never a pantheist.[3] The very terminology may seem somewhat inappropriate to discussions of Wordsworth; since he was a poet rather than a metaphysician, it is not easy to describe his convictions accurately with the abstract

---

[2] Thomas M. Raysor, "The Themes of Immortality and Natural Piety in Wordsworth's Immortality Ode," *PMLA*, LXIX (September 1954), 861–75.

[3] Norman Lacey, *Wordsworth's View of Nature* (Cambridge, 1948), p. 30; Herbert Read, *Wordsworth* (London, 1949), p. 134; and Willard L. Sperry, "Wordsworth's Religion," in *Centenary Studies*, ed. Gilbert T. Dunklin (Princeton, N. J., 1951), p. 153, to name only three.

labels of philosophy. The question of whether or not he was a pantheist is nevertheless an important one, because the moments of mystical exaltation on which he based his worship of nature were both a product and a cause of a particular concept of the physical world. That he did at one time firmly believe in the actual presence of a spirit in nature is inescapably apparent in passages from the first two books of *The Prelude*, and more clearly still in "Tintern Abbey," which traces all stages of the process by which he attained direct communion with that spirit.

According to "Tintern Abbey," written in 1798, the first and most elementary of his experiences with nature was a "dizzy rapture" that he had felt as a child in the presence of sensory beauty, when the sounding cataract haunted him like a passion, and when all visible forms and colors were for him "an appetite, a feeling, and a love" that had no need of any charm or support "unborrowed from the eye." These animistic joys of his youth are no longer possible for the Wordsworth of 1798, but the memory of them has comforted him in maturity, and has also enabled him to achieve even more exalting experiences. During the five years since his first visit to this scene, he has learned to hear "the still, sad music of humanity" when he contemplates natural beauty; and that music, together with the sensory stimulus of his surroundings, has power to chasten and subdue him for that "serene and blessed mood" in which the affections lead him on until he is "laid asleep in body" and becomes "a living soul," able to see into the life of things. Similar moments of revelation are described in the parts of *The Prelude* which were written by 1800. He had felt "gleams like the flashing of a shield," and the earth "and common face of Nature" had spoken "rememberable things" to him.[4] Characteristically, these bursts of vision begin, but only begin, with his awareness of a vivid sight or sound while he is made alert by a strong emotion; he is able to see into the life of things only "when the light of sense / Goes out, but with a flash that has revealed / The invisible world."[5] "Tintern Abbey" is still more specific: with the immediate sensory awareness of a natural scene, and with the receptivity induced by his simultaneous awareness of remembered beauty and of humanity's still, sad music, he can feel "a presence" that disturbs him

---

[4] *The Prelude*, ed. Ernest de Selincourt (London, 1925), Bk. I, lines 585–88. Unless otherwise identified, citations from *The Prelude* are to the text of 1805–1806.

[5] *The Prelude*, Bk. VI, lines 600–602. This passage is taken from the 1850 version, but it accurately describes the process of his early experiences.

> . . . with the joy
> Of elevated thoughts; a sense sublime
> Of something far more deeply interfused,
> Whose dwelling is the light of setting suns,
> And the round ocean and the living air,
> And the blue sky, and in the mind of man:
> A motion and a spirit, that impels
> All thinking things, all objects of all thought,
> And rolls through all things.
>
> (ll. 95–102)

Because of such experiences, he is a lover of nature, pleased to recognize "in nature and the language of the sense" the "anchor" of his "purest thoughts," "the nurse, the guide, the guardian" of his heart, and the "soul" of all his moral being. And in an address to his sister and companion, Dorothy, he voices his conviction that nature can so affect the true votary that no pain of experience, not even "the dreary intercourse of daily life," can disturb his "cheerful faith" that all that he beholds "is full of blessings."

To recapitulate, then, visionary seeing is the first step toward seeing into the invisible life of things, literally "life" because nature is animate; the presence, the motion and the spirit, is not just in the mind of man, nor is it in some distant, eternal realm, but actually interfused with the whole corporeal world. This is a monistic and a pantheistic view of the universe, not thoroughly systematized and elaborated in an abstract way, but deeply felt and firmly believed. According to it, the senses of man and the material world can unite to form a bridge by which the human soul can make contact with the universal spirit of which it is a part. The visionary faculty works "but in alliance with the works which it beholds" (*Prelude*, II, 260); the whole manifold of sense data is merely an aspect of the invisible world, not a separate essence. In fact, the need for making such distinctions simply did not occur to Wordsworth in 1798; what mattered was his assurance that reality was fundamentally spiritual. Furthermore, it was wholly good. Evil can have no real existence in a universe ultimately full of blessings: in such a universe even the still, sad music of humanity is ontologically unimportant.

The world view implicit in the Immortality Ode is vastly different from this earlier one, as is the epistemological process that it conditions. In the Ode, external nature is composed of heavy, unintelligible material, which can be vitalized only by the creative energy that a human soul projects upon it. The "eternal mind" that haunts the newborn child of the Ode is not *in* the visible world—not in the blue sky, not in the light of setting suns. The world of this poem is that of "Tintern Abbey," with the deity removed from it. As a result, the rapture man can feel in the contemplation of natural beauty is limited to that joy of animistic perception which, in the earlier poem, had been considered merely the first step toward attaining oneness with the spirit of the universe. The Ode does not even hint at mystical experience made possible by cooperation of the human soul and a spirit in nature; the only manifestation of divinity it describes is the creative power which had enabled the poet, in his childhood, to see nature with a visionary gleam. He does not say that the earth actually was "apparelled in celestial light," but that it once seemed thus to him. The eternal spirit, the source of man's soul, is no longer a presence to be felt, but an object of deliberate faith, whose existence is only *intimated* to the adult by his recollection of the "glory and the dream" of his childhood visions.

The Ode is composed of three main parts: in the first four stanzas, which were written at least two years before the rest of the poem, Wordsworth laments the loss of a visual power and asks why it has been lost; in the next four stanzas he gives a semi-Platonic answer to his question; and in the last three stanzas he tries to find sustaining hope in conclusions reached by reasoning about the fact that his imagination was once creative. In form the poem is endowed with a kind of unity by one primary and pervasive metaphor: the career of the human soul is symbolized by the passage of the sun from dawn through midday to sunset. Complementing this fundamental image, and in fact dependent upon it, is the use of light to suggest spiritual energy, and of the sense of sight to stand for creative intuition. This imagery serves a dual purpose; it not only gives sensory vividness, but also supports the abstract statements of the poem by furnishing a cosmic background for them.

The first four stanzas, which set the physical scene and establish a mood, provide both a tangible context and a logical preparation for the philosophical myth which follows. On a May morning, in the presence of singing birds, bounding lambs, and happy children, the poet is oppressed by a sense of something lost. He can see the beauty of the landscape, hear with delight the many happy sounds, and even feel vicariously the bliss of the youthful merrymakers; yet in spite of his determination not to "wrong" the season with voluntary grief, he is reminded by all that he beholds of the absence of the visionary gleam, the dreamlike radiance that formerly cloaked his perceptions. To him, moreover, the gleam is more precious than a mere visual phenomenon; it was the sensory product of a primal sympathy which, whatever it may be, links the human soul to the external world, and is therefore the chief proof of the new-born child's divine origin. Now in "Tintern Abbey" this primal sympathy sprang from a power in nature as well as in the human being, and it had led the mature nature-lover to mystical insight into invisible reality. In the Ode, however, magical sympathy flows exclusively from the soul of man. Earth, the homely nurse, does her best to make man, "her Foster-Child," forget the glories of his previous existence. The child, who at first feels blank misgivings because he moves about "in worlds not realised," learns to reject his instinctive identification of himself with material objects. Imitating adults, he gradually adopts their fixed categories of perception, until finally "custom" lies upon him "with a weight, / Heavy as frost, and deep almost as life!" The "vision splendid" of the infant gradually fades "into the light of common day" as he learns to accept the separation of himself from the visible world. The heaven of primal sympathy that lies about him in his infancy is gradually shut out by the prison walls of customary distinctions.

Considering the import of the entire poem, one is inclined to believe that the myth was chosen by Wordsworth because it expressed his changing ontological convictions, and thus to reverse the causal order of the suggestion that the "mythology of the Ode . . . by shifting all the 'glory' into pre-existence and super-nature," forced him "to degrade earth into a foster-mother, and Nature into a medium to which the heaven-born visitant is gradually subdued."[6] It is worth remembering that in the first part of the poem, written at least two years before the Platonic section, Wordsworth grieves over the loss of the perceptual gleam but does not mention that mystical insight so exultantly hailed as a more sublime gift in "Tintern Abbey," and that in the last three stanzas he clearly implies that no vital spirit pervades nature. Whether consciously or not, he had lost his former sense of the nearness and accessibility of the deity, and this poem is a record of his impassioned effort to salvage spiritual value from his lost sense of identification with what he now believed to be an essentially dead and alien world.

Deprived of the sustaining force of mystical experience, he sought comfort in reasoned conclusions about his past; somehow he had to

---

6 Willey, pp. 284–85.

adjust his religious beliefs to the difficulties of his adult life. His interest in personal immortality is itself Christian, rather than pantheistic, and it shows a painful awareness of mortality which he had not felt in 1798. The "faith that looks through death" had not been necessary when he could feel his oneness with the spirit of the universe. In "Tintern Abbey" the fading of instinctive perceptual power and the discouragements of growing up had been treated as necessary preparations for mystical insight. In the Ode no such compensation comes from keeping watch over man's mortality; growing up is simply a process of subjugation of the divine element in man, of the closing in of prison walls about the creative spark brought from his real home. Hence the child really is the spiritual father of the man.

It cannot be overemphasized that the consolations Wordsworth offers to himself in the last part of the poem are derived from thought, not feeling. Memory and reason have replaced immediacy and intuition. It is "the thought" of his past years that "doth breed" in him "perpetual benediction"; he finds some basis for hope in the conclusion that the primal sympathy, having once existed, must still exist in some form, that "those first affections" must be "a master-light" of all his "seeing," but "the truths that wake, to perish never" are truths only inferred from "shadowy recollections" of childhood. The attainment of "the philosophic mind" requires conscious and deliberate effort. Remembering his former sense of possible sublimity, and calmed by "the soothing thoughts that spring / Out of human suffering," he can acquire a "faith that looks through death." Because this faith is founded upon thoughtful gratitude for past moments of vision, natural beauties can now exercise a "more habitual sway" over him; but that sway is voluntary and mediate, not direct and overwhelming. In other words, as one critic has noted. "natural piety has not worked"[7] for the poet. Whatever piety he feels is neither spontaneous nor satisfying; the lines which form the epigraph to this poem express a wish that was not fulfilled for Wordsworth, as is evident in the concluding stanza of the Ode. "The meanest flower that blows" can arouse in him "thoughts that do often lie too deep for tears," but the flower has no intrinsic power; it can merely suggest memories to "the human heart by which we live."[8]

Clearly, Wordsworth was attempting to resign himself to more than

---

[7] John Crowe Ransom, "William Wordsworth: Notes Toward an Understanding of Poetry," in *Centenary Studies*, p. 112.

[8] Raysor, p. 871.

the loss of a visual power. It was becoming impossible for him to retain his belief that all that he beheld was full of blessings. By the time he finished the Ode in 1806, he had kept watch over man's mortality in a number of ways. One of the greatest shocks he had endured was the death of his brother, John, in the preceding year. There had also been his gradual, bitter disillusionment with the French Revolution, especially after the renewal of war between England and France in 1803, and with that disillusionment had come doubt of the hopeful principles on which the Revolution had been based. It seems probable, however, that the major reason for his inner turmoil was the loss of his mystical capability. The philosophic mind was a cold substitute for pantheistic rapture; and until he resumed regular attendance at Church in 1807, he lacked the secure sense of order which usually comes from sharing the beliefs and practices sanctioned by the society in which one lives. Thrown back entirely upon himself, he longed for more rest and support than reason and memory could provide. The "Ode to Duty," composed in 1805, makes clear his need for some guide other than himself:

> Me this unchartered freedom tires;
> I feel the weight of chance-desires:
> My hopes no more must change their name,
> I long for a repose that ever is the same.

(ll. 36–40)

And another poem, also written in 1805, indicates how much he longed for human fellowship now that he could no longer believe that nature throbbed with divine life:

> Farewell, farewell the heart that lives alone,
> Housed in a dream, at distance from the Kind!
> Such happiness, wherever it be known,
> Is to be pitied; for 'tis surely blind.[9]

It is not surprising that he soon afterward sought the repose of orthodox Christianity.

At the time of the Ode, however, he had most certainly not achieved the repose he longed for. Lionel Trilling interprets the poem as a "welcome of new powers and a dedication to a new poetic subject";[10] the grief expressed in the first four stanzas, so he believes, "is

---

[9] "Elegiac Stanzas, Suggested by a Picture of Peele Castle," lines 53–56.
[10] Lionel Trilling, "The Immortality Ode," in *The Liberal Imagination* (New York, 1951), p. 151.

not of long duration."[11] This interpretation, in my opinion, confuses Wordsworth's wishes with his convictions, and ignores the tone of the poem. A morality unsupported by a metaphysic had already proved unsatisfying for Wordsworth during his Godwinian days a decade before; and in 1805 he had not yet been able to give full assent to the doctrines of Christian theology. "The faith that looks through death" rests on his personal experience, not on historical revelation. The religious aim of this poem is to fit vestiges of pantheism into a dualistic but not really Christian view of the universe. For Wordsworth that aim is not realized, nor could it be until he had given up his dislike for conventions. Paradoxically, the rigidity of custom which he condemned in the Ode was identical, on a different level, with that ritualistic order for which he was beginning to feel a strong need; and the poem derives much of its intensity from this unresolved conflict within him. In any case, it is not a convincingly cheerful welcome of new powers. That Wordsworth was trying to discover reasons for optimism is undeniable, but the mood of the last stanzas is as different from joy as is the sober coloring of "the clouds that gather round the setting sun" from the glorious brightness of those that accompanied the newborn child on his journey from celestial realms. The Ode is dominated by "a sense of loss and alienation, in spite of the claims of the concluding lines."[12] Reasons for gratitude and hope can not balance the sadness Wordsworth feels at the dying away of a glory from the earth; the palms of grim wisdom are accepted sadly by a lonely man who is desperately trying to learn to live "in reconcilement" with his "stinted powers"[13] in a world bereft of spirit.

ROBERT L. SCHNEIDER

[11] Trilling, p. 134.
[12] Willey, p. 285.
[13] *The Prelude*, Bk. v, line 541.

MARK TWAIN REVISES *OLD TIMES ON*
THE MISSISSIPPI, 1875–1883

SINCE his death in 1910, Mark Twain has come to be recognized as one of the great stylists of the English language. His skill is acknowledged even by those impervious to his humor. Modern scholarship is interested in the development of Mark Twain as a literary artist, and has sometimes regretted that he did not, in the manner of Henry James, revise some of his early writings late in life—if for no other reason than to provide alternate texts for comparison.

Although we are denied the opportunity to study in this way the progress of Mark Twain across the decades, in one instance we *are* provided with a considerable work which he revised after a period of about eight years. *Old Times on the Mississippi* appeared in seven installments in *The Atlantic Monthly* from January to July, 1875. Eight years later in 1883 was published the volume, *Life on the Mississippi*. Chapters IV–XVII of the book, contrary to popular belief,[1] include all the material from *The Atlantic Monthly*. These fourteen chapters contain approximately 36,000 words, just about twenty-five percent of the entire volume. (The rest of the book was inspired by Twain's trip down the river in 1882.) To the best of my knowledge, until now no one has troubled to make a close comparison of these chapters with the original magazine version.

At the outset it might be asked whether William Dean Howells, then editor of *The Atlantic Monthly*, himself revised the manuscript pages as they arrived from his good friend in Hartford. After all, Mark Twain did give him a free hand. With the first installment came a note: "Dear Howells,—Cut it, scarify it, reject it—handle it with entire freedom. Yrs. ever, Mark."[2] But Howells replied that the piece was "capital"—adding, "I don't think I shall meddle much with it even in the way of suggestion."[3] It would seem that Howells kept his word. Mark Twain professed to feel quite comfortable in writing for

---

[1] Both Mark Twain's official biographer and his bibliographer are guilty of carelessness on this point. Albert Bigelow Paine writes: "The first twenty chapters were contributed to *The Atlantic Monthly* in 1875 . . . ." Introduction to *Life on the Mississippi*, Definitive Edition of *The Writings of Mark Twain* (Gabriel Wells: New York, 1923), XXXI, xi. Merle Johnson repeats this error, even implying that *Old Times on the Mississippi* formed the first twenty-one chapters of the book. *A Bibliography of the Works of Mark Twain*, rev. ed. (Harpers: New York, 1935), p. 43.

[2] *Mark Twain's Letters*, ed. Albert Bigelow Paine, Definitive Edition of *The Writings of Mark Twain*, XXXIV, 230.

[3] *Life in Letters of William Dean Howells*, ed. Mildred Howells (Doubleday, Doran: New York, 1928), I, 196.

the *Atlantic* audience. The result, therefore, was doubtless a product which the tasteful magazine could print just as it came from the author's pen. One thing is fairly sure. If Howells *did* make any revisions in Twain's manuscripts, Twain incorporated them into his book. The differences between the two texts are mainly of a stylistic nature beneath the notice of a busy editor. (Such was not the case ten years later when Richard Watson Gilder printed sections of *Huckleberry Finn* in *The Century Magazine*—carefully pruning and polishing the powerful book.)[4]

When we inspect the revisions in *Life on the Mississippi*, we are not surprised to find several dozen which might be the work of a conscientious proofreader. Commas are deleted; quotation marks are placed around unspoken comments; boat names are italicized; paragraphing is altered; and spelling is modernized or corrected in many words like "brim full," "centre," "cuspadores," and "any way." There are also ten alterations necessitated either by the change of publication date or by the change from serial to book form. For example, "Twenty-two years ago" becomes "In 1853," (p. 149)[5] while words like "numbers," "papers," and "articles" are changed to "chapters" (94, 107, 119). In 1883 Mark Twain also feels free to refer to his old friends by their real names (Bixby, Ealer, etc.), instead of by mere initials. Such revisions, however, are all of a routine sort not pertinent to our study.

More significant are the forty-five additional changes which can be broken down into the following categories:

Word substitutions	16
Deletions	10
Changes of tense or number	6
Additions	6
Changes of fact	3
Changes of expression	3
Division of a speech	1
	45

The first and largest category shows Mark Twain's increasing concern for the *right* word—to replace what he called "the approximate word, a second cousin to the right word." Thus, the profanity of the big stormy mate is no longer "perfect," but "sublime" (41); and a mere "shout" of laughter becomes a "thundergust" (117). New Or-

---

[4] For detailed information on this subject, see my forthcoming study in *American Literature*.

[5] Page numbers refer to the Definitive Edition, *op. cit.*

leans "pavements" are now more exotic "banquettes" (122). The more exact and alliterative "dims" replaces "fades" as the lantern now "dims away in the remote distance" (101). Rereading also made Mark Twain self-conscious about several of his pet words, for the overworked "gaudy," "marvelous," and "execrable" are on occasion replaced by the more appropriate "dashing," (137) "great," (148) and "troublesome" (80). Style is simplified and tightened, moreover, by changing "down the slant of" to "athwart," (143) and by substituting the pronoun "them" (32) for the awkward locution italicized in the sentence: "Before these events, the day was glorious with expectancy; after *they had transpired*, the day was a dead and empty thing." Of the sixteen cases of word substitution, the only one which fails to strengthen the prose is the change of the oath "hell" to "h--l" (40)— and this may simply have been a rule of the publishing house.

In the matter of deletions, too, the changes improve the style. Twice the unneeded word "very" is dropped (37, 145); and gone are the redundant words "else," (46) "in order" (from "in order to," 71), "was" (verb made active, 146), the adjective "gentle-spirited" (from the expression "good old gentle-spirited Captain Y," 123), and the conjunction "and" (from "packed and black," 144). "Milk-teeth" becomes merely "teeth," (91) the paranthetical "(some sixteen or seventeen years ago)" is excised entirely (155), and the qualifying introduction, "I am informed that," is eliminated to make the statement a positive assertion of fact (155)—of fact perhaps verified during the author's recent trip on the river.

The six changes of tense or number are not significant. It makes no difference whether chairs are tilted back against the "wall" or against the "walls" (33). And three of the verbs are put into the past tense simply for the sake of consistency (50, 55, 78). As for the fourth verb change, purists might argue that the original subjunctive "were" is preferable in the sentence: "If the theme was hackneyed, I should be obliged to deal gently with the reader. . . . " (82) But these are small matters.

The first three chapters of the book give a brief history of the great river and its explorers, and then describe raft life by means of a chapter lifted from the unpublished manuscript of *Huckleberry Finn*. These chapters were not in *The Atlantic Monthly*, but were written later to provide a more literary introduction to the book. Also added to the book were two and a half pages of statistical tables: "The Record of Some Famous Trips" (150-52). Mark Twain most likely acquired these tables during his visit to the river in 1882. A third addition is that of a footnote explaining that some authorities dispute a

sailing record the author has just cited (149). Two other additions
are of the emphatic word "ever" (32) and of the phrase "of the reversed bench" (100)—the latter necessitated by an altered comparison
we shall note in a moment. Artistically, only one addition is important.
At the end of Chapter 14, a penny-pinching captain is conversing with
Stephen, an impoverished pilot whom he has signed on for half wages.
When the smug captain finally complains that the pilots on another
boat up ahead are saving time and fuel by taking short-cuts through
chutes, Stephen replies:

> "*They!* Why, *they* are two-hundred-and-fifty-dollar pilots! But don't
> you be uneasy; I know as much as any man can afford to know for a hundred
> and twenty-five!"
> The captain surrendered. [This sentence is new.]
> Five minutes later Stephen was bowling through the chute and showing
> the rival boat a two-hundred-and-fifty-dollar pair of heels. (126)

It would seem that Mark Twain believed that the less select audience
of the book required a more definite, less subtle indication of the
captain's capitulation.

Rather interesting are the three changes of fact, which suggest
that the author's romantic memory of 1875 was corrected by his
direct observation of 1882. In Chapter 6, the shores by Mr. Jones's
plantation were at first "not much more than a mile apart." Twain
later cut this distance in half (48). Again, one dark night Mr. Bixby
told him that he should keep the steamboat "within twenty feet" of
the shore when going upstream. No doubt it *seemed* like only twenty
feet to the frightened apprentice pilot, but Mark Twain later had the
honesty to increase the distance to "within fifty feet" (64). In the
same manner, his sense of drama and his desire to impress caused
Twain at first to speak in awe of the "two thousand shoal places between St. Louis and New Orleans." In the book these shoals have
diminished in number to "five hundred" (70)—and it is doubtful that
the reduction was an alluvial one.

The three times that Mark Twain meddles with larger elements
of writing, his style changes from spontaneity to artifice—a dubious
improvement. In the book, the first time he took the wheel of a steamboat his "heartbeat fluttered up into the hundreds" (45). This is
precise, yes, and avoids cliché. But is it, after all, more apt than the
simple original comment: "my heart went down into my boots"?
A chapter later, the terse "Talk was going on, now, in low voices"
burgeons into a flowery "Out of the murmur of half-audible talk, one
caught a coherent sentence now and then—such as . . . "(60). The
third change of expression probably represents the search for a more

descriptive metaphor. In describing a sounding buoy, Twain at first called it "a reversed boot-jack." No boot-jack is mentioned in the book, where the buoy now is described as "a reversed school-house bench, with one of the supports left and the other removed" (100). The clarity of the comparison depends upon the reader's own personal experience, but there is no doubt as to which metaphor *reads* better.

The final change tabulated above is merely the attributing to two successive speakers of a bit of dialogue originally given, thus, to only one (as the boat goes over a dangerous shoal): " 'Her stem's coming down just *exactly* right, by *George!* Now she's in the marks; over she goes!'" (60) The change is an improvement, since it suggests—as does the sense of the words—that a few anxious seconds have elapsed between the two exclamations.

What is the significance of all these revisions? They show, I believe, that Mark Twain disliked revising any more than necessary. His friend, James R. Osgood, who was to publish *Life on the Mississippi*, probably requested him to read over the *Atlantic* pieces with a view toward correcting errors, making those changes required by the passing of time and by the different form of publication, and in general polishing up the style wherever it seemed too rough. A comparison of the two texts indicates that Mark Twain made these revisions with a minimum of effort—perhaps in the wide margins of the magazine itself. Also, he seems to have followed his early practice of revising sporadically.[6] Of the 45 revisions catalogued above, 30 occur in the first and last quarters of *Old Times on the Mississippi*, while only 15 occur in the middle half. This fact, considered together with the triviality of most of the revisions, is further evidence that Mark Twain's approach towards editing his own printed works was casual, perfunctory, and bored.[7] A popular writer, at the height of his creative power in 1882–83, Mark Twain wrote for the present. And the present loved him as he was. Never did he show a Jamesian desire to spend laborious months reworking his published writings for the sake of posterity. Many students of literature may regard this reluctance on Mark Twain's part as being additional proof that he really *was*—as he has frequently been called—"the divine amateur."

ARTHUR L. SCOTT

[6] See Arthur L. Scott, "Mark Twain's Revision of *The Innocents Abroad* for the British Edition of 1872," *American Literature*, xxv (March, 1953), [43]–61. These earlier revisions ,too, might well have been made in the margins of the American edition.

[7] This does not apply to his newspaper travel letters (1867), where a different problem was involved. See Leon T. Dickinson, "Mark Twain's Revisions in Writing *The Innocents Abroad*," *American Literature*, xix (May, 1947), 139–57.

A SEPTEMBER DAY IN CANTERBURY: THE VEAL-BARGRAVE STORY

THE TABLES have been turned in the famous case of Mrs., or as we would say, Miss Veal of Dover, who died on 7 September 1705 and, according to her friend Mrs. Bargrave, came the next day to Canterbury and talked with Mrs. Bargrave for nearly two hours. In 1821 Sir Walter Scott thought that readers of the *True Relation of the Apparition* (July 1706) were taken in by Defoe. Today Mr. Rodney M. Baine thinks that Defoe was taken in by Mrs. Bargrave.

The *True Relation* differs from out-and-out fiction in an important way. Defoe pretended that Crusoe and Moll Flanders wrote their own stories; but one could not have gone to them (as an anonymous interviewer went to Mrs. Bargrave in 1714) and asked whether their stories were true. The Bargraves and the Veals were real people, with an existence independent of Defoe's pages. Mrs. Bargrave told, and retold, the story of Mrs. Veal's appearance. The *True Relation* was not published until ten months after the "event" and six months or more after another printed account. As a consequence, it is now difficult to consider the *True Relation* apart from the historical facts behind it and from four parallel accounts. All of us are interested in what happened to Mrs. Bargrave on that eighth of September. I for one welcome all the light we can get, provided we are not blinded by it and that we keep clear whether we are studying the mind of Mrs. Bargrave or the mind of Defoe. In this paper I intend to trace the growth of our knowledge of the characters in the story, present further information about these characters, and, in offering some conclusions of my own, correct others which I regard as unsound.

I

Several of Defoe's contemporaries claimed to have interviewed Mrs. Bargrave, and Dr. Johnson in 1772 implied a general recognition that she was a real person. But the impression was already widespread that her story was, as Toplady called it, "a fabulous legend." From this it is not a long step to the belief that the characters also were inventions. Not until 1895 did Aitken rediscover the factual basis of the story. He identified Mrs. Veal and found, as we might expect of one said to have died 7 September 1705, that she was buried at Dover on 10 September of that year. He identified her brother William, also, and "Old Mr. Breton," who (Defoe quotes Mrs. Veal as telling Mrs. Bargrave) had secretly allowed Mrs. Veal £10 a year. Aitken tentatively (and wrongly) identified Mrs. Bargrave as the wife of a Richard Bargrave, maltster.[1]

Aitken's friend, Sir Charles Firth, published in 1931 the first of two accounts of the apparition known to have preceded Defoe's account. It was in a letter of 9 October 1705 from a Lucy Lukyn in Canterbury to her aunt in London. It gives some details not in the *True Relation*, with which, on the whole, it agrees. Later in 1931, in a paper which shows how misleading a fact may be, Dorothy Gardiner discussed the Canterbury setting of the story. Having found that in 1726–31 a Mrs. Bargrave (presumably the widow of the maltster cited by Aitken) lived two doors away from a William Watson (almost certainly the Captain Watson, uncle to Mrs. Veal) and near the Lukyns, Mrs. Gardiner thought she had iron-clad proof that here was the scene of the visitation. Her conclusions, amplified with a map of the area and a photograph of the Watson and Bargrave sites in Watling Street, reappeared still later in 1931 in Wright's biography of Defoe.[2]

In 1954 Mr. Baine reprinted the latest of the known eighteenth-century versions of the Veal story. It purports to have been taken from the lips of Mrs. Bargrave in London in 1722 by an Exeter clergyman named Payne, but it was not published until 1766. Like the *True Relation*, which appeared first as a separate pamphlet, it was prefixed to a translation of Drelincourt's *Consolations de l'âme fidèle contre les frayeurs de la mort*. Still another version of the Veal story prefaced John Spavan's 1720 condensation of Drelincourt. The Payne account, though largely rehashed from Defoe's, has some fresh details, which Baine uses to identify more completely the persons in the story and to introduce some suggestions about its origin.[3]

Professor Arthur H. Scouten has found and is currently reprinting in *RES* the most important of all the accounts paralleling Defoe's *True Relation*—important because it preceded the *True Relation* and, unlike the Lukyn letter, it was available to Defoe in print. It appeared anonymously in No. 14 (21–24 December 1705) of a very rare periodical, the *Loyal Post*. It asserts that many Londoners had received

---

[1] George A. Aitken, "Defoe's Apparition of Mrs. Veal," *Nineteenth Century*, XXXVII (1895), 95–100; Boswell, *Johnson*, ed. Hill-Powell (1934-50), II, 164.

[2] Sir Charles Firth, "Defoe's *True Relation*," *RES*, VII (1931), 1–6; Dorothy Gardiner, "What Canterbury Knew of Mrs. Veal and Her Friends," *RES*, VII (1931), 188–97; Thomas Wright, *Life of Daniel Defoe*, rev. ed., pp. 112 (opposite), 129–38.

[3] Rodney M. Baine, "The Apparition of Mrs. Veal: A Neglected Account," *PMLA*, LXIX (1954), 523–41; "Defoe and Mrs. Bargrave's Story," *PQ*, XXXIII (1954), 388–95.

letters carrying the story and that several from "Persons of Good Repute have reached our hands, besides Relations we have had by Word of Mouth. . . . " It agrees with the Lukyn letter in crediting the story to Mrs. "Bargrove," but, though slightly briefer than the letter, it has a few independent details.[4]

II

Mrs. Bargrave. As we have seen, Aitken and Mrs. Gardiner thought the Mrs. Bargrave we are interested in was the wife of Richard Bargrave, maltster. But *that* Mrs. Bargrave (born about 1657) is not known to have lived in Dover, and she is not likely to have been the girlhood friend of Mrs. Veal, who was eighteen years or so younger. The late Mr. William Minet, a descendant of Mrs. Veal's sister-in-law, correctly identified our Mrs. Bargrave as the daughter of John Lodowick, a Dover clergyman.[5]

Payne corroborates Minet, and Baine has further details about John Lodowick and his daughter. Payne adds that Mr. Bargrave was a barrister. The earlier account in the *Loyal Post* says that he was an attorney living near St. George's Gate. All this corrects the Aitken-Gardiner mistake and exonerates Defoe from the charge by Thomas Wright (of all people!) of having tampered with fact when he says that, in leaving Mrs. Bargrave's house to go to the Watson's, Mrs. Veal faced the (cattle) market and that Mrs. Bargarve watched "till a turning interrupted the sight of her." St. George's Gate, at the intersection of St. George's Street and the city wall, was right at the cattle market. And to go from there to the Watsons in Watling Street required at least one major turn.

---

[4] Professor Scouten has allowed me to see the *Loyal Post* account in typescript. As this is written (June 1955), the printing of it in *RES* is still to come. See also Scouten's *"The Loyal Post*, A Rare Queen Anne Newspaper, and Daniel Defoe," *Bulletin of the New York Public Library*, LXIX (1955), 195-97.

[5] As a president of the Huguenot Society of London and an editor of several of its publications, Mr. Minet had learned about the Lodowicks (or Lodwiks or Lodwicks), who had come to England in an early wave of Huguenots. He left his notes on Mrs. Bargrave in the British Museum with an offprint of his "Daniel Defor and Kent" (1914). I used them in 1949 in an attempt to find whether the Dover Lodowicks were related to the Charles Lodwick who sponsored Defoe's application for a marriage licence and the John Lodwick who was chaplain of the ship upon which Drury went to India in 1701. There are other possible links between the Veal and Drury stories. William Minet has called attention to the fact that William Veal in November 1705, six weeks after the death of his sister, married Elizabeth Hughes, daughter of Drury's captain, William Young, and succeeded to the captain's estate, the manor of Capel-le-ferne near Dover. The Captain's widow, who survived till 1750, was born Alice Watson. Could she have been related to Mrs. Veal's uncle, Captain Watson?

The Veals, the Haslewoods, and the Hydes. The Veles, Veels, or Veals were a family of distinction. Their ancestors had come over with the Conqueror and had intermarried with the Berkeleys. In the late sixteenth century a Nicholas Vele purchased the manor of Alveston in Glouchestershire. His son, Thomas Veel, a colonel in the Civil War and the grandfather of Mrs. Veal, leased from the Berkeleys the nearby manor of Simondshall and passed it on to his oldest son. A sketch of Colonel Veel's career is in the *DNB*, and it is surprising that Defoe scholars have not found it earlier. At some time after 1623 he married, as his second wife, Margaret, "daughter of . . . Hide of Hatch." This last was possibly Lawrence Hyde (died 1590), father of Chief Justice Nicholas Hyde and grandfather of the first Earl of Clarendon, but more probably he was Lawrence's oldest son Robert, who inherited the estate at West Hatch near Tisbury in Wilts. Margaret was the widow of Robert Culliford of Purbeck, Dorset. By this marriage—a marriage into the most powerful law family then in England—Thomas Veel had a daughter and two sons, Nicholas and Thomas, Jr., father of Mrs. Veal.[6]

Colonel Veel and these two sons were hot royalists. The Colonel was governor of Berkeley Castle in 1644 and commander of a regiment of horse at the battle of Worcester. Later he had letters from Charles II authorizing him to enlist troops. With Sir Edward Massey, to whom he was related, he took part in the unsuccessful uprising in Gloucestershire in 1659, which resulted in the seizure of his property and that of the two sons.

At the Restoration, with Clarendon as Secretary of State and Lord Chancellor until 1667, the Veels quite naturally expected to repair their ruined fortunes. All three seem to have haunted the court to see what could be got. In 1662 Clarendon cited their extraordinary loyalty and approved a request made by the Colonel. But, though

---

[6] Baine called attention to Gloucestershire as the home of the Veals and to the marriage of Thomas Veal into the Hyde family. Other sources are: *Visitation of the County Gloucester . . . 1623* (1885), ed. John Maclean and W. C. Heane, pp. 173–74, and *Visitation of . . . Gloucester, 1682–3* (Exeter, 1888), ed. T. Fitz-Roy Fenwick and Walter C. Metcalfe, pp. 191–92; *Visitation of . . . Dorset . . . 1623* (1885), ed. Paul Rylands, p. 72—this gives Margaret Hyde as wife of Robert Culliford; *DNB* (under Robert Veel); Sir Robert Atkyns, *Ancient and Present State of Gloucestershire*, 2nd ed. (1768, from 1712 printing), pp. 110–12, 449–50; *Cal. of the Proceedings of the Committee for Advance of Money, domestic, 1642–1656*, Part II, 746; *Cal. of the Proceedings of the Committee for Compounding . . . 1643–1660*, pp. 85, 748, 865, 2079–80, 3248; *CSP*, d.s., 1661–62, p. 386; *CSP*, d.s., 1665–66, p. 482; *CSP*, d.s., 1670, p. 668; *Cal. of Treas. Books*, I–VIII (see indexes).

the king expressed gratitude, he threw the Colonel only a scrap or two before the latter's death in 1663. The sons were somewhat more successful. In 1665 they were named to collect certain taxes in Gloucestershire, and in June, 1666, Thomas Veel and a Matthew Black (elsewhere called Bluck) purchased the reversion of the office of collector of customs at Sandwich port in Kent. But for two decades misfortune dogged the brothers, whose inefficiency, or worse, in handling the tax money is reported in the Calendar of Treasury Books, I–VIII. Among their sureties were Edward Hyde of East Hatch (either their mother's brother or their cousin) and Robert Culliford (probably their half-brother and possibly comptroller of customs at Southampton). For a while Thomas and possibly Nicholas Veel were under arrest. Defoe alludes to this time when he tells us that Mrs. Veal's father so neglected his children that they wanted both food and clothing.

Not until 1687 were the brothers released from their bonds. Meantime, in 1674, the post at Sandwich was vacated, and, as Baine points out, Thomas Veel and Richard Breton (*vice* Black) received the patent for that office. As we shall see, the patent included the ports of Dover and Deal also. They held this patent indefinitely, though Thomas Veel's troubles in Gloucestershire disqualified him in 1676 to be deputy, or actual, collector of Dover port. Of Veel's first wife nothing is known; she may have been the Mary Butler of Dorset whom Baine, following sources which he does not recognize as "doctored," identifies with the second wife Amy. At any rate, he was a widower when, in December 1666, he married the widow of a London merchant, Amy Farewell of St. Andrews Undershaft. By her he had a son William and a daughter, the famous Mrs. Veal (born *ca.* 1675), probably named Margaret.[7]

---

[7] *Allegations for Marriage Licences . . . from the Faculty Office of the Archbishop of Canterbury* (1886), entry for 12 December 1666; *Visitation of . . . Gloucester, 1682–3,* p. 191. In the latter we find the following:

> Thomas Veel of Dover, Kent, mar. *Mary,* widow of . . . Farewell of London, Merchant, living 1682, *dau. of Henry Butler (of Hanley, co. Dorset. She died 1658, aet. 24. M.I.)*

Baine has accepted this statement without question, but it has serious errors in it. In the first place, the editors have amplified their documents by inserting names and by extending genealogies beyond 1683; some Veel entries come down to 1851. These amplifications are in italics.

Examination of the statement about Thomas Veel and his wife suggests that the parts in roman typeface are fact and that the editorial insertions in italics are guesswork. All the other evidence we have indicates that the widow Farewell was named Amy, not Mary. The marriage allegation, cited above, calls her Amy; she named her

The identity of Mrs. Veal's sister, who with her husband came to Dover just as Mrs. Veal was dying, has not been known. Lucy Lukyn gave her name as Haslewood, and Payne called her a half-sister. Mrs. Gardiner thought that she may have been Mrs. Bargrave's sister rather than Mrs. Veal's. The Haslewoods turn out to be Londoners of some importance and to have an interesting link of their own with the Hyde family.

Thomas Veel's wife Amy had, by her first marriage, a daughter also named Amy. This Amy Farewell of Low Layton, Essex, was described as a spinster of about thirty when, in 1694, she married a bachelor of forty-six, the Rev. John Haslewood, B.A., M.A., B.D., and D.D., rector of St. Olave Southwark. His father, John Haslewood of Oxford, "pharmacopolae," was doubtless the viol player and apothecary to Sir Thomas Clayton whom Anthony à Wood disliked. Before his marriage to Mrs. Veal's half-sister, Dr. Haselwood had been chaplain to Henry Hyde, second Earl of Clarendon, when the latter was lord lieutenant of Ireland, and then and afterward he was an intimate family friend in the Clarendon home. Whether this association had anything to do with Haslewood's marriage to the stepdaughter of Clarendon's cousin, Thomas Veel, I cannot say.[8]

William Veal and the Customs at Dover. Defoe says that the friends of Mrs. Veal's brother William got him a place in the custom house

daughter by Farewell Amy, and the one by William Veal, Margaret after his mother. If, as the interpolations say, she died in 1658, she could not have been living in 1682 nor have married William Veal in 1666.

Since such interpolations usually have some basis in fact, I suggest that Mary Butler was Thomas Veel's first wife. Veel is described as a widower in his marriage allegation of 1666. *The Calendar of . . . the Committee for Compounding* mentions the deposition of a Mary Veel, 24 November 1659, who, in the index, is called the wife of the Colonel. But, unless the Colonel was married three times, he had no wife Mary, though he had a daughter by that name. Assuming that this older daughter had already married a Mr. Coppinger of Winchester, and that the interpolated date of Mary Butler's death (1658) in the *Visitation* is inaccurate, the Mary Veel of the 1659 deposition may have been Mary Butler, first wife of Thomas Veel, Jr. The three Thomas Veels mentioned in the *Calendar* (p. 3248) are the Colonel, his son Thomas, Jr., and his grandson, Thomas, son of William Veel of Simondshall.

[8] *Allegations for Marriage Licences . . . by the Vicar-General of the Archbishop of Canterbury, July 1687 to June 1694* (1890), p. 290. Luttrell's *Brief Relation* (VI, 341) announces on 21 August 1708 that Dr. Boulter has succeeded to the living of Dr. Haslewood deceased (£300 a year) at St. Olaves.

See, also, *Alum. Oxon . . . 1500–1714*, ed. John Foster (1891) II, 670; Anthony à Wood, *Ath. Oxon*, ed. 1813, I, xxvi, xlvii, and IV (Fasti, II), 398; *Corr. of Henry Hyde* (London, 1828), II, 271, 285, 287–88, 292. This Earl of Clarendon refers to the Edward Hyde (security for the Veels) as Cousin Hyde. The index to this work gives Harlewood instead of Haslewood.

at Dover. Payne amplifies this. He tells us that William's father had been collector of customs at Dover and that William was made comptroller of the customs there by Queen Mary because of his relation "by the [grand]mother" to the Hyde family. Baine discovered that William and his father held these posts at the port of Sandwich, but no one has found confirmation that they held them also at the port of Dover. A careful reading of the records, however, shows that an appointment to Sandwich included appointment to Deal, Dover, and perhaps other nearby ports.

Richard Breton, Mrs. Veal's benefactor, claimed in 1708 that he and Thomas Veel had been "constituted joint patentees of the office of Collector of Sandwich port & members 'of which Dover is one, which office was to be executed by deputy . . . '." The Customs Commissioners in London replied that the Breton-Veel patent of 1674 "did not apparently intend the collection at Dover." But Lord Treasurer Danby, who had authorized that patent, had directed the Commissioners on 27 April 1676 "to depute Richard Breton (he and Thomas Veel being the patent customers of Dover port) as deputy collector of said port *loco* Mr. Stockdale . . . ." There can be no doubt that in his own mind and, in that of the public, Thomas Veel was joint collector of Dover as well as of Sandwich.[9]

Analogous evidence makes William Veal comptroller of the port of Dover from the 1692 fiat appointing him to succeed Walter Breame (Breames or Braems) as comptroller of Sandwich. Between 1663 and 1692 a series of warrants were issued for Breame's annual salary of £15 6s. 8d. (the same as William Veal's after him) as comptroller of Sandwich. Without any other recorded authorization, however, Breame is referred to in the Treasury Book of 1679 as comptroller of Dover. And when William Veal died 19 November 1729, the *Political State*, possibly under the direction of Defoe, described him as having been "Comptroller-General to the Custom-House of Dover, Deal, Sandwich and Feversham, which places he held by a Patent granted by Queen Mary for life." The published Treasury Books do not indicate payment to anyone for these additional ports. Probably, like the deputy collector at Dover, the comptroller deducted his salary before money was forwarded to London.[10]

[9] *Cal. of Treas. Bks.*, IV, 625, 634; V, 198, 398; XXII, pt. II, 245.

[10] *Cal. of Treas. Bks.*, I, 542; II, 623, V, 398; VI, 266; VII, Part I, 106 (the index to this entry calls Walter Breame Comptroller of Dover); IX, Pt. II, 709, Pt. IV, 1627, 1819. *Political State*, XXXVIII (1729), 496.

William Veal and Queen Mary were cousins, and Mrs. Bargrave's remark in the Payne account that she got a relative of hers, a gentleman named Boyce, to introduce William to Archbishop Tillotson, who in turn introduced him to Queen Mary, would seem to be questionable. Baine intimates that Mrs. Bargrave's relationship to the Boyce family may have been through the marriage of John Boys, Dean of Canterbury, to an Angela Bargrave. That ancient marriage of 1599 (1604?) was, however, in Mr. Bargrave's family. If there is any truth in Payne's statement, the Mr. Boyce was probably from a Huguenot family named Dubois, a number of whom in Kent anglicized the name to Boyce or Boys.

Major-General Sibourg. Payne thought that Mrs. Veal's illness and death were owing to fits brought on when her brother forbade her to receive the addresses of "Major-General Sibourg (a natural son of the the Duke of Schomberg) sinced killed in the battle of Mons." As General Charles Sibourg seems to have died of natural causes in 1732/3, we have some details which could not have been communicated by Mrs. Bargrave in 1722, but which must have been introduced by Payne or his publisher. Perhaps, however, General Sibourg has been confused with his brother, Colonel Frederick Sibourg, who was killed in a famous explosion at Alicant in 1709.[11]

III

Authorship of the True Relation. Though the *True Relation* has been in the Defoe canon for over 150 years, Mr. Baine, in a second article, raises the question of authorship and traces the history of the attribution. What he found evidently satisfied him, for this article which he announced as "Did Defoe Write *An Apparition of Mrs. Veal?*" he later published as "Defoe and Mrs. Bargrave's Story." The earliest implication of Defoe as the author Baine found in an anonymous passage in the *Universal Spectator* of 1734, three years after Defoe's death—a comparatively early date. The same problem exists for nearly all of Defoe's narratives. The novels do not mention his name, and, so far as I know, *Robinson Crusoe* is the only one attributed to him in his lifetime. The *Memoirs of a Cavalier* was vigorously maintained to be the journal of a real soldier until 1895.

A prefatory statement in the *True Relation* attributes the narrative to a Maidstone justice of the peace. But this is like many other state-

[11] See David C. A. Agnew, *Protestant Exiles from France*, 2nd ed. (1871), III, 183 n.; *Proceedings of the Huguenot Society of London*, IX (1911), 52, 482–83, 507.

ments by Defoe. The adventures of Robinson Crusoe were "Written by himself," and those of Moll Flanders "from her own Memorandums." The *History of Charles XII* was by a "Scots Gentleman in the Swedish Service." These are only a few of the many works which Defoe pretended were by someone else, and there is now no reason to question his authorship of this one, especially since in tone and style it is universally felt to be his.

Mrs. Bargrave's Story. Baine admits that Defoe's skill in dramatizing the *True Relation* made it famous. But he thinks "the whole problem of authorship alters considerably" with what he regards as his discovery that Mrs. Bargrave was probably lying. "Mrs. Bargrave, not Defoe [he says], must be given the credit for the original fiction. It was she who invented the themes discussed and dreamed up the minute evidence for the reality of the apparition."

I confess myself puzzled by this. Who but Mrs. Bargrave has been given credit for the story? She was the only witness to the apparition and the source of all the accounts. Defoe and the others deny for lack of motive that she invented the story, but they tell us over and over that they are reporting only what she told them. Naturally that included the topics discussed at the meeting and details advanced to make the story credible. Since this has been widely known for sixty years, I cannot see how it alters the problem of authorship.

What Baine does have, it seems to me, is a plausible motive for the hoax and some interesting comments upon Mrs. Bargrave's ingenuity and courage. All the accounts agree that Mrs. Bargrave had a bad husband, and Lukyn and Payne say that some hours after the apparition he came home in a temper and put her in the garden (Lukyn: a wet washhouse) to spend the cool September night. This treatment, says Baine, "if it did not cause an actual hallucination, might easily have provoked a story told partly out of malice, partly from a desire for notoriety."

On any interpretation, Mrs. Bargrave was a woman of remarkable powers. Her story was not of events remote in time and place, or even of contemporary nobodies. Though Sir Walter Scott referred to Mrs. Bargrave as a seamstress and to the Veals as an exciseman and his housekeeper, the Veals were people of station and birth—cousins of Queen Anne herself. To challenge the story in London were the Haslewoods; in Canterbury, the Watsons and Mr. Bargrave, an attorney trained to weigh evidence; and in Dover, William Veal and

Mr. Breton. Under the circumstances, it could not have succeeded if its fiction had not been blended skillfully with fact.

A hoax is seldom if ever without some basis in fact. And no matter how lively her imagination, Mrs. Bargrave did not, as Baine suggests, fabricate her story out of nothing. It was convincing because, as Scott says, it sobers "the whole supernatural visit into the language of middle or low life:" or, to put it in other words, because it consisted so largely of commonplace realities. The Haslewoods did come to visit Mrs. Veal as she was dying; Mrs. Veal did have fits; she did have a scoured silk dress; she did have a purse of gold pieces and other valuables and a cabinet in which they may have been kept; she and Mrs. Bargrave did have childhood memories in common—among them, doubtless, recollections of their reading in Drelincourt and similar books of devotion; Mrs. Bargrave was ill on Sunday, and on Monday she must, as she said, have gone to the Watsons inquiring for her friend and astonished them with the minuteness of her knowledge. How she acquired this knowledge may in part be explained by the early account which Scouten is reprinting from the *Loyal Post*.

The *Loyal Post*'s account tells us that Mrs. Veal had visited Canterbury just a week before her death—on which occasion she may have communicated to her old friend many of the obscure facts which the Watsons thought only they shared. It tells us also, and in a context to suggest a recent association of the two friends, that on the famous Saturday night, Mr. Bargrave, "in the midst of some Angry Words, told her, now her Friend Mrs. Veal was dead," and that not until the next day did Mrs. Bargrave tell her husband "that she saw Mrs. Veal Yesterday." When, therefore, Bargrave put his wife into the garden, she had all the details she needed for the story except the apparition itself, the inspiration for which we shall probably never know. It is at least possible that, in fabricating the counterfeit conversation with Mrs. Veal, she used a real one of the week before.

Was Defoe Taken in by Mrs. Bargrave? Defoe, according to Baine, was convinced by Mrs. Bargrave that her story was true, and, disgusted at finding out later that he had been gulled, he omitted it from his 1727 anthology of apparitions. There were, however, much more cogent reasons for the omission than irritation at Mrs. Bargrave. By 1727 her story was, on Baine's own evidence, shopworn and controversial; and doubtless it was too closely identified with Defoe to risk in a work which he was publishing under a pseudonym. We are, then, dependent upon what we know of Defoe generally and upon the *True Relation* to discover how far he believed Mrs. Bargrave.

His interest in the supernatural might dispose us to believe him gullible if we ourselves did not share it. Was he not like journalists of today who exploit popular interest in King Tut's curse and Friday the 13th? And was he any more gullible than Professor J. B. Rhine? He himself perpetrated some remarkable hoaxes in his time, of which the *Shortest Way* is only one.

We shall learn little more about the gullibility of Defoe from the *True Relation*. This is because the problem of making it convincing was the same, whether he himself believed it or not. He no doubt listened sympathetically to Mrs. Bargrave and presented her story as something she at least believed; and he tried to make his readers believe it. He did the same thing in his novels, and in the *Shortest Way* he identified himself so completely with the "high-flyers" that readers were blinded to his irony. It is naïve, however, to suppose that he was unaware of what he was doing. Possibly he made a distinction between what Mrs. Bargrave thought (or pretended to think) she saw and what she really had seen.

At the end Defoe remarked: "This thing has very much affected me, and I am as well satisfied, as I am of the best grounded matter of fact." Even though this may be construed as a rather confused statement of belief in the truth of Mrs. Bargrave's narrative, some of his arguments for her integrity sound more plausible than convincing. They explain why Swift called him sententious and dogmatical, and why Sir Walter Scott spoke of "his art of recommending the most improbable narrative, by his specious and serious mode of telling it."

Though for a half-century it has been the fashion to smile at Scott's views, one of his comments upon Defoe's method in the *True Relation* is still valid:

The narrative [says Scott] is drawn up "by a gentleman, a Justice of Peace at Maidstone, in Kent, a very intelligent person." And, moreover, "the discourse is attested by a very sober and understanding gentlewoman [his relation], who lives in Canterbury, within a few doors of the house in which Mrs. Bargrave lives." The Justice believes his kinswoman to be of so discerning a spirit, as not to be put upon by any fallacy—and the kinswoman positively assures the Justice, "that the whole matter, as it is related and laid down, is really true, and what she herself heard, as near as may be, from Mrs. Bargrave's own mouth, who, she knows, had no reason to invent or publish such a story, or any design to forge and tell a lie, being a woman of so much honesty and virtue, and her whole life, a course, as it were, of piety." Scepticism itself could not resist this triple court of evidence so artfully combined, the Justice attesting for the discerning spirit of the sober and understanding gentlewoman his kinswoman, and his kinswoman becoming bail for the veracity of Mrs. Bargrave.[12]

Defoe may have been serious when he suggests that a woman of such honesty and virtue had no reason to forge and tell a lie, and that he had been unable to find any deceit in her face. But other circumstantial evidence introduced seems to have little bearing on the question of validity. How, for example, her story is validated, as Defoe implies it is, by what he calls her cheerful disposition, even "under her husband's barbarity, which I have been a witness to," this writer does not see. Such details justify Scott in feeling that Defoe was enjoying his cleverness. He could hardly have been straightforward in suggesting that William Veal's attempts to stifle the story were hypercritical. He asks why Mr. Veal should object when it was generally agreed that his sister was "a good spirit" and that "her discourse was so heavenly." If people urged these reasons upon Veal, we can well understand his irritation at the whole business.

ARTHUR W. SECORD

[12] Scott, *Miscellaneous Works* (ed. 1880), IV, 266–74. Some believe John Ballantyne to be the author of this. A careful reading, however, reveals that Ballantyne's death interrupted him at p. 274 of this edition. Much of Scott's comment is weakened by the general ignorance of his time about the circumstances of the Veal-Bargrave story. He thought Defoe was perpetrating a hoax about middle- and lower-class characters. But even Defoe, in 1706, seems not to have known how high the Veals stood by birth and station.

BERNARD SHAW'S "BAD QUARTO"

EVERY biographer of Shaw has related the amusing circumstances of the genesis of his first play, *Widowers' Houses*. The story was first told by William Archer, and has been modified and supplemented in various details by Shaw himself.[1] There were the first meetings of Shaw and Archer in the British Museum Reading Room in 1885, where Archer was fascinated by the "young man of tawny complexion and attire," deeply and daily engrossed in alternative study of *Das Kapital* and the score of *Tristan und Isolde*. Then came Archer's proposal that they collaborate in writing a play, Archer to furnish the plot and Shaw the dialogue. Archer fancied himself a master of dramatic construction and Shaw claimed he could "write dialogue by the thousand yards." Archer tells us that he "drew out, scene by scene, the scheme of a twaddling cup-and-saucer comedy, vaguely suggested by Augier's *Ceinture Dorée*," which contained "two heroines, a sentimental and a comic one, according to the accepted Robertson-Byron-Carton formula," and a hero who, having proposed to the sentimental heroine, discovered her to be the daughter of a slum-landlord (or a sweater)—"and I know he was to carry on in the most heroic fashion, and was ultimately to succeed in throwing the tainted treasure of his father-in-law, metaphorically speaking, into the Rhine."

For six weeks Shaw worked away, putting "exquisite shorthand" into his notebooks. Then one day he dumbfounded Archer by telling him that he had finished the first act of "our play" and hadn't yet come to the plot—in fact, he'd forgotten it, and begged to hear it again. A few days later he complained that three pages into the second act the plot was all used up, and Archer must give him more to go on with. Here, or hereabouts, Archer renounced the collaboration, claiming that his plot was "a rounded and perfect organic whole, and that I could no more eke it out in this fashion than I could provide him or myself with a set of supplementary arms and legs." Shaw read him what he had written. What happened at that session we shall never know: Archer claims that "the process was too lingering and painful for endurance" and that he had to ask for a narrative outline to ascer-

---

[1] William Archer's account appeared in *The World*, December 14, 1892, and was reprinted by Shaw in his Author's Preface to the 1893 edition. To this account Shaw added details of his own. For further embellishments see, e.g., Archibald Henderson's *Bernard Shaw, Playboy and Prophet* (1932); Hesketh Pearson's *G.B.S., A Full Length Portrait* (1942); William Irvine's *The Universe of G.B.S.* (1949). The following résumé derives from all these sources.

tain that Shaw had simply abused the material; but according to Shaw's account Archer, as was his habit at great performances of great plays, simply went to sleep. At any rate, the collaboration ended, and Shaw put away his notebooks and forgot about them for several years.

In 1891 came the founding of the Independent Theatre by J. T. Grein, and the bombshell production of Ibsen's *Ghosts*, which filled London with screams of anguish from the conservative bench of critics; then Grein's long, fruitless search for "a single original play of any magnitude by an English author." Although Shaw was not yet a dramatic critic, he propagandized for Grein whenever he could,[2] and finally "in this humiliating national emergency" he offered to provide a play himself. "I had rashly taken up the case; and rather than let it collapse, I manufactured the evidence."[3] In the summer of 1892 he resurrected the discarded notebooks, completed the play, and called it *Widowers' Houses*. Grein accepted it sight unseen. It was produced December 9, 1892 (there were only two performances), and published as Number One of the Independent Theatre Series of Plays in March, 1893.[4]

Everyone who writes on Shaw reckons with *Widowers' Houses* critically, either minimizing it, as Shaw himself tended to do in after years, or as Eric Bentley does, claiming it, for all its faults to be "the most revolutionary act in modern English drama."[5] It would seem, however, that no critic in the last half century or so has read the play in the form that Shaw first wrote it and as it was produced and pub-

---

[2] See, e.g., *Music in London* (Standard Edition), I, 142, 160.

[3] Henderson, *op. cit.*, p. 355.

[4] The title-page reads: WIDOWERS' HOUSES. A COMEDY BY G. BERNARD SHAW. FIRST ACTED AT THE INDEPENDENT THEATRE IN LONDON. LONDON: HENRY AND CO. BOUVERIE STREET, E.C. 1893. The gilt title on the board cover reads WIDOWERS' HOUSES, BY G. BERNARD SHAW. BEING NUMBER ONE OF THE INDEPENDENT THEATRE SERIES OF PLAYS. EDITED BY J. T. GREIN. It will be noted that Shaw still retains the initial G. In due time his *nom de théâtre* became simply Bernard Shaw. The contents of the 1893 volume are as follows: pp. v–vii, "The Editor's Preface to the Independent Series," by Grein, dated, "LONDON, *Ides of March*, 1893"; pp. ix–xix, "The Author's Preface," containing Archer's story of the writing of the play, Shaw's comments and corrections, and general prefatory matter not elsewhere reprinted; pp. 1–102, the text of the play; pp. 103–14, Appendix I, "The Author to the Dramatic Critics"; pp. 115–24, Appendix II, being extracts from letters by Shaw to the press, to record the "commotion" caused by the play; pp. 125–26, Appendix III, being a news-item reporting a fatal fall of a charwoman on a defective slum staircase; and two pages of advertisements of the Series and of "Works by the Same Author."

[5] Eric Bentley, *Bernard Shaw* (1947), p. 102.

lished by Grein. It is now read only in the much altered version issued in 1898 as the first member of *Plays: Pleasant and Unpleasant*, or the still further polished version in the Standard Edition of 1930. A review of the 1893 edition will provide some astonishments in the art of playwriting and some curious sidelights on Shaw's own development toward mastery of the form.

After 1893 and before 1898, Shaw served his full apprenticeship in the theatre, not only by writing half a dozen more plays, but by studying the theatre from every thinkable point of view as dramatic critic for the *Saturday Review*. By 1898 he was thoroughly ashamed of his first version of *Widowers' Houses*. In the Preface to *Plays: Pleasant and Unpleasant*, he wished it out of existence.

The volume. . . . is still extant, a curious relic of that nine days wonder, and as it contains the original text of the play with all its silly pleasantries, I can recommend it to collectors of quarto Hamlets, and of all those scarce and superseded early editions which the unfortunate author would so gladly annihilate if he could.[6]

Anyone who has tried to make a prompt-copy of an early Shaw play—say *Candida* or *Arms and the Man*, matching early editions against the Standard Edition or reprints therefrom, is aware of the pervasive, detailed, and sometimes drastic revisions which Shaw effected in his dramatic works just before 1930. But he made these revisions quietly and without public announcement, much as, say, Henry James reworked his early novels and tales for the "New York Edition," simply to bring them into consonancy with his maturest sense of the *mot juste*. The 1893 text of *Widowers' Houses* is the only text that Shaw ever deplored so heartily as to wish he could "annihilate" it.

The reasons for this wish are not far to seek. A good look at the "premature" text of *Widowers' Houses*, will reveal that it reads, in parts, more like the work of a Robertson or Taylor, a Pinero or Jones, than like Bernard Shaw.

Basically, of course, the play is from the very first established as we now know it. The fable is the same. The anti-idealist, anti-romantic, anti-melodramatic attitude is the same. The Socialist economics, the implied directive "to vote on the Progressive side at the next County Council election," is all there. The second and third acts (the portions written last) are quite superior to the first act, and especially it should be noted that the great discussion scenes featuring Sartorius and Lickcheese are nearly identical with the versions we are used to.

[6] See Preface to *Plays: Pleasant and Unpleasant*, vol. i, p. xiii.

The differences are simply matters of workmanship: stage direction, stage management, details of characterization and motivation, and brightness of dialogue in the more casual and relaxed portions of the play.

The first astonishment to catch the reader's eye on a casual turning of the pages of the 1893 edition is a typographical one—the affectation of the continental style of numbering scenes within the act with heavy capital letters whenever there is any change of personnel. Thus in the first act we get

SCENE I

COKANE,   TRENCH

and two pages later

SCENE II

TRENCH, COKANE, WAITER, SARTORIUS,
PORTER, BLANCHE

and presently

SCENE III

TRENCH,   BLANCHE

This sort of thing runs on to the number of ten attention-bumps in the first act, thirteen in the second, and twelve in the third, This was not standard English· play-publishing practice at the time, and we can only assume Shaw meant by it to flaunt his affinities for the continental drama. Of course he abandoned it as soon as he came upon the doctrine that plays are to be *read*.

In the Preface to *Plays: Pleasant and Unpleasant*, Shaw spends several pages declaring the case for the literarization of plays in print. Few people, he argues, actually go to see plays as a regular practice—therefore we must make it congenial for them to read plays. But how can they be expected to do so

when they find nothing in them except a bald dialogue, with a few carpenter's and costumier's directions as to the heroine's father having a grey beard, and the drawing-room having three doors on the right, two doors and an entrance through the conservatory on the left, and a French window in the middle?[7]

Shakespeare and Sheridan and even Ibsen, he says, would have made

[7] *Ibid.*, p. xxiii.

their points much more effectively if they had bothered to write out the intended action of their plays. The actors would profit from more explicit directions and explanations. And since no one but the author can visualize a perfect and complete rendition of his intentions, he had better do his best to supply it himself.

The case, then, is overwhelming for printing and publishing not only the dialogue of plays, but for a serious effort to convey their full content to the reader. This means the institution of a new art; and I daresay that before these volumes are ten years old, the attempt that it makes in this direction will be left far behind, and that the customary, brief, and unreadable scene specifications at the head of an act will by then have expanded into a chapter. . . . [8]

Shaw, of course, became a master of this art of "conveying the full content"—after whom, to be sure, James Barrie and the like almost spoiled the game by overdoing it.

But look at the first stage direction of Shaw's first published play.

ACT I

Garden of a Hotel at Remagen on the Rhine, on a fine afternoon in August. Tables and chairs under the trees. Entrance to garden from riverside, L. Entrance to hotel, R. Entrance to Table d'Hote, RC. Waiter in attendance. . . . Enter from hotel Trench and Cokane, in tourist dress.

The style is undistinguishable from that of a run-of-the-mill Robertsonian farce. Never again would Shaw commit himself to the miserable telegraphy of R, L, and RC. By 1898 the bulk of these scrappy phrases are translated into readable sentences, and the last one is expanded into nine lines of specific, vivid description of Trench and Cokane.

Even such easy shop-terms as "enter" and "exit" become tabu with Shaw, and he learns to add everywhere to his directions of doing and going the distinctive qualifier indicative of purpose, mood, and manner. He would obviously rather save readers' attention than printers' ink. Here is a handful of small but telling specimens from 1893 with their 1898 revisions.

Exit Waiter into hotel.—The Waiter goes for the beer.
Enter Sartorius from the hotel.—Sartorius appears on the threshold of the hotel.
Exit R.—He walks away and disappears into the garden to the right.
They sit.—Trench, half-hypnotized by his own nervousness and the impressiveness of Sartorius, sits down helplessly.

These expansions of shop-work into literature are drawn from only the

[8] *Ibid.*, p. xxiv.

first few pages of the play: their number as the play goes on is count-less—their increase of meaning is immense. This meaning, too, is quite as valuable in terms of the theatre as in terms of the study. The actor-waiter who merely "exits into hotel" is a dead nineteenth-century actor, merely getting off the stage when no longer needed; the actor-waiter who "goes for the beer" is an Antoine-Grein-Stanis-lavsky actor who goes for a purpose.

Certainly one of the highest dramatic moments of the second act is the conclusion of Sartorius' long speech in which he so thoroughly justifies his resistance to the depradations of his irresponsible tenants, and then suddenly shifts about to crush Trench with a question.

No, gentlemen: when people are very poor, you cannot help them, no matter how much you may sympathize with them. It does them more harm than good in the long run. I prefer to save my money in order to provide additional houses for the homeless, and to lay by a little for Blanche. (*He looks at them. They are silent: Trench unconvinced, but talked down; Cokane humanely per-plexed. Sartorius bends his brows; comes forward in his chair as if gathering himself for a spring; and addresses himself, with impressive significance, to Trench.*) And now, Dr. Trench, may I ask what *your* income is derived from!

How much of the drama of this moment would be perceived by read-ers, by directors, or by actors without the precise and exciting indica-tions of these stage-directions? But not one word of them—not even an indication of a moment's silence before the question—occurs in the text of 1893.

Next we should take note of what may be loosely called "stage management"—the getting of characters on and off stage as needful for setting up the ensuing conversations, and the conduct of business on the stage so as to bring the characters into proper contact with each other. Even in the revised version one may be aware of some pretty obvious shuffling of characters in and out of doorways to ar-range for the "scenes." And at least once or twice rather intimate dialogues are encumbered by the unavoidable presence of a silent third party. Late in the first act, for instance, Blanche and Trench have to conduct a quarrel *sotto voce* while Cokane sits by preoccupied with his letter writing. Shaw can't get rid of Cokane, but in the revised version he minimizes the problem by shortening the quarrel by several speeches.

The entrances and exits provide numerous examples of the play-wright learning his business. Take, for instance, the first entrance of Blanche and Sartorius. In the 1893 version, Trench announces them with "Too late, by Jove: here she comes with her governor." Sartorius entering, orders his porter to "Place those things on that table." The waiter, bringing beer for Cokane and Trench, corrects him. "These gentlemen are using this table, I think, sir. Would you mind—" Sartorius rebukes him for "not having told him before," apologizes to Cokane, and retires to a farther table. Nothing could be more barren. In the revised version Shaw animates and motivates this contretemps, and "makes a little play of it." Trench's announcement of their arrival is less slangy and fulsome, but more properly breathless: "Oh, I say. Here they are." Cokane, the ever-ready companion, catches his arm and warns him: "Recollect yourself Harry: presence of mind, presence of mind." Then Cokane proceeds to fix the situation with the waiter, in language which he knows Sartorius cannot understand: "Kellner, ceci-là est notre table. Est ce-que vous comprenez Français?" The waiter agrees in broken English. When Sartorius gives his order to the porter to "Place those things on that table," the waiter naturally intercedes with his well-spelled "Zese zhentellmen are using zis table, zare. Would you mind—"

The next problem of the scene is to draw the two parties into conversation, and the initiative is Cokane's. In the 1893 version his management is merely clouterly. He begins by engaging Sartorius with "We are fellow-travellers, if I mistake not," and is abruptly snubbed. Then he calls for the waiter to bring him the *visitors' book*, explaining loudly that he wishes to ascertain whether this is the hotel where Trench's aunt, Lady Roxdale, stays. Then in an aside he urges Trench to try a conversation with the old man, to offer him a *newspaper*. Trench fetches out the *Lancet*, then under protest from Cokane finds, instead of the medical journal, a more acceptable offering—an old copy of *Tit Bits*. Cokane passes it over. Sartorius (who has come alive at the mention of Lady Roxdale) accepts it, and responds with a rather stupidly farcical repetition of Cokane's earlier line, "We are fellow-travellers, I believe." The revised version is much cleaner, bolder, and more relaxed. The heavy machinery of the visitor's book and the newspaper are dispensed with. As soon as Cokane and Trench have taken a sip of their beer, Cokane springs the social trap with "By the way, Harry, I've often meant to ask you—is Lady Roxdale your mother's sister or your father's?" Sartorius comes alert at once, and Cokane then rambles on freely and tantalizingly about Trench's need to marry, Lady Roxdale's interest in his marrying, and the social importance of having one's wife properly floated in London

society. "You don't know the importance of these things," he adds
with a flourish, "apparently idle ceremonial trifles, really the springs
and wheels of a great aristocratic system." All this is such tender bait
to Sartorius that Cokane needs only to offer to exchange tables with
him and the desired conversation gets under way.

The dialogue next following is in the 1893 version painfully skimpy
—a quick rattle of introductions and a proposal to have a look at the
river before dinner, Shaw's technical objective being to clear our Sartorius and Cokane and leave the hero and heroine alone. It consists
of but twenty bare-bone speeches. In the revised version there are
forty-three speeches, which make up a pleasant little social occasion
with tea-drinking, chat about tourism, readings from a Baedeker, remarks on the Sartorius' home-arrangements at Surbiton and Bedford
Square, and some amusing discussion of the local Apollinaris church
—which, rather than the uninteresting "river," becomes the goal of
the excursion before dinner.

In the second act the first on-stage encounter of Blanche and
Trench, after Trench has learned from Lickcheese the shocking truth
about his prospective father-in-law's business affairs, shows a remarkable development from one version to the other. In 1893, Blanche
enters and "*Trench, seeing her, gives up the attempt to explain, and
collapses into a chair.*" Her opening remark is an incredible banality:
"Polite of you, Harry, isn't it, to receive me seated?" At which he
begs her pardon, rises, offers her a chair, and apologizes for his absorp-
tion in his own thoughts. In the revised version he is left on-stage alone
for a moment, and "*collapses into a chair, shuddering in every nerve.*"
Blanche appears unseen by him. "*Her face lights up when she sees that
he is alone. She trips noiselessly to the back of his chair and clasps her
hands over his eyes. With a convulsive start and exclamation he springs
up and breaks away from her.*" She cries "Harry!", astonished, and he
distractedly apologizes and invites her to sit down.

At the end of their dialogue they have developed a dreadful quarrel
and Blanche rushes away to pack up his "false letters" and "hateful
presents," being "very glad" to be rid of him forever. In the 1893
version Trench is left alone for an inept soliloquy:

"Very glad!" Then, by George, so am I very glad. "Very glad!" That
settles it. I always warned Cokane against women; and I was right. A woman
who could say such a thing to a man who loves her—or who did love her when
he was a fool—may be pretty, but she has no heart. Not that I care—still—.
"Very glad!" It is I who am glad to be out of it, and with more reason: just
as glad as she. She cannot pretend that I said anything to hurt her feelings.

Some day, perhaps, she will find out how much I have spared her, and what an old rascal her father is. Then she will learn the value of the affection—no matter! I am well out of it: there can be no doubt of that. I had better not see her again: at all events I hope I shant. . . .

He is interrupted by Cokane, who rushes in to tell him that Sartorius has met Blanche offstage and being "a keen old bird, *rusé*, as the French say, *très rusé*" has sensed that there's trouble and will be here presently to make a row. In the revised version all this bumbling sardoodledom is replaced by an exciting scene of conflict. Sartorius enters at the very climax of Blanche's scolding, orders her to be silent, hears her scream out that Trench has thrown her over, dismisses her with a further admonishment to control her temper, calls in Cokane, pitches into Trench, and develops the discussion scene. The main lesson Shaw has learned here, and in many another transition passage, is to dovetail and overlap the goings and comings and to avoid the empty stage or the forced transitional soliloquy.

Immediately after the play's production Shaw fought a voluminous paper war with his critics, even going so far in one letter to the press as to point out certain errors which he had committed in the political and economic details of the play and which they had ignorantly failed to notice. One of these was the error of making Sartorius a resident of suburban Surbiton but a vestryman of St. Giles parish. By 1898 he managed to correct this slip, and indeed to capitalize on it. In the second act he shows Sartorius at home in his *summer* house at Surbiton (chosen because it is built on gravel and has a low death rate); in the third act he is at home at his proper and sumptuous legal residence in Bedford Square. Thus the impression of Sartorius' wealth is enhanced, and his care for his own health is slyly contrasted to his indifference to the squalor of his tenement dwellers. The third act removal to London proper also helps minimize, though it does not dispel, the queer coincidence that Trench's residence is just "around the corner" from the Sartorius'.

In 1898 Shaw repudiated the "silly pleasantries" of the earlier version, and one is glad to see that a number of idle puns and quibbles have been expunged. "No, my dear boy," cries Cokane, just after he has come upon Trench and Blanche embracing. "No, No." "What the deuce are you No-ing at?" asks Trench. "Nothing," is the response: "I am the last man in the world you could describe as knowing at anything," et cetera. This is not Shavian wit, but Robertson-Jones wit, and long before 1898 Shaw learned to avoid such raw silliness.

Perhaps the most interesting aspect of the play's revision is the increased cleanness and precision with which Shaw projects his characters. Lickcheese alone of the *dramatis personae* appears to have come through at first writing just as Shaw wanted him: except for a few additional descriptive details in the stage-directions and in the speeches a few vulgarizations of spelling to indicate pronunciation, and a few cuttings of redundant arguments, Lickcheese does not change. All the others do. Even the little Parlour Maid loses a little and gains a lot by the 1898 revision. Shaw suppressed the pointless name of Annie which he had first sent her out with, and he markedly accentuates her cringing, timorous subservience.

Trench's Horatio, Mr. William de Burgh Cokane, is quite altered. In 1893 he was a young man, evidently about Trench's own age. "I may mention that Trench is the friend of my boyhood," he says to Sartorius; "I may say that he is my other self." Yet, as Trench points out in the first act, Cokane is not only married but has five children. Further, he is apparently a sort of libertine. He scolds Trench for having stolen a march on him with Blanche and cut him out. When Trench reminds him of his marital status, he counters with "Do you suppose a married man has no feelings?" And in the last act he still thinks that Blanche rejected Trench because she was "attracted in another quarter"—meaning himself. In the revision Shaw suppresses the libertine motif—wisely, for it only clutters the characterization—and specifically makes him much older: "*probably over 40, possibly 50—an ill-nourished scanty-haired gentleman, with affected manners, fidgety, touchy, and constitutionally ridiculous.*" The wife and children are also suppressed. Indeed, throughout the play one would take him to be the standard stage-joke about the sexless bachelor. That he is a married man appears only in one line of Lickcheese's very near the end: "Come, Mr. Sekkatary: you and me, as married men, is out of the 'unt as far as young ladies is concerned." The retention of this line may perhaps he regarded as an oversight in the revising process.

Dr. Harry Trench is not much changed except to be economized on. Considering Shaw's perennial delight in spoofing the medical profession, which was to find lively expression in the satiric sketch of Dr. Paramore in his very next play, *The Philanderer*, one wonders why Shaw made Trench a doctor at all if he could not make more satiric use of the characterization. Trench's stupidity, ignorance, and social irresponsibility are generalized beyond the limits of a specific profession, and he might as well be any young London man-about-town.

We can only guess that Shaw at first intended something more than he found time in this play to achieve, for in the 1893 version Trench's professional affinities are emphatically detailed early in the first act. His friend Cokane is quite hypochondriacal about the "frightful draught" under the trees and the "northerly aspect" of the place they're sitting in, and Trench jocularly assures him, "as a medical man of three weeks' standing, that you will not get rheumatism from the sun here at five o'clock on an August afternoon." He carries the *Lancet* in his pocket. His conversations with Blanche on the river-boat had largely been shop-talk, "especially about the new germ theory." But these details occur only in the first few pages, and once Shaw gets a good grip on his main theme, the medical references are almost entirely dropped. In the 1898 version none of the specifics cited above appear at all. It is as if Shaw foresaw *The Doctor's Dilemma* even thus early, and chose to hold fire until ready. In any case *Widowers' Houses* is tightened and improved by the excisions.

One of the marvellous things about Sartorius as we now know him is his dignity, his sincerity, his self-respect, and, from his own point of view, the unshakable validity of his position—no moustache-twirling villain he. It is amusing therefore to discover that in the 1893 version Shaw had not yet quite been able to free him from taints of melodrama. At the end of the first-act love scene, in 1898, Harry sees Sartorius coming and breaks the embrace in time (we are supposed to think) to escape detection: in 1893 Blanche is still in Trench's arms as "*Sartorius enters, and observes them with quiet satisfaction.*" In 1898 when Sartorius learns that Cokane is to write Trench's letter to Lady Roxdale, he responds blandly, "Indeed, Mr. Cokane. Well, the communication could not be in better hands"; in 1893 his reaction is a startled snarl: "Oh, he has left the letter to you, sir, has he? Hm!" At the end of the first act, in 1898, Cokane happily shows his completed draft of the letter to Sartorius for his approval; in 1893 Sartorius tries to wheedle a look at the letter by the clumsy device of offering to stamp it for mailing, and when that doesn't work he waits until Cokane is gone, "*then deliberately opens the visitors' book; takes out the draft letter; and proceeds to read it as the act drop comes down.*" In the second act, in 1898, Sartorius speaks plainly and openly to Trench about Blanche's "strong temper"; in 1893 he stoops to the euphemism of her "not wanting in seriousness of character." In short, the original Sartorius is more than a bit of a conniver, obviously seeking to impose his own pattern for his own ends; the revised Sartorius is actually

much more threatening a figure because Shaw makes him operate behind an inscrutable mask of seeming disinterestedness. The ultimate
Shavian touch in the 1898 version is embodied in two sentences of
Sartorius' near the end: "Dr. Trench puts the case frankly as a man
of business. I take the wider view of a public man." Thus with devilish
ingenuity Shaw has learned to make the worse appear the better
cause.

The emergence of Blanche into the firmly imagined predator that
we now know her to be is a remarkable development from one version
to the other. Her final scene, in which she gobbles up Trench as a
spider any fly, was completely conceived and nearly perfected from
the first. But as we work backward through the play there are many
signs that Shaw did not at first know surely just what he was getting
at. In 1893 he thought it necessary, for instance, to "excuse" the final
gobbling by conceding a latent idealism in Blanche. Early in the third
act Sartorius is made to explain to her that Trench had rejected her
fortune because he had thought it tainted, and "that is why he first
wanted to support you on his money alone." The effect of this is to
"justify" Blanche and to soften the point of the play. By 1898 this
explanation is suppressed. and she gobbles the young man simply because she is hungry for him. In the second act, the notorious scene in
which she mauls and strangles the Parlour Maid is simply crude as
Shaw first wrote it; by 1898 it is not only better linked in by transi-
tions fore and aft, but it is better imagined, motivated, and written.

It is in the love scene of the first act that the most astonishing differences appear. In the 1893 version the dialogue ambles along, like
a rather vague scene in a novel, to the number of sixty-two speeches;
by 1898 it is compressed to thirty-eight speeches, all taut with psychological significance, and exploding with half a dozen dramatic surprises. A sample from the beginning of the 1893 version will suffice to
indicate its general aimlessness:

Trench. I believe I have had the pleasure of meeting you before, Miss Sar-
torius.
Blanche. (*ironically*) Indeed?
Trench. (*injured*) I thought you might have remembered it.
Blanche. I believe I have had the pleasure of conversing with you for an hour
or so on three different occasions, Dr. Trench. I thought you might
have remembered it.
Trench. I do remember it very well, of course.

One cannot tell, from this or any of the rest, *whose scene it is.* The progression, through vague sarcasms and chaffings and pleadings and affections and embarrassments until they are in each other's arms, is a soft social bibble-babble—two rather pleasant, purposeless, characterless young persons talking their way into a kiss. How amazing the difference when Shaw has seen his way backward from the spiderish ending of the play and rewritten this scene; when he has crystallized Trench into a bumbling male idiot-victim and Blanche into the predator supreme. Blanche opens the scene with a crashing surprise line: "Well! So you have done it at last." And she ends it with a crashing clincher: "But Harry . . . when shall we be married?" And from first to last she takes the initiative, stinging him with contempt, luring him with false pathos, checking him with anger, forcing him with every ace in her deck into the final declaration. For sheer delight in comedy of character the scene stands in Shaw's works as a little masterpiece, but as of 1893 he didn't know how to write it, because he had not yet comprehended the fun and dramatic potential in the predatory-female theme.

Probably a full collation of Shaw's earlier plays with the text of the Standard Edition will sometime have to be done, so that we can measure his growth between 1898 and 1930. But in a general way, we may recognize that by 1898 he had found his grip. By study of the chance and "premature" publication of *Widowers' Houses* we can appreciate the amazing amount of technical skill he discovered during the years of his apprenticeship.

CHARLES H. SHATTUCK

CHRISTOPHER SMART, FREE AND ACCEPTED MASON

WITH THE publication of W. F. Stead's edition of Christopher Smart's *Rejoice in the Lamb* (London, 1939) another name was added to the roll of famous eighteenth-century Masons, for in that curious poem Smart unequivocally states, "I am the Lord's builder and free & accepted MASON in CHRIST JESUS";[1] in the same edition there is announced the discovery of a Masonic song by "Brother C. Smart, A.M." (p. 25). As early as 1934, Odell Shepard and Paul Spencer Wood had attempted to solve the problem of the Greek letters assigned to the seven pillars in *A Song to David* in terms of Masonic symbolism,[2] but it is my conviction that the *Jubilate Agno*, not the *Song*, affords greater opportunities for uncovering possible Masonic symbolism and associations. I am not myself a Mason, and the more closely guarded secrets of that Order are unknown to me, but there is a vast Masonic literature upon which to draw. Since the connection between Masonic history and legend and the Old Testament is so close, one can rarely be sure that an allusion is to be interpreted as solely Biblical or solely Masonic—or as both. Nowhere do I insist that lines in *Jubilate Agno* must be interpreted solely in the light of Masonic symbolism or legend. And it should be apparent from this study that when Stead insists, as he does, on Smart's knowledge of occult literature other than that of Freemasonry, his belief becomes suspect when particular lines, explained by him in terms of occultism, are equally understanble against a Masonic frame of reference.

It is in the *Jubilate Agno* that Masonic symbolism and associations seem most apparent. There is even the possibility, one that must remain highly conjectural, that parts of this poem were conceived and must be interpreted on two levels, the literal and the Masonic. The title and opening section of the poem best lend themselves to illustration. The lamb is an important Masonic symbol for innocence and, in the high degrees, for Christ. The aprons worn by Masons are made of lambskin. The first two lines of the poem read

Rejoice in God, O ye Tongues; give the glory to the Lord, and the Lamb.
Nations, and languages, and every Creature, in which is the breath of Life.

---

[1] The line is B1, 119 (*For*) in the edition of the same poem by W. H. Bond (London and Cambridge, Mass., 1954). All line references will be to Bond's edition, titled *Jubilate Agno*.

[2] *English Prose and Poetry, 1660–1800* (Boston, 1934), p. 1020. The statement that the "seven pillars are themselves a Masonic emblem. Alpha and Gamma, taken together suggest the Compasses and Square; Eta may stand for Jacob's Ladder, Theta for the Eye, and Iota for the Plumb-line" is not confirmed in any Masonic volume I have examined.

Although the most immediate "source" for these lines is the liturgy in the Book of Common Prayer and Rev. 7.9–10 (quoted by Bond in a note), it should not go unremarked that in "The Charges of a Free-Mason . . . " one finds the words "we are also of all *Nations, Tongues, Kindreds,* and *Languages.*"[3] The fourth line of the poem is particularly interesting: "Let Noah and his company approach the throne of Grace, and do homage to the Ark of their Salvation." Translated into Masonic language this reads "Let the Masons (descendants of Noah and sometimes called Noachidae) approach the seat of the Grand Master in the Grand Lodge of England (called the throne) and do homage to the Ark of Safety (part of the ritual in the American Royal Arch Degree)."[4] In this same section (A) of the poem the names of Biblical persons are coupled with animals, birds, and insects in 110 of the 113 lines; at least twenty-one of these names figure in Masonic history and symbolism.[5] Although these parallels and possible allusions are suggestive of Masonic influence they would not, in isolation, be sufficient to establish the presence of Masonic symbolism in *Jubilate Agno*. In what follows, lines in the poem will be quoted and their Masonic significance indicated. I have used the text of Bond's edition, giving line references to his arrangement first and then to Stead's. Albert G. Mackey's *Encyclopaedia of Freemasonry*, revised edition, 2 vols. (New York and London, 1916) is my chief Masonic authority.

B1, 35 (*For*)—vii, 35
"For there is a traveling for the glory of God without going to Italy or France."

"In the symbolic language of Masonry, a Mason always travels from west to east in search of light—he travels from the lofty tower of Babel, where language was confounded and Masonry lost, to the threshing-floor of Ornan the Jebusite, where language was restored and Masonry found" (Mackey II, 792).

B1, 64 (*For*)—vii, 64
"For I bless God in behalf of TRINITY COLLEGE in CAMBRIDGE & the society of PURPLES in LONDON."

Certain high degrees of Masonry wore purple collars and aprons and were called "purple brethren" (Mackey II, 601).

B1, 71 (*For*)—vi, 1 and D206—xxxi, 12
"—God be gracious to the house of Stuart"
"—God be merciful to the house of Stuart"

---

[3] *The Constitutions of the Free-Masons* . . . (London, 1723), p. 54.

[4] One may ask if Smart knew anything of the American rituals, but American Masonry is often a modification of English Masonry.

[5] A4, 5, 6, 7, 9, 10, 15, 16, 25, 26, 33, 42, 54, 58, 64, 69, 78, 87, 101, 112, and 113.

"Stuart Masonry" was invented by adherents of that family as a political instrument for the restoration of the Stuarts to the throne of England (Mackey II, 730). This may explain Smart's sympathies.

B1, 176 (*For*)—ix, 26
"For Fire . . . purifyeth ev'n in hell."

"And in the high degrees of Masonry . . . there is a purification by fire."[6]

B1, 84 (*For*)—viii, 14
"For I bless the Lord Jesus for the memory of Gay, Pope and Swift."

Pope and Swift (and Arbuthnot as well) were Masons;[7] one could suspect Gay of being one if only out of sheer good fellowship.

B1, 129 (*For*)—viii, 59
"For I have the blessing of God in the three POINTS of manhood, of the pen, of the sword, & of chivalry."

"Three points in a triangular form ($\therefore$) are placed after letters in a Masonic document to indicate that such letters are the initials of a Masonic title or of a technical word in Masonry" (Mackey II, 785). "In Masonry, the use of the sword as a part of the Masonic clothing is confined to the high degrees and the degrees of chivalry" (Mackey II, 750). The Recorder or Secretary in Masonic Lodges wore crossed pens as his "official jewels" (Mackey I, 369).

B1, 137 (*For*)—viii, 67
"For I am descended from the steward of the island . . . "

(Smart's father was steward of Fairlawn, the estate of William, Viscount Vane.) Bond suggests St. George for the steward. The Grand Stewards in Masonry were officers whose duty it was "to prepare and serve at the Grand Feast . . . " (Mackey I, 308).

B1, 167 (*For*)—ix, 17
"For the Glory of God is always in the East . . . "

This is obviously a recollection of Ezekiel 43.2, "And, behold the glory of the God of Israel came from the way of the East," but Smart may also have been thinking of the Master in Freemasonry who always presides in the East and of the rule that a Masonic lodge must stand due east and west. Atheists, it may be necessary to note, could not join the Masonic Order.

B1, 217 (*Let*)—xiii, 67
"—My DEGREE is good even here, in the Lord I have a better."

Is Smart thinking of his Masonic degree?

B1, 225 (*Let*)—xiv, 4
"—St Paul is the Agent for England."

---

[6] Mackey I, 266. See also Dudley Wright, *England's Masonic Pioneers* (London, n.d. [1925?]), p. 61, who quotes, as part of an early Masonic ritual ("At giving the Fire"), the words "as Fire purifieth all things."

[7] See Rae Blanchard, "Was Sir Richard Steele a Freemason?" *PMLA*, LXIII (Sept. 1948), 911.

Bond conjectures that Smart is thinking of St. Paul's Cathedral. If this is so, it might be added that some Masonic writers look upon the building of St. Paul's as one of the seven sources of Masonry (Mackey II, 660–61).

B2, 317–319 *(For)*—xi, 22–24
"For the SUN is an intelligence and an angel of the human form.
For the MOON is an intelligence and an angel in shape like a woman.
For they are together in the spirit every night like man and wife."

The sun and moon are Masonic symbols, masculine and feminine respectively (Mackey II, 491). Stead finds evidence of Smart's knowledge of occult literature in many lines of the poem; his note (p. 212) on the two lines quoted is interesting: " 'The Sun and Moon are two Magicall principles, the One active, the other passive, this *Masculine,* that *Foeminine,*' Eugenius Philalethes [i.e., Thomas Vaughan], *Anthroposophia Theomagica* (1650), p. 24." This is to disregard the possible Masonic symbolism as well as, more obviously, Biblical imagery. See *Psalm* 19.4–5 and Smart's version of that *Psalm*. It is my belief that there is almost no real evidence for Smart's interest in any other occult literature. His borrowing of Iamblichus' *Life of Pythagoras* from the University library is the sole fact that can be advanced, but the schools founded by Pythagoras "have been considered by many writers as the models after which Masonic Lodges were subsequently constructed." Iamblichus' own philosophical system "assimilates him most . . . to the mystical and symbolic character of the Masonic philosophy" (Mackey III, 602 and I, 362).

B2, 327 *(For)*—xi, 32
"For I am the Lord's News-Writer—the scribe-evangelist"

In English Masonry there are two scribes who act as secretaries (Mackey II, 672), and as Smart mentions the "pen," the official jewel of the Recorder or Secretary, in B1, 129 *(For)*, one might conjecture that he served the order in that capacity.

B2, 329 *(For)*—xi, 34
"For in the divine Idea this Eternity is compleat & the Word is a making many more."

The "True Word" is very important in Masonry as a symbol of life eternal (Mackey II, 856), and the verb "to make" is synonymous with "to initiate" in early Masonic literature (II, 461).

B2, 422 *(For)*—xv, 12
"For Preferment is not from the East, West or South, but from the North, where Satan has most power."

The north is the place of darkness in Masonry, and Satan is, of course, the Prince of Darkness (II, 518). Stead states that *"The North, where Satan has most power* again shows Smart's acquaintance with occult lore" (p. 228). It is hardly necessary to point out that this idea occurs in the Bible, Shakespeare, and Milton, and that the first part of the line is nothing more than a recollection of *Psalm* 75.6, "For promotion cometh neither from the east, nor from the west, nor from the south."

B2, 490 (*For*)—xvi, 38
"For ♄ is in the stars the sun and in the Moon."
The sun, moon, and stars are part of the insignia or symbols on the
carpet of "all modern Masters" of Masonry. Sun and moon are symbols
in the First Degree; the stars in the high degrees (Mackey II, 737).

B2, 603–615 (*For*)—xviii, 21–33
In these lines the twelve cardinal virtues are coupled with the names of
the twelve sons of Jacob. There were "twelve original points in Masonry
which form the basis of the system and comprehend the whole ceremony of initiation." The initiation "was divided into twelve parts, in
allusion to the twelve tribes of Israel," each tribe bearing, of course, the
name of one of the sons of Jacob.[8]

B2, 609 (*For*)—xviii, 27
"For Naphtali is sublime—God be gracious to Chesterfield."
Naphtali is probably a place name. The mother of Hiram Abif, architect
of the Temple and an extremely important figure in Masonic history and
legend (Mackey I, 329–32), was of Naphtali. There is a "sublime" degree
in Masonry (Mackey II, 732). And Chesterfield was a Mason.[9]

C145 (*For*)—xxiv, 65
"For when they get their horns again they will put them on the altar."
"In the Jewish Temple, the altars of the burnt-offering and of incense
had each at the four corners four horns of shittim wood. . . . As the
Masonic altar is a representative of the Solomonic member, it should be
constructed with these horns" (Mackey I, 337).

C153 (*For*)—xxiv, 73
"For the horn is of plenty."
The jewel of the Steward of a Masonic Lodge is called the Horn of Plenty
(Mackey II, 717).

In section D Smart lists names; many remain unidentified.
Among those that can be identified are the following who were Masons: the Duke of Newcastle (D39—xxvi, 7), Sir Isaac Newton (D170
—xxx, 9), and Thornhill and Hogarth (D193—xxx, 32).[10] One wonders
how many more of the names in this section, and elsewhere in Smart's
work, recall Masonic associations.

There is little discernible Masonic symbolism in Smart's other
poetry. But one stanza of Smart's version of *Psalm* 118 catches the
eye in this connection. Smart's practice in "translating" the *Psalms*

---

[8] Mackey II, 810. See also George Oliver, *Historical Landmarks . . . of Freemasonry*, 2 vols. (New York, 1855), I, 215–16.
[9] For Chesterfield as Mason, see A. F. Calvert, *The Grand Lodge of England*
(London, 1917), Plate 14.
[10] For the Duke of Newcastle and Thornhill and Hogarth, see Blanchard, *PMLA*,
LXIII (Sept. 1948), 911, 906, and 907; for Newton, see Oliver, *Historical Landmarks*,
I, 59.

was to expand one verse of the original into an entire stanza. The version of the *Psalms* he used was that in the *Book of Common Prayer* where *Psalm* 118.22 reads "The same stone which the builders refused: is become the head-stone in the corner." Smart makes of this

> That rock neglected and unknown
> Is now become the corner stone
> Ev'n of the house of God;
> Which all the builders to a man
> Refus'd, from him that drew the plan,
> To him who bore the hod.

The Masonic allusion in this stanza resides in the last two lines with their references to the architect and the bearers of the hod.

Possibly there is more symbolism of the Masonic order in the *Psalms* and in the other poetry, but it is far from clear to the uninitiate, even with the aid of Masonic literature. There are, however, very evident Masonic associations in the names of persons to whom or upon whom Smart wrote poems. *A Solemn Dirge, Sacred to the Memory of his Royal Highness Frederick Prince of Wales* was written to mourn the death of the highest ranking Mason in England. The poem *On being asked by Colonel Hall to make Verses upon Kingsley at Minden* celebrates the bravery of another Mason, Maj. Gen. William Kingsley, Col. of the 20th Regiment of Foot, at the battle of Minden. Smart dedicated his verse translation of Horace (1767) to another Mason, Sir Francis Blake Delaval, Grand Warden in 1753, the same Francis Delaval for whom, and for whose brother, Smart had provided a prologue and epilogue when an amateur performance of *Othello* was put on in 1751. The poem *Female Dignity* was "Inscribed and Applied to Lady Hussey Delaval," another member of the same family.[11] It is possible that Smart's connection with this family prompted his entry into the Masonic order. Since, according to the *Constitutions of the Freemasons* (1723), one had to be at least twenty-five years old, the earliest possible date for Smart's initiation would be 1747 or 1748.

At least two conclusions seem warranted from this study which, I feel, has only broken the ground: many lines which have resisted explanation may now be explained in terms of Masonic symbolism, ritual, and history; and Stead's contention, evident from his notes, that Smart was interested in occult literature—other than that of Freemasonry, of course—needs close examination.

Arthur Sherbo

[11] For the Prince of Wales as Mason see R. F. Gould's *History of Freemasonry*, 5 vols., revised by Dudley Wright (London [1931]), II, 231; for Kingsley and Delaval see Calvert, *The Grand Lodge of England*, Plates 101 and 91 respectively.

ORIGINES ARTHURIANAE: THE TWO CROSSES OF SPENSER'S RED CROSS KNIGHT

Ac yna y gwisgawt Arthur . . . atharean aelwit Gwenn adelw yr Arglwides Veir yndi. ("And then Arthur put on . . . a shield that was called *Gwenn* [White], with the image of the Lady Mary on it.")
—*Brut y Brenhinedd,* Cotton Cleopatra MS, fol. 79, ed. John Jay Parry. (See Note 46, below.)

IN A RECENT article in this *Journal*,[1] the cross borne by Spenser's Red Cross Knight is considered in the light of Catholic symbolism as "not merely decorative, but as 'a protection,' " in a tradition centuries older than Elizabethan Puritanism. Whitaker, distinguishing between the crosses on the breast and on the shield,[2] had associated their joint function with the Anglican rite of baptism. The symbolism of the Knight's armor (based, as we are informed in Spenser's letter to Raleigh,[3] on *Ephesians*) would thus have the Knight "put on the whole armor of God," including the "breastplate of righteousness" and the "shield of faith," in order to "stand against the wiles of the devil"[4] in the shape of the dragon.

Much has been written about the romance sources of the Knight's

---

[1] Beatrice Ricks, "Catholic Sacramentals and Symbolism in Spenser's *Faerie Queene*," *JEGP*, LII (1953), 322–31; see especially pp. 325–27. In support of her position Miss Ricks might have cited the words of Irenius, who consistently speaks for Spenser in the *View*, in urging the rebuilding of churches in "better forme" (Var. ed., *Prose Works*, lines 5097–5100): "The outward show, assure yourself, doth greatly draw the rude people to the reverencing and frequenting thereof, whatever some of our late too nice fools say that there is nothing in the seemly form and comely order of the Church." For microfilms of unpublished material, I am indebted to the generosity of the University of Illinois.

[2] "The Religious Basis of Spenser's Thought," *Stanford Univ. Publ.: Lang. and Lit.*, VII (1950), 199; "The bloody cross on his breast might pass muster as a mere memorial, although not with extreme Puritans; but never the cross on his shield . . . [T]hat cross is itself a protection; . . . a symbol of the protection of Christ." Compare line 185, "Cristes croos was his proteccion," in *The Life of St. George* by Lydgate, ed. Hammond, *Englische Studien*, XLIII (1910–11), p. 19, also lines 5 and 16.

[3] Variorum ed., *F.Q., Book I* (1932), 169: "In the end the Lady told [that clownish person] that vnlesse that armour which she brought, would serue him (that is the armour of a Christian man specified by Saint Paul v. Ephes.) that he could not succeed in that enterprise, . . . he seemed the goodliest man in al that company . . . "

[4] The phrases, from Ephesians 6:11–16, are those of the King James Version. In Cranmer's Bible (the "Great Bible") of Spenser's boyhood, which strongly influenced his later writing (see Landrum, *PMLA*, XLI [1926], 524), they read: "Put on all the armoure of God, that ye maye stande agaynst the assautes of yᵉ deuyll, . . . the brest plate of ryghtwesnes, . . . the shylde of fayth" (1st ed., 1539; the later editions through 1562, when Spenser was ten years old, show no significant variations).

armor.[5] In addition to the St. George legend, which Spenser appears to have had in mind in at least two passages of Book I,[6] there are compelling parallels in the *Perlesvaus*[7] and the related *Queste del Saint Graal*.[8] On the assumption that the *Perlesvaus* is of earlier date, I shall refer to it rather than the *Queste*, without necessarily suggesting that Spenser drew upon either work directly.[9] The reference to "that armor which she brought" in the letter to Raleigh (note 3 above) may be compared with the shield which the damsel brought (*Perl.*, I, 610–11: *e portoit un escu . . . e une croiz vermeille*), which the hero has inherited from Joseph of Arimathea (9566) and with which he is to achieve the Grail (627: *E de cest escu conqerra il le Graal*). But where Spenser's Knight has a silver shield,[10] the shield of Perlesvaus is silver and blue (*bendé d'argent e d'azur*).[11] Neither shield can be used by anyone but the hero: Spenser's Knight is told that unless the armor would *serve* (i.e., suit, fit [of clothing]: *NED verb*, 30) him, "he could not

[5] See Var. ed., *F.Q.*, I, 379–401 and ff. Cf. Tuve, "The Red Crosse Knight and Mediaeval Demon Stories," *PMLA*, XLIV (1929), 710 ff.

[6] *Ibid.*, I.2.11–12; 10.61. Spenser mentions St. George nowhere outside of Book I, except for the rhyme at the end of the Harleian version of *A Brief Note of Ireland* (Var. ed., *Prose Works*, p. 245, note), In addition to Percival's note on the cross in *The Birth of St. George* (Var. ed., I, 177–78), see Percy's version of *St. George and the Dragon*, where the hero swears vengeance on his foe:

> "And lo! by Christ his cross I vow,
> Which here is figured on my breast. . . . "

See Padelford and O'Connor, "Spenser's Use of the St. George Legend," *SP*, XXIII (1926), 142–56.

[7] Ed. Nitze and others, 2 vols. (1932–37).

[8] Carman, *Univ. of Kansas Humanistic Series*, V (1936), in an excellent study of the relationship between *Perlesvaus* and the *Queste*, offers convincing evidence that the latter drew for its inspiration upon the *Perlesvaus*, written about 1200. (So Nitze, II, 89; Loomis, *Rom. Rev.*, XXVIII [1937], 352).

[9] But see Hall, "Spenser and Two Old French Grail Romances," *PMLA*, XXVIII (1913), 539–54, for the "probability that Spenser drew directly" from the *Perlesvaus*.

[10] I.1.1.2: "Ycladd in mightie armes and siluer shielde." Later (II.1.18) Archimago disguised himself to look like the Red Cross Knight, and

> "in his siluer shield
> He bore a bloudie Crosse, that quartred all the field."

There are, of course, many silver shields apart from the Arthurian or Grail traditions. The *sciath arggdide* of the Irish heroic cycles (cf. *Lebor na hUidhre*, ed. Best and Bergin, 6907, 7556, 8601–2, 10663, etc. and *JEGP*, XLV [1946], 6, line 11) is not to be confused with the *gelsciath* or "chalked shield" (Stokes, *Acallam na Senórach*, Irische Texte, IV, notes on ll. 1564 and 7588).

[11] Elsewhere Perlesvaus is furnished with three other shields (Nitze, II, 224); cf. the three shields of King Arthur (Robinson's *Assertion of King Arthure*, 1582, p. 13, ed. Mead, with *Middleton's Chinon of England*, EETS, 1925). With Arthur's "shield *Azure* (blew), three crownes *Or* (gold)," compare Lancelot's "*Siluer* Shield, *Three Bandes* of *Blew*" in Robinson's *Auncient Order*, 1583 (reproduced in Millican, *Spenser and the Table Round*, between pp. 64 and 65).

succeed in that enterprise, which being forthwith put vpon him with dewe furnitures thereunto, he seemed the goodliest man in al that company";[12] similarly of Perlesvaus, *nus no porroit oster se cil non, ne pendre a son col* (626). In order to invest the shield with authority, the author appears to have invented its association with Joseph of Arimathea.[13] As for the knights themselves, Spenser's Knight, who like Chaucer's Sir Thopas "was chaast and no lechour," closely resembles Perlesvaus (16: *car il fu chastes e virges de son cors*); both knew that grace and faith must be supplemented by good works.[14] And Perlesvaus' white mule starred on the forehead with a red cross (*Perl.,* 2997–99: *une blanche mule . . . estelee enmi le front d'une croiz vermelle*) is evidently transferred to Una, "Vpon a lowly Asse more white then snow."[15] Not the least among the advances of Arthurian scholarship during the past twenty years is the realization of the importance of the *Perlesvaus*, directly and indirectly, for later writers.

In their search for religious symbolism and moral or political allusions, the source-hunters have failed to uncover the realities of actual contemporary events in Spenser's poem. As M. M. Gray wrote concerning the Pollente episode in Book V,[16] "Spenser's use of Irish material in a very transparent allegory has been easily recognized; but the absolute fidelity to the facts of Irish warfare has not perhaps been sufficiently emphasized." A further source, neither religious nor romantic but politico-military, is to be seen in a Munster proclamation issued by Sir William Pelham,[17] who on September 7, 1580, soon after Spenser arrived in Ireland as Grey's secretary, presented the sword of state to the new Lord Deputy in a delayed ceremony.[18] As Judson

---

[12] Letter to Raleigh, I, 169.

[13] As Carman (p. 52) observes, "it seems quite improbable that he was imitating a source." *Perl.* 9566–67: "Il ot a non Josep Abarimacia; mes il n'avoit point de croiz en l'escu devant la mort Jhesu Crist." In 1505 John Coke, drawing upon Hardyng, tells how Joseph converted Arviragus and "gave hym a whyte shelde with a red crosse in it for his armes" (*Le Débat des Hérauts d'Armes,* ed. Pannier et Paul Meyer [Paris, 1877], pp. 71, 163).

[14] *F.Q.,* I.1.19.3, 12.18.3, etc.; cf. *Perl.,* 6164–69.

[15] Little or no attention has been given to Una's steed: see Var. ed., I, 496–500.

[16] *RES,* vi (1930), 416.

[17] Pelham's unpublished 108-page Diary, or Breviate, is calendared in *Carew MSS, 1575–88,* pp. 312–14; most of the documents numbered 129–479 (pp. 157–312), from Oct. 16, 1579 to Sept. 7, 1580, are preserved in this collection only; 26 (probably originals) are calendared in *CSPI 1574–85,* pp. 191–243; 15 others in *CSPI* are not contained in the Letterbook. On Pelham, see "A Note on 'Good Sir Sergis' " below.

[18] *Liber Munerum Publicorum,* ed. Lascelles, I, ii, 4. Jenkins (*PMLA, LII,* 342) has suggested here an influence on *The Faerie Queene:* "Spenser was undoubtedly pres-

has pointed out, "Upon Spenser, who adored fine weapons and armor, Grey's ceremonious receiving of the sword amid almost regal pageantry probably made a deep impression."[19] Spenser's early months in his new surroundings were crowded with "deep impressions." He doubtless heard about Pelham's proclamation soon after his arrival, and later he was in a position as Bryskett's deputy and as clerk of the Munster council,[20] not only to make copies of state documents but to peruse the records for himself. Pelham issued the proclamation from Limerick on November 6, 1579. Within the year, Spenser was destined to march over Pelham's route, stopping at Limerick[21] on his way to Smerwick, where he witnessed the bloody massacre which also made a deep impression upon him,[22] as also, we may almost certainly assume, the execution of Murrough O'Brien had done at Limerick[23] in the summer of 1577.

The proclamation is here reproduced complete. A marginal caption reads: "A proclamation that / euery horsmane should / were redd Crosses. Dated / at limiricke the vj / Nouember 1579."[24]

---

ent at this solemn ceremony when Grey took the oath and received . . . the Sword of State. In the *Legend of Justice* the aged knight, Sir Sergis, is probably . . . Pelham, the hardy old campaigner who was worn out in the Queen's service. And Chrysaor, Artegal's sword of justice, must symbolize this Sword of State."

[19] Variorum *Life of Edmund Spenser* (1945), pp. 88–89.

[20] Jenkins, *PMLA*, XLVII (1932), 109–21; LIII (1938), 350–62.

[21] Jenkins, *PMLA*, LII (1937), 343.

[22] Var. *Prose Works, View*, 3355–88 (pp. 161–62), also pp. 524–30.

[23] For Spenser's eyewitness account, see *ibid.*, p. 112, Judson's *Life*, p. 46, and Renwick's edition of the *View*, p. 224.

Drury's report of the execution of Murrough is still unprinted, though it was calendared in 1868. Gottfried (*Prose Works*, p. 344) states that Spenser's presence is "still open to doubt," but it should be noted that Ware's remark in 1639 carries no weight. The pertinent part of Drury's letter follows: "the ferste day off thys moneth I adiorned the sesstyons [*sic*] for thys cowntie off lymeryke, vntill a nu warnyng, and haue caused one murough o bryen a second piller off Jemes fitz morisch is late rebellyon and a praktyser off thys nue combination a man off no less fame then James hym selfe) [*sic*] beyng orderly Indited arraygned condempned & Iudged for late offences wythyn these iiij monethes (because I woold not seame to unrypp old matters) to be ther executed thre hundred powndes was offered for hys lyfe and more woold haue been geuen but thre thousand schoold not haue saued hym / thearle of dessemond made greate acompte of hym and so did all the discontentid for he was a fyte Instrument to execute an euell enterpryse, he was amongest the people In greate extymation he was holden the best & forwardest horseman off Ireland / he was greatly off the good feared hys dethe was farre better then hys lyffe, and he confessed he had deserued dethe /"

[24] Calendared in *Carew MSS, 1575–88*, No. 154, pp. 166–67, where it is labeled "Contemp. copy; Signed by Pelham at the beginning." This proclamation appears to be preserved only in Pelham's Letterbook, where it occurs at fol. 102v f., though not so recorded (*Carew*, p. 313).

By the lo: Iustice. /

William Pelham

fforasmuch as the said lo: Iustice expresse plea = / sure is, that all horsemen that are to intende / her Ma^{tis}: service in this assemblid Armie, shalbe / knowne from others: Not beinge of the same retinewe / his lo: ordereth, publisheth, and Comandeth in her Ma^{tis}: / Name, that all the said horsemen both Englishe and / Irishe, shall presentlie provide in redines two rede / crosses, either of Silke or Cloth, the one to be / fastened on the breste, and the other on the backe / of Eache such horseman as is vsuall, and to conteyne / in lenght viij inches, and in bredthe one Inche, and / a halfe, to be Worne vpon every horsemans vpper = / moste garment wch he purposeth to serve in, be it / habergine, Iacke or other vpper garment, for / defence, What so euer, vpon paine for not havinge / such a crosse, as is before mentioned by Wensdaie / morninge[26] next, eache horseman to forfaicte xx^s, & / that the provoste Marshall of her Ma^{tis}: Armie / shall leavie, and take vpp eache such forfaiture / to be disposed at the pleasure of the said lo: Iustice / Yeuen at Limiricke the vj Novembr 1579. /

God saue ye quene. /

In characteristic fashion, Spenser alters his historical source to make it conformable with romance traditions.[26] He retains the first cross "on the breste"[27] but transfers the second cross from the horseman's back to his Knight's shield[28]—the silver shield of the Grail symbolism. The size of the crosses specified in the proclamation is suggested by both terms used by Spenser: the usual "crosse" as well as "croslet" (1.6.36.6). The "habergine, Iacke or other vpper garment" named in the proclamation recalls the passage in the *View* where Spenser asserts that "the Leather quilted Iacke" and "all these which I haue rehearsed to youe be not Irishe garmentes but Englishe,"[29] as may be seen in Chaucer's rime of Sir Thopas; Spenser's "hacqueton and haberi[ci]on" (*View* 2185) are Chaucer's "aketoun" and "haubergeoun."[30] The proclamation clearly states that the insignia are "for

[25] "Nov. 11" (*Carew*).

[26] Upton was the first editor, 200 years ago, to suggest that Book I "shadows forth the outstanding events of the English reformation" (Var. ed., p. 449). On 1.4.14.7–9 he commented: "[Spenser's] poem is to be considered always with more than one meaning" (p. 215). As Millican (p. 114) observes, "The Arthurian legend was to Spenser epic in scope, but the bulk of its substance reached him in the form of romance."

[27] 1.1.2.1: "But on his brest a bloudie Crosse he bore,"

[28] 1.1.2.5: "Vpon his shield the like was also scor'd." Cf. note 10 above.

[29] *View*, 2147, 2177–78. But the "olde Englishe" terms were still current in Spenser's Ireland: Bryskett, for example, writes to Walsingham in 1581 (Plomer and Cross, *Life and Correspondence of Lodowick Bryskett*, p. 21) of Feagh MacHugh's "Jack and haubergeon." See the discussion of the native Irish army by Seán O'Domhnaill, "Warfare in Sixteenth-Century Ireland," *Irish Historical Studies* (1946), especially pp. 36–45.

[30] Chaucer, *Canterbury Tales*, Group B, 2050–51.

defence"; Spenser, as both Whitaker and Miss Ricks point out, as unmistakably labels them for "protection."[31] It is in the protective function of the crosses, and in the proposal whereby her Majesty's horsemen "shalbe knowne from others not of the same retinewe" that longstanding traditions are symbolized. In Hardyng's *Chronicle* (1543), upon which Spenser drew elsewhere, this recognition motif is emphasized and the legend of Arviragus' conversion is traced to Nennius; twice within ten lines[32] we are told how Joseph of Arimathea made Arviragus incline to Christ's law, "by Nennius' information":

> And gaue hym a shilde of siluer white
> A crosse endlong and ouerthwart full perfecte:
>
> These armes were vsed through all Britain
> For a cōmon signe eache māne to know his nacion
> From enemies whiche now we call certain
> Sainct Georges armes, by Nenius enformacion
> Full long afore sainct George was generate
> Were worship there of mikell elderdate.[33]

Without entering into the vexed problem of the connection between the *Perlesvaus* and Nennius, we may consider the tacit assumption in the Pelham proclamation that the wearing of red crosses in her Majesty's service was "vsuall." An extensive reading I have made of P. R. O. and Carew documents relating to Ireland has thus far yielded no other mention of such a custom.[34] Nor can I find any trace of an earlier proclamation in Ireland on the same subject.[35] But an English statute does offer a precedent, though it requires not two crosses but one and is less specific concerning the dimensions of the cross, which must be "suffysaunt and large"; like Pelham's proclamation, it provides penalties:[36]

---

[31] See the opening sentence of this article, and note 2 above.

[32] Chap. xlviii, fol. xli. See also the lengthy prose chapter heading. On Spenser's indebtedness to Hardyng, see C. A. Harper, *The Sources of the British Chronicle History in Spenser's Faerie Queene*, especially on Joseph, pp. 112–15 (where these lines are not cited). Cf. note 13 above.

[33] *The Faerie Queene*, ed. Church (1758), I, 3, note.

[34] Barnaby Googe's pen-and-ink sketch of the interview between Essex and Turlough Lynagh at the Blackwater in 1574 does, however, show the English horsemen displaying the guidon of St. George: see *Notes & Queries*, ser. 3, III (1863), 182b.

[35] I can find no mention of the wearing of the cross of St. George in the 20 vols. of the Irish *Statutes at Large* (Dublin, 1786–1801); see vol. VIII, Index.

[36] "Certayne Statuts and Ordenaunces of Warre" (1513), =Short Title Catal. 9333, fol. c.ii.recto, quoted in part by Todd (Var. ed., *F.Q.*, I, 177). Thus, as an enemy disguising himself in the "vainely crossed" arms, Archimago (1.2.11; 1.3.34–35: both without commentary, Var. ed., pp. 199, 210) is guilty not only of deceit but of treason, "vpon payne of dethe."

¶for them that bere nat a bonde.
or a crosse of seynt George.
¶Also that euery man goynge in ostynge or batayle of what estate condy-
cyon or nacyon he be of ye kynges partie and hoste / except he be a bus-
shop or offycer of armes / bere a crosse of seynt George. Suffysaunt and
large vpon the payne that if he be wounded or slayne in the defaute
therof he that so woundeth or sleeth hym / shall bere noo payne therfore
/ And if he for any cause passe the bondes of the felde that then he bere
openly a crosse / of seynt george with his capitaynes conysaunce / vpon
payne to be emprysoned and punysshed at the kynges wyll.
And that no souldyour bere no conysaunce but the kynges & his capitaynes / vpon payne of dethe / & that none ennemy bere the sayd signe
of seynt George but if he be prysoner & in warde of his maister / vpon
payne of deth.

If the Irish records are silent, the Scottish chronicles reveal that
as early as 1544 it was not only "vsuall" but "the note of the English"[37] to "bere a crosse of seynt George" for purposes of recognition.
In that year, according to the *Diurnall of Remarkable Occurrents*, "the
Inglismen . . . causit all thame that thai fand betuix [Kirktown and
Sowtray] weir ane reid croce."[38] According to Lindesay of Pitscottie,
many Scots took the oath of assurance.[39] Later the assured Scots were
required to wear red crosses "fast sewed" on their jacks[40] or coats,
under penalty of being taken for enemies. But these Scottish records
of 1543–48, unlike the Pelham document thirty years later, make no
mention of more than a single cross. The Irish records before 1579, on
the other hand, appear to offer no parallel for the expedient of "assurance."

The wearing of two crosses, however, is demonstrably earlier than
the sixteenth century. Although the earliest citation of the term
"red-cross" in *NED*, drawn from a poem on the battle of Agincourt,[41]

[37] The Scottish Chronicle in Holinshed's 1587 edition (p. 337b, 24–29), draws upon
Leslie for its account of the Scottish "bordirmen, quha in a gret number bure the rid
croce, quhilke was noted to the Jnglis men of weir, and was as a takne to ken thame by"
(*Historie of Scotland*, STS, II, 286).

[38] Bannatyne Club ed., 1833, p. 35.

[39] *Croniclis of Scotland*, STS, II, 29 and 42; see note, p. 419. On the "assured Scots,"
see Burton, *History of Scotland* (ed. 1905), III, 190–214. Cf. Maxwell's alternative of
serving "with the red crosse on his cote" (*State Papers Henry VIII*, V, 479).

[40] "Instructions for John Brende," *Calendar of Scottish Papers*, I, 114 (May, 1548).
The word *jack* does not appear in Spenser's poetry, but its diminutive *jacket* occurs
three times. It will be recalled that in *Mother Hubberd's Tale* (205) the Ape disguises
himself "souldierlike" in a "blew iack(et) with a cross of redd" and perhaps also significantly, "an old Scotch cap" (209). See note on *jack* in the *View* (Var. ed., *Prose Works*,
p. 352).

[41] Here St. George's "crosse rede" is borne not on the battlefield but by the English
fleet.

is dated 1430, Sir Harris Nicolas, in his detailed account of that battle, printed from MS Harl. 1309 an ordinance of Richard II (1386) "for the Government of the Army." It contains the following clauses:

> Also that non be so hardy to sett forth and displaie any banner or pendon of Saint George, nor non other, for to cause men to withdrawe them from the hoste for to goo any wher . . .
>
> Also that everi man of what estate, condicion, or nation thei be of, so that he be of owre partie, bere a signe of the armes of Saint George, large bothe before and behynde, upon parell that yf he be slayne or wounded to deth for defaulte of the cross that he lacketh. And that non enmy do bere the same token or crosse of saint George, notwithstandyng if he be prisoner, upon payne of dethe.[42]

Comparison will make it clear that this ordinance offers an ultimate source for the phrasing of the sixteenth-century statute.[43] But the discrepancies are significant. Where the 1513 document prescribes a single cross "suffysaunt and large," the 1386 ordinance calls for two crosses, "large bothe before and behynde." Thus the symbol worn by Spenser's Red Cross Knight belongs to a tradition more than two centuries old.

It is surprising that Pelham's proclamation, which has been in print since 1868, has gone unnoticed in Spenser criticism. If the first book of *The Faerie Queene* has long been subjected to interpretation as twofold and threefold allegory, it is because the poet saw and seized upon many diverse opportunities to make dark his conceit. Of recent years the role of the contemporary Irish scene in providing him with source material for his poem has become increasingly evident.[44] A number of notes and articles revealing the poet's use of Irish history and legend have been written too late for inclusion in the Variorum edition of *The Faerie Queene*, of which the sixth and last volume appeared in 1938. More may confidently be expected.

A NOTE ON THE VICISSITUDES OF ARTHURIAN SHIELDS. Spenser's interest in armor and heraldry, both antiquarian and Elizabethan has been ably discussed by Millican in *Spenser and the Table Round*; on Arthur's "sacred arms" and a possible Nennian influence in 1586, see pp. 62–65, 195–96. The magical, Ariosto-like shield which Spenser invented for Arthur, "all of Diamond perfect pure and cleene" (*F. Q.*,

---

[42] Nicholas Harris Nicolas, *The History of the Battle of Agincourt* (1827), p. 110,

[43] On the frequent confusion between laws, statutes, and ordinances, see *JEGP.* XLIX (1950), 414.

[44] On Spenser's use of such historical allusions and events, see particularly Josephine W. Bennett, *The Evolution of "The Faerie Queene"* (1942), pp. 117–18.

I.7.33), is as far removed from Arthur's "shield Azure (blew), three crownes Or (gold)" of 1583 (cf. note 13 above), as the latter differs from the unpretentious shields of the early histories:

Octavum fuit bellum in castello Guinnion [White —?] in quo Arthur portavit imaginem sanctae Mariae perpetuae virginis super humeros suos . . . (Nennius, §56)

Bellum Badonis in quo Arthur portavit crucem domini nostri Iesu Christi . . . in humeros suos,[45] et Brittones victores fuerunt. (*Annales Cambriae*, Harleian MS 3859)

Humeris quoque suis clipeum, uocabulo Pridwen [White Form], imposuit . . . (Geoffrey of Monmouth, IX. iv)

From these brief selections the complete and striking metamorphosis of Arthur's shield between the earliest extant texts and Spenser becomes apparent. It might seem that Arthur was not provided with a shield (*clipeum*) before Geoffrey. Yet even here we are beset by textual obscurities of a sort which call for more investigation than they have received. What, for instance, is to be inferred from such phrases as *super humeros suos* ("upon his shoulders," rendered in the Irish *Lebor Bretnach* by *fora gualaind*, ed. Van Hamel, p. 73) and *humeris suis?* If we accept the repeated claims of Nennius that he drew upon a *vetus traditio seniorum nostrorum*, presumably a written tradition (from *veteres libri*, as he states) in Welsh as distinct from the Roman tradition, and if we accept Geoffrey's dependence upon a very ancient book (*liber vetustissimus*, perhaps Nennius) in the Welsh language (I, i; XI, i; XII, xx) as translated by Walter the Archdeacon into Latin, the question of the form of these Welsh originals is bound to arise. Did they contain any reference to Arthur's "shoulders"?

The Welsh word for "shoulder" is *ysgwydd*, pl. *ysgwyddau:* as in *ar ei ysgwydd*, Isaiah 9: 6; *ar ei ysgwyddau*, Luke 15: 5. It is cognate with Ir. *sciath*, "shoulder blade, wing:" cf. Lat. *scindere*. The modern Welsh word for "shield" is *tarian*, which occurs in the *Brut y Brenhinedd* passage quoted at the beginning of this article.[46] But an old

---

[45] As Wade-Evans has pointed out, the "portage of Christian symbols on Arthur's shoulders" is transferred here to the legendary Badon from Nennius's eighth battle (*Nennius's History of the Britons*, pp. 75, 86).

[46] The need for, and the value of, Professor Parry's edition of the Welsh *Brut*—"a most useful piece of work excellently carried out," as Idris Bell has called it—are nowhere more apparent than in the striking divergences of the Cotton Cleopatra version from the more famous *Red Book of Hergest*, which reads: *Taryan a gymerth ar y ysgwyd, yr honn a elwit Gwenn, yn yr hon yd oed delw yr arglwydes Veir yn yskythredic.* Did both *taryan* and *ar y ysgwyd*, "on his shoulder," have their ultimate origin in the single Welsh word *ysgwydd?*

word, now obsolete, was *ysgwyd* (**sqeit-*: Lat. *scūtum*, Ir. *scīath*, "shield"), which was more than once confused in early Welsh with *ysgwydd*, "shoulder." (On the two roots see Walde-Pokorny, II, 543–44.) It thus appears likely that the Welsh word for "shield" was incorrectly translated *humeros* in the Latin texts, and that there is no justification for seeing in pre-Geoffrey texts a more "primitive" type of fighting. Indeed, a tale is not *necessarily or inevitably* earlier merely because it seems less influenced by the prevailing tone of chivalric romance. From the oldest writings available to us, as in the earliest traceable Finn stories in Irish[47] and perhaps in the corresponding Gwynn ap Nudd tradition in Welsh, Arthurian warriors and their prototypes have been furnished with shields.

There is, moreover, the matter of the late interpretation of the shield *Gwenn* (*Brut*, ed. Parry, fol. 79, note) as "blessed" rather than in its original sense of "white,"[48] which would account for Lewys Dwnn's reference in 1586 to the *arfau kyssegredig* ("sacred arms") of Arthur. Similar transferences may result from misreadings (as when John Coke, following Hardyng, writes *felde* for *shelde*) or may be due to artistic "improvements" by a romanticizing poet. Like textual corruptions of various kinds, they appear at every turn. So in Nennius, Pridwen—originally Arthur's ship—becomes his shield; so his horse Cafal (<Lat. *caballus*) becomes his dog, much as the name Dormarch (*march* = "horse") may have been transferred from Gwynn ap Nudd's horse to his dog. So the Irish CúChulainn's sword Caladbolg is handed over to Arthur; so the Grail, borrowed by or from Chrétien, and the Round Table, borrowed by or from Wace, become completely transformed long before Spenser's time, not to mention ours.

That Spenser knew Robinson's 1582 translation of Leland's *Assertio* is the more likely in view of its triple dedication to Lord Grey (while still Lord Deputy in Ireland), Sir Henry Sidney, his more popular predecessor, and "Master" Thomas Smith, "customer" of the port of London (not to be confused with Gabriel Harvey's benefactor, Sir Thomas Smith of Saffron Walden, whose *De Republica Anglorum* was

[47] In the third volume of the *Duanaire Finn* (Dublin, 1954), ed. Gerard Murphy, a book which Arthurian scholars cannot afford to overlook, the problems of Celtic origins are once more considered, and new approaches suggested. The earlier Finn material, however, is not that listed on p. cxvi of this volume, but on pp. xvi ff. of Kuno Meyer's *Fianaigecht*, Todd Lect. Ser., vol. xvi (Dublin, 1910).

[48] In "The Dream of Rhonabwy" (*The Mabinogion*, transl. Gwyn Jones and Thomas Jones, p. 145) *Gwenn* is the name of Arthur's magic mantle. On *Gwenn* as a proper name, see further Ifor Williams, *Canu Aneirin* (Caerdydd, 1938), pp. 150–51.

published in 1583). Both Latin original and English translation of the *Assertio* drew upon Nennius in listing Arthur's twelve battles by name, even though they omitted the details of the eighth battle given above. John Coke, on the other hand, merely remarked that Arthur fought twelve battles but added ambiguously: "he bare in his armes the pycture of the blyssed virgyn Mary, with Christ her sone." And if Spenser was not familiar with Robinson's *Auncient Order* of 1583, he "certainly knew" (Millican, p. 64) of the London Round Table of the sixteenth century which that book was intended to publicize. Even Camden, who disparaged Arthur's glory, wrote in his *Remaines:* "I onely read among the britans that the victorious Arthur bare our Ladie in his shield, which I do the rather remember, for that Nennius who liued not long after recordeth the same."[49] Indeed, it is not necessary to assume that Spenser borrowed directly from Nennius in order to believe that the shield and crosses of the Red Cross Knight may be traceable ultimately, in part at least, to the *imaginem sanctae Mariae* of Castellum Guinnion or to the *crucem Iesu Christi* of the *Annales Cambriae*. And in the descriptions in *The Faerie Queene* Spenser intended a magnificence which was not to be found in the Scythian "longe broade shieldes made but of wicker rodds" reported in the *View* (1771–74) to be still "comonlye vsed amongest the Northerne Irishe." Finally, if we accept Mrs. Bennett's belief that Spenser introduced Prince Arthur into his poem as a late "afterthought," it is reasonable to suppose that the poet, having already drawn upon Arthur's armor for his Red Cross Knight, was forced to invent a newer, more sumptuous armor for his Prince Arthur (*F.Q.*, I.7.29–36).

A NOTE ON "GOOD SIR SERGIS." Renwick has proposed Pelham as the original of Spenser's "old Sergis" (*F.Q.*, V.11–12), and Jenkins has supported the identification.[50] Earlier Walsingham and Sir Henry Sidney had been suggested, without good reason; more recently Mrs. Bennett (*Evolution*, pp. 196–99) has identified the "old knight" with Sir Henry Wallop.

Spenser describes Sergis (V.11.37–38) as an "aged wight" who "long since aside had set / The vse of armes" and who "whilome did

---

[49] Ed. 1614, p. 178; ed. 1623, p. 158. The section on "Armories" did not appear in the 1605 edition.

[50] *PMLA*, LII (1937), 342: see note 18 above. It may not be sheer coincidence, as Jenkins has suggested, that Pelham, like Spenser, had by his second marriage an only son named Peregrine.

attend / On faire *Irene* [Erin] in her affliction." Artegall [Grey][51]
salutes him with the words:

> "Haile good Sir *Sergis*, truest Knight aliue,
> Well tride in all thy Ladies troubles . . . "

An examination of unpublished documents supports the identification of Sergis with Pelham. The facts are briefly these. Wallop,
who accompanied Pelham, wrote to Walsingham on September 9,
1580, telling of their arrival in Dublin on the sixth and explaining that
Wallop would have brought the sword in accordance with Grey's instructions had not "her Maiesties lettre willed him [Pelham] to deliuer
the sworde to my Lo: Greye upon sight of the Commission." This
caused Pelham "to repaire hither him selfe," leaving Bourcher in
charge of the Munster forces. Wallop concludes: "The vij[th] herof
S[r]. William Pelham in his owne person deliuered the sworde to my
Lo: Deputie, moste willinge to be dischardged of it." Wallop's account is in agreement with Pelham's diary (July 27 to September 7).

Pelham was born at least ten years before Wallop, who was only
12 years older than Spenser himself. Pelham asked to be relieved of
the justiceship as early as November 4, 1579; his age was no doubt the
prime reason for his request: "for as much as I . . . do finde the burden of this service to heavie for me" (January, 1580) and "farre aboue
my powre to deall with" (December 15, 1579). He often dwells upon
his "longe sute to be disburdened of this place" or to be "realesed
ffrom this charge," which he terms "the greatteste happines that could
light vnto me." He had been "attending on fair Irena" before Wallop
set foot in Ireland; for almost thirty years his military skill was highly
regarded by Grey, Leicester, and others. In a letter dated August 23,
1580, his mention of "myne auntient bond of love to your lo[rdship],"
doubtless alludes to the siege of Louth in 1560, when Grey was
wounded and Pelham was praised for his "stout and valient endeav-
our." His virtues were extolled later not only by Grey and Wallop,
but by such dissonant personalities as the Fentons, Gerrard, Anthony
Power, Waterhouse, and Nicholas White. Edward Fenton wrote that
"the people of this realm are much affected" to Pelham, and admired
him for his "zealous disposition to advance God's glory" as well as
his "greate and honorable care" to supply any want of his soldiers,

---

[51] Heffner (Var. ed., *F.Q.*, v, p. 326), it will be noted, makes no claims for the
identification of Artegall with Essex prior to the Burbon episode, which begins with
stanza 44 of Canto ii.

"together with his grave perswacions and his owne liberalitie," which made them "the more willing in this accion."

Pelham's loyalty to Grey[52] was unwavering. As early as November, 1579, when he wrote Walsingham that he would "stand beste satisfied with a quiett privat life," he asserted that he was "glad of that good choice wch I here of my lo: graie: A man euery Waie so well accomplished, as shalbe fitte for the place, and the office for him." To the Queen he wrote that he was rejoiced "by the Choice of suche a governoure, as hath in him Wisdom to deserue in all causes of Iustice, so have your souldiours reasons to reioyce in such a leader, both for honour and experience meete to be their generall." He gives Grey his "assuraunce of firme frendshipe," being "second to none in true affection and honowringe of yow." Since he addresses Grey as "My verie good lo:" and "My good lo: and Captaine," and writes to others of "my verie good lo: Lo: Graie," it may be that Spenser is returning the compliment when he has Artegall address "good Sir Sergis." Pelham signs himself "Your Lordships true [*or* verie assured] frend *and Souldioure*."

In the light of Spenser's interest in word-play and "changeable letters" (*View*, 1383 ff., P.R.O. text, lines 7–8), and assuming that he was aware that Anglo-Norman *servant* and Central French *sergeant* were variant forms, one may wonder whether "old Sergis" is not, perhaps, the poet's "dark conceit" for "old Service."[53] For Pelham's

---

[52] Dunlop's article on Pelham in *DNB* needs revision, particularly in the account of the sword episode: "But Pelham was offended at the lack of courtesy shown him by the deputy's secretary, Edmund Spenser, and determined to go himself to Dublin." Pelham had decided upon a personal meeting as early as Aug. 14. Nor is there any evidence that Pelham's irritation extended to Grey or that the secretary whom Pelham wanted to "teach good manners" was Edmund Spenser. So far as I can discover, the letter which offended Pelham has not been preserved. The earliest letter written for Grey in Spenser's Italian hand is that of Nov. 12 from Smerwick to the Queen. (After examination I am confident that Spenser wrote this letter as well as the later letter to the Queen from Dublin dated November 6. Not only is the hand identical with the endorsement of July 10, 1581 reproduced by Plomer (*MP*, XXI [1923], p. 204, Fig. 2), but it has all the regularities and peculiarities of Spenser's spelling [so different from Mulcaster's] seen in his many other letters.) The earliest letter in Spenser's secretary hand is the Smerwick letter of November 28 printed by Jenkins (*PMLA*, LII, 338–39). As the earlier Grey letters preserved in the Public Record Office were written by others, Spenser may have been serving in some other capacity between his arrival in Ireland and November 12. At all events, there is no surviving evidence to suggest that Spenser wrote any letters for Grey (or for himself) upon arriving in Dublin or at Glenmalure, at the sword ceremony, at Drogheda, or from Kilkenny, Cork, or Limerick en route to Smerwick.

[53] Spenser, like his printer, regularly spells this word *service* (*seruice*). Other Elizabethans, like Sir Richard Bingham, as regularly spell it *servis*.

reputation for being "truest Knight aliue"[54] puts him on the same pedestal as his contemporary Philip Sidney dying at Zutphen—as "verray, parfit gentil knyght" as Chaucer's Knight and as "*servys-able*" as Chaucer's Squire.

In marked contrast to this old campaigner is Wallop, who presented no heroic or lovable figure, and was less the soldier than the politician. From his arrival in Ireland he complained of his bad health. In April, 1581, he recommended Pelham for the Munster presidency because his own infirmities rendered him unfit for that office. He is neatly characterized by Mathew: "His concentration on business had brought its rewards, but he was without friends, a rather humorless man 'in nature and condition somewhat sour,' as Malby described him, and not one who could royster through his extortions."[55]

ROLAND M. SMITH

[54] Anthony Power, whom Sentleger commended as "the most ancient soldier in England or Ireland," wrote on July 26, 1580: "That noble gentleman Sir William Pelham hath had good success in all his attempts." See also Morgan Colman's verses (*Carew MSS, 1575-88*, p. 296) on "the travels of Belona's knight" and "worthy Pelham's fame." Few English leaders in Ireland have ever been so completely and so invariably free from censure and abuse.

[55] *The Celtic Peoples and Renaissance Europe* (1933), p. 213.

AN APPROACH TO *THE PEARL*

ALTHOUGH there are some basic agreements about *The Pearl*, the area of critical accord is surprisingly small. Beyond a few trustworthy suppositions about the manuscript itself (MS. Cotton Nero A.x., British Museum), the record of the Pearl Poet and the historicity of the Pearl Maiden are lost in the fogs of time and conjecture. Since Schofield's attempt to lift the significance of the poem above the narrative level of elegy, there has been a heated, running controversy concerning *The Pearl* as an elegiac, allegorical, or symbolic construct.[1] Stemming from studies like J. B. Fletcher's, which points out that elegy and allegory are not mutually exclusive, there has been a growing critical unity in accepting the poem as something more than pure elegy.[2] But still, as a recent article concludes, "to date, the symbolic interpretation has . . . been weakly argued."[3]

Accordingly, students have had to "explain" the poem using the standards of medieval conventions as they are exposed within *The Pearl* itself. It is not within the scope of this brief study to evaluate the claims of rival approaches and exegeses, but rather to recall attention to two well-known conventions that can aid interpretation. One is a consideration of the multiple levels of meaning discovered in traditional Scriptural exegesis according to the four senses,[4] and the second is a consideration of the gemological meanings found in the lapidary tradition. When the poem is explicated in the light of these traditions, specific details of meaning emerge which provide a basis for such analyses as those by John Conley, Sister Mary Vincent Hillman, and Wendell S. Johnson.[5]

---

[1] Three articles by W. H. Schofield form a convenient center for the growth of controversy about *The Pearl*. See "The Nature and Fabric of *The Pearl*," *PMLA*, XIX (1904), 154–203; "The Source of *The Pearl*," *PMLA*, XIX (1904), 203–15; and "Symbolism, Allegory and Autobiography in *The Pearl*," *PMLA*, XXIV (1909), 585–675. Factual and conjectural aspects are summarized in the introductory material of E. V. Gordon's edition of *The Pearl* (Oxford, 1953), which furnishes the text used for this study.

[2] "The Allegory of the Pearl," *JEGP*, XX (1921), 1 ff.

[3] John Conley, "*Pearl* and a Lost Tradition," *JEGP*, LIV (1955), 333.

[4] The literal or historical, the allegorical, the moral, and the anagogical. The most convenient study of the four senses is by Walter J. Burghardt, S.J., "On Early Christian Exegesis," *Theological Studies*, XI (March, 1950). I am indebted to Dr. Arnold Williams for suggesting Burghardt's article and this double approach to *The Pearl*.

[5] Conley insists that *The Pearl* is primarily a Christian *consolatio*. "The theme of *Pearl* . . . might be called the sovereign theme of the Christian tradition . . . : the nature of happiness, specifically false and true happiness." ("*Pearl* and a Lost Tradition," *ibid.*, p. 341). Hillman views the poem as a symbolic statement about the need for

Although the four senses and gemology cannot limit explication, they provide a set of directive suggestions apparent in the first few stanzas. (Some critics have noted that the structure and theme of *The Pearl* are implicit in the introduction, but there is still a paramount need for patterned examination of details.) For instance, Pearl at once is associated with the noblest metal (gold), and with the Orient, which is the eastern direction literally representative of the most priceless gems and anagogically representative of sun, light, Christ and Jerusalem.[6] Immediately the singularity and spotlessness of the Pearl remove it from the domains of earth. The narrator, however, loses his Pearl through the literal medium of grass and earth, and it becomes evident that the poem grows out of the medieval rage for order which struggled to create an orthodox Christian unity from the Platonic duality of world and ideal. The narrator's plaint,

> *O moul, þou marreȝ a myry iuele,*
> *My priuy perle wythouten spotte.*[7]

discloses the tension within the unified duality: the narrator is unable to maintain his earthly existence in union with a Pearl-value which is the basis of Christian happiness. At the same time, life without that value is torment. Consequently, although the meaning of Pearl is not yet specified, apparently it will reside largely in the third or moral sense, because the narrator's loss of Pearl is synonymous with loss of happiness.[8] The fundamental tension becomes an opposition of the meanings of earth and Pearl, and discovery of those meanings is discovery of the significance of the poem as well as of a particular medieval mind.

---

renunciation ("Some Debatable Words in *Pearl* and Its Theme," *MLN*, LX [1945], 241–48). Johnson perceives that *The Pearl* is centered about "a ubiquitous sense of contrast between the nature of heaven and the nature of earth, the relevation of which seems . . . to be the poem's main purpose." ("The Imagery and Diction of *The Pearl*," *ELH*, XX [1953], 161–80.)

[6] Almost all the lapidaries agree in placing the greatest value in eastern gems. Orientality is specified as highly significant.

[7] *Pearl*, ll. 23–24.

[8] The narrator loses no time in establishing the relationship between himself and the Pearl:

> *Syþen in þat spote hit fro me sprange,*
> *Ofte haf I wayted, wyschande þat wele,*
> *þat wont watȝ whyle deuoyde my wrange*
> *And heuen my happe and al my hele.*
> *þat dotȝ bot þrych my hert þrange,*
> *My breste in bale bot bolen and bele . . .* (lines 13–18).

The third, fourth, and fifth stanzas complete the introductory evaluations of Pearl. The gem, as symbol, creates fruitful and reproductive qualities without which earthly life would wither. The reader is introduced to the garden arbor of the Pearl's grave in *"hyȝ sesoun,"* in August, during the day of the Assumption of the Virgin on the fifteenth of that month—a fruitful time *"Quen corne is coruen wyth crokeȝ kene."*[9] The moment of introduction to the Pearl in her arbor is charged with suggestions of the Virgin and consequently of the Virgin's qualities: faithful chastity, humility, holiness, and servitude as a submissive instrument of God's will—all qualities of the renunciation of earth and human will. The generative and cleansing powers of the ideal are then linked with the Virgin Mary-like Virgin Pearl by the last few lines of stanza three, wherein the generality of "spices" is given concrete significance by the enumeration of certain spices in the garden arbor. The gilliflower was considered an aromatic and *healing* clove; the ginger an aromatic and *energizing anti-irritant;* the gromwell bears polished, white, stony nutlets very much like *pearls;* the peony is transmitted to medieval medicine from antiquity as the emblem of Παιάν, the Greek god of healing. The "spices" are earthly manifestations of heaven's beneficence, and the anagogy parallels the literal level, wherein the bodily decay of the earthly Pearl Maiden enriches the ground for new growth. Briefly, in implications that suggest the doctrine of works (which undercuts the *visio's* argument for the doctrine of grace), the poem suggests that the proper Christian behavior must continue to result in peace and rejuvenation. Good must continue to come of good:

> *Of goud vche goude is ay bygonne;*
> *So semly a sede moȝt fayly not,*
> *þat spryngande spyceȝ vp ne sponne*
> *Of þat precios perle wythouten spotte.*[10]

The Pearl, as equated with the ideal, is to be associated with that one foundation for all being, faith in the perfect, unified order of the divine creation.[11] The chaos resulting from rejection of all that the

[9] Charles Osgood, "Introduction," *The Pearl* (Boston, 1906), p. xvi.

[10] *Pearl*, ll. 33–36. The poem can be treated fruitfully as a revelation of the tension (often unconscious) between the desire to follow a rationally founded order of behavior, which triumphed in the official acceptance of Thomism, and the more idealistic Pauline doctrine of greater renunciation and fideism. For instance, *The Pearl* is a valuable medieval art-document for a discussion of such doctrines as the nominalist heresy.

[11] Although the narrative-level image of stanza three is only that of putting grains in barns for storage, it is highly probable that a medieval poet would keep a sharp eye out for all tropological possibilities in interpretation. At least the image almost certainly would suggest Joseph and the Parable of the Tares.

Virgin Pearl symbolizes is to be equated with Satanic evil as mani-
fested in mankind by sin. The most direct key to the opposition of
earth and Pearl appears in a determination of the Satanism exemp-
lified by the narrator in his revelation of his own personality.

The Pearl-ideal is the purity of spotless faith, the unswerving
devotion and submission to the will of God which results in perfect
order and regeneration. But without any observations about good or
bad, the narrator simply states that the fears and longings of his
earthly mind almost overpower his faith in the ideal. His man's will
attempts to question the nature of Christ and the will of God. Such a
revealing statement would need no moralizing for the medieval reader
or listener. The narrator's basic negative sin is lack of faith, accompanied by its positive consequence and Satanic counterpart, Pride—
the first of the Seven Deadly Sins.

> Bifore þat spot my honde I spenned
> For care ful colde þat to me caȝt;
> A deuely dele in my herte denned,
> Thaȝ resoun sette myseluen saȝte.
> I playned my perle þat þer watȝ spenned
> Wyth fyrce skylleȝ þat faste faȝt;
> Þaȝ kynde of Kryst me comfort kenned,
> My wreched wylle in wo ay wraȝte.[12]

The inability to accept God's will and grief over the loss of the historical Pearl have made the narrator lose the allegorical, moral, and
anagogical Pearl as well. The narrator falls from the medieval ideal
of the ignorant man who, with limited knowledge, has a faith more
valuable than all the intellection in the world. And it is faith, symbolized by jasper, that is the first foundation for all the other fundaments of the Heavenly City, which the narrator is permitted to
glimpse.[13] The narrator is unable to retain the one "spice," faith,
which is the only effective medicine for his torment. Had he been able
to say, "The Lord giveth and the Lord taketh away," and to add with
complete acceptance, "Blessed be the name of the Lord," the poem
never could have been written.[14]

As the association with the Virgin makes plain, purity is more than
simple sexual chastity. It is the abstract spotlessness typified by faithful maidenhood.[15] The *visio's* debate about innocence versus righteous-

---

[12] *Pearl*, ll. 49–56.

[13] The early fifteenth century *London Lapidary of King Philip* comments: "*The
veray bokes tellen vs that the gode Iaspe is grene & of grete grenehed, & signifieth the trewe
peple of man that ben of the lesse vunderstandyng in the ffader & the sonne & the holy gost;
thei be lewde men, that yef a gode clerc opposed hem thei couth not answere hym, for thei ben*

ness emphasizes that heaven's decision, as stated by the Pearl, is decisively in favor of grace and God's sovereignty as opposed to the good works of a mortal will that cannot escape vitiation because of its postlapsarian condition. And so in accordance with the general (albeit early) preference for the *vita contemplativa*, the poem insists that purity is born of unspoiled faith. Pure faith becomes the quintessential and innocent avoidance and ignorance of earth and its ways. Insofar as the simple, ignorant, or extremely young person is the purest, *The Pearl* is in agreement with medieval literature's general estimation of earth: Adam's fall made it inevitable that the best mind and will shall become corrupted in time. Argues the Pearl,

> *Where wystez þou euer any bourne abate,*
> *Euer so holy in hys prayere,*
> *þat he ne forfeted by sumkyne gate*
> *þe mede sumtyme of heuenez clere?*
> *And ay þe ofter, þe alder þay were,*
> *þay laften ryzt and wrozten woghe.* . . . [16]
> *I rede þe forsake þe worlde wode,*
> *And porchace þy perle maskelles.* [17]

---

bounden, and signifien Iaspe. Moyses seith that this stone is ful gode ayeins temptacion of fendes, of Iewes, & sarazins. Seint Iohn seith vs in the Appocalipce that [in] *the fundament of the heuenly kyndgome of Ierusalem the Iaspe is first, and therefore hit signifieth thre vertues that shulde be in euery gode man. Iaspe is that stone that is cleped feith, the second hope, & the thridde charite, & he that grene Iaspe beholdeth ayeins day, of the feith of Ihesu Xrist he shoulde haue mynde."* Reprinted in Evans and Serjeantson, *English Medieval Lapidaries* (1933), pp. 23–24.

[14] The fact that the poem *was* written (and was written in a manner that emphasizes the very faith the narrator could not accept) strongly suggests that the Pearl Poet's intention was the creation of extended *exemplum* rather than elegy, which was utilized as the vehicle and not the burden of the poem.

[15] Schofield calls attention to the Pearl Poet's exhortation to his maiden readers (*Clanesse*, 1110–32) that they become spotless pearls in order that they may enter heaven. "To speak of maidens in this similitude was . . . no new thing. Long before our poet's time they had been so described. A notable instance is one that occurs in the famous tract of the English Saint Aldhelm, *De Laudibus Virginitatis* (written A.D. 706): at the end the author salutes the maidens whom he had particularly in mind as '*Margaritae Christi, Paradisi gemmae.*' Maidenhood, moreover, was frequently written about in England as a 'gemstone' more precious than any other in God's esteem, which, if preserved clean, would insure participation in the highest bliss of paradise." Schofield also cites the *Love-Rune* of the thirteenth-century Franciscan, Thomas de Hales, who describes abstract purity of maidenhood as a gem of all-surpassing beauty which "shineth bright in heaven's bower . . . " (*Old English Miscellany*, ed. Morris, Early English Text Soc. [1872], 93 ff.) "The Nature and Fabric of *The Pearl*," *PMLA*, XIX (1904), 167.

[16] *Pearl*, ll. 617–24.

[17] *Pearl*, ll. 743–44.

The stains of faithlessness and pride ruin the purity of the mortal narrator. The no-longer *"maskelles"* mortal cannot enter the kingdom of heaven until the stains have been washed from the soul by faith and repentance. And in concurrence, there is a tremendous concentration on whiteness and spotlessness in the vision of heaven.

But the narrator persists in willful pride. He attempts to cross the water barrier and enter the Heavenly City by storm. The stream which separates the narrator from heaven is a traditional death-and-rebirth water symbol, one of the mystical and conventional borderlines between the natural and supernatural worlds, in this case between earth and ideal.[18] In context, in the moral sense the stream represents the waters of absolution, purification by faith and repentance. More especially is this interpretation tenable when the jewels of the streambed are considered as gemstones of virtue. The jewels are "adubbement" in all the connotations of the word: the soul must "'walk'" on virtue in crossing the barrier between earth and heaven. But the prideful narrator finds the barrier too deep and turbulent. In his urge to reclaim the Pearl, he is not permitted to enter heaven using as footing virtues which he cannot claim and has not earned.

Although the streambed is packed with various jewels, only three are specified. Beryl, described in the lapidaries as having the color of pure water, is an emblem of the entrance into heaven of the sum of all virtue—it is symbolic of the Resurrection. Emerald is symbolic of chastity, faith, and good works. Sapphire signifies hope and the saving of a good man by Jesus. The enumeration of only these three gems among all the others in the streambed would seem to indicate that the Pearl Poet quite consciously intended to make his poem one huge typological metaphor of orthodox Christian behavior. And as we have been led to expect from the relationship of the Pearl to the narrator, the theme of behavior is based upon the moral sense of the Pearl's significance. The meaning of the loss of Pearl on the historical level can be only an educated guess. But allegorically, loss of Pearl becomes loss of spiritual peace, perhaps loss of ability to receive spiritual sustenance from the church.[19] Morally, loss of Pearl is loss of faith. And in the consequent anagogical sense, loss of Pearl is loss of heaven. The total loss of happiness is dependent upon the moral loss,

[18] Howard R. Patch, *The Other World* (Cambridge, Mass., 1950), *passim*.

[19] Sister Madeleva suggests that the meaning of the poem exists on this level. But such restriction of meaning as well as the application of the pertinence of the poem to those in religious life seems too exclusive. See *The Pearl: A Study in Spiritual Dryness* (New York, 1925), *passim*.

and it is salient that when the narrator speaks of his former peace and joy in faith and submission, he speaks in terms almost identical to those used by the Pearl in describing her present state in heaven.

The resolution of the tension between earth and Pearl is a typification of Pauline doctrine. The best purification of will, the best exercise of will, and the best choice of moral conduct is the renunciaton of will. Such renunciation is a consequence of submission to God and a withdrawal from earth. The withdrawal is retention of total purity and so becomes a retention or a regaining of Pearl in all the four senses.

It is not necessary to prove that the Pearl Poet consciously based his symbolism upon lapidary material. Gemology was so common in exegetical tradition that it is hardly possible that the poet did not take his jewel symbolism for granted. A curious parallel within the poem itself provides internal evidence that the poet blithely did use such material in a manner that, for a modern, would require deliberate effort in choice of materials. When the Pearl lectures the narrator, she lists attributes of the complete virtue which the narrator must regain in order to find peace. First, she emphasizes the doctrine that man must have *faith* in the grace and sovereignty of God.[20] Second, the statement is recast in terms of the resultant necessity for *hope*.[21] Third, the good that can be obtained by the loss of pride is demonstrated. Specifically, for the narrator, the proper acts to which will must be bent are the meekness and charity of speech and behavior which he so patently lacks. More inclusively, the third attribute of *charity* is the generality of *good works*.[22] Fourth, the youth, innocence, and purity of the Pearl are reintroduced, recalling again the *chastity* or *cleanliness* of the Virgin.[23] Fifth, there is a statement of the need for *repentance*.[24] Sixth, Jesus is suddenly introduced as the open gate through which innocents pass to eternal bliss. For human behavior, the necessary attribute is the *meekness and love of Jesus*.[25] Seventh, the miracles of Christ are recounted. The discussion of metamorphosis from sin to virtue, from stain to whiteness, and from grave to life focusses attention upon the miracles of the *holy gift* of redemption and the formative spirit of love, or *the Holy Ghost*, which is not named as

---

[20] Stanzas 25, 26.
[21] Stanzas 27–29.
[22] Stanza 34.
[23] Stanzas 36–40 (especially line 426).
[24] Stanzas 51, 52.
[25] Stanzas 57, 58, 60, 61.
[26] Stanzas 63–71.

such in the Pearl's *exhortatio*.[26] Eighth, there is a reminder of the translation of the state of the Lamb in the historical Jerusalem to the state of the Lamb in the anagogical Jerusalem. The reminder is a statement to man about the rewards of virtue, *the Resurrection*.[27] Ninth, the narrator discovers that because he has not been purified by the travail of repentance, he cannot enter heaven. The final need of the narrator is patient *travail*, and indeed, because of his impatient pride he is forced back to earth to spend the rest of his days in the travail in which he was first introduced, when his *"breste in bale bot bolne and bele."*[28] It is not until he reaches the purified state suggested by the tone of the last stanza that he can utter words of peaceful resignation.[29]

The poem then builds rapidly to the crescendo of the beatific vision, and in immediate juxtaposition to the lessons the narrator has learned in the conventional debate, the fundaments of the Heavenly City are enumerated. The medieval and Renaissance lapidaries generally evaluate the fundament stones, in order, as follows: jasper is faith; sapphire is hope; chalcydon is good works; emerald is chastity; sardonyx is repentance; ruby is Jesus; chrysolite is the miracles of Christ, the holy gift, and the Holy Ghost; beryl is the Resurrection;

[27] Stanzas 68–75.

[28] Stanzas 79–100.

[29] The final statement of stanza 101 constitutes one of the poem's major flaws. The journey of the narrator extends from ignorance to enlightenment in methods of regaining the Pearl. The narrator's last action is a rebellion. His last speech (stanzas 99, 100) is a realization and acceptance. The expectation is fully developed that he will be cast back to earth to enter his period of enlightened travail. Stanza 101, however, has the narrator utter words which properly belong to the completion of that period. In fact, were it not for the mystagological statement in lines 1209 and 1210, there would be no difficulty in believing that the narrator actually is now in heaven. His language and attitude are identical with that of the Pearl during the debate. At this point a statement of glory gained is unnecessary. The reader already has digested one hundred stanzas of such statement and implication, and our expectations for the narrator have been defined fully: either the narrator will continue in pride and be denied heaven, or, as stanzas 99 and 100 make more probable, he will embark upon a new life of purification. The purpose of the poem has been fulfilled. Its instruction and theme are complete. On the one hand the final stanza is not prepared for by any passage of earthly time in the poem —there is not even a transitional passage between stanzas 100 and 101 as there is between the introduction and the *visio*. On the other hand inclusion of a passage of earthly time would necessitate the writing of a new poem, perhaps much like the Book of Job thematically, in which it is shown *how* the narrator overcomes the obstacles of earth and time, and earns the right (morally as well as structurally) to make the statement of lines 1201 and 1202:

> *To pay þe Prince oþer sete saȝte*
> *Hit is ful eþe to þe god Krystyin . . .*

Appearing as it does, the 101st stanza of resolution and reconciliation is gratuitous and facile.

topaz is the nine orders of angels; chrysoprase is travail; jacinth is safety in far places; and amethyst is Christ's robe.[30] The fact that the poet has not paralleled the plight of the narrator with the stones of the fundaments in the cases of topaz, jacinth, and amethyst indicates that the poet did not order the parallel consciously. But the extent of the parallelism that does exist makes it difficult to doubt that he was fully conscious of and immersed in the traditions with which he worked.

An approach to *The Pearl* governed by exegetical traditions may leave much to be desired in the quantity of material it explains. But it is an important approach, for, because of the lack of a demonstrable historical level, the student is faced with a necessity for not confusing the unknown intentions of an unknown poet with the discoverable intentions of a known poem. And the exegetical traditions demonstrate that no matter what degree of elegy obtains in *The Pearl*, the result is still a revelation of a medieval mind working out a moral instruction and a religious attitude.

MILTON R. STERN

[30] The most important of the medieval lapidaries is the Latin Lapidary of Bishop Marbodus, with its many Latin and vernacular derivatives. Also noteworthy are the *Etymologiae* (Bk. xvi) of Isidore of Seville, the *Steinbuch* of Volamar, the Latin Lapidary of Albertus Magnus, the commentary on Aaron's breastplate by St. Epiphanius, the *Explanatio Apocalypsis* of Bede, the *Commentarium super Apocalypsim* by Primasius, the *De Expositione Veteris et Novis Testamenti* of St. Paterius, the *De Universo* of Rabanus Maurus, the *Summa de Exemplis* of St. John a St. Geminiano, and the collections of L. Pannier, *Les Lapidaires Francais*, and J. Evans and M. Serjeantson, *The English Medieval Lapidaries*. Among Renaissance lapidaries, some of the most important are the *Speculum* of Leonardus, *De Gemmis* of Ruet, *De Subtilitate* of Cardan, *Le Lapidaire* of Mandeville (pseudo), *Gemmarum et Lapidum Historia* of Boodt, *Trattato della Gemme* of Dolce, *Rerum Naturalium* of Scribonnius, *Universae Naturae Theatrum* of Bodin, *Magicae Naturalis* of Porta. Don Cameron Allen, who lists the foregoing Renaissance lapidaries, suggests that all the Renaissance works were in the medieval tradition except the seventeenth century Dolce and Boodt, who exhibit a scientific scepticism "coupled with a suggestion of seventeenth century rationalism." See "Drayton's Lapidaries." *MLN*, LIII (1938), 93.

THE LANGUAGE OF LOVE IN CHAUCER'S
MILLER'S AND REEVE'S TALES AND IN
THE OLD FRENCH FABLIAUX

E. T. DONALDSON has demonstrated Chaucer's device, in the *Miller's Tale*, of sprinkling the characterizations and conversations "with clichés borrowed from the vernacular versions of the code of courtly love—phrases of the sort we are accustomed to meet, on the one hand in Middle English minstrel romances and, on the other, in secular lyrics such as those preserved in Harley MS 2253—but phrases that are not encountered elsewhere in the serious works of Geoffrey Chaucer"[1]—for example, the "oore" (=mercy) for which Absolon begs his sovereign lady, l. 3726.[2] We have in such a phrase a contrast between elegant or would-be-elegant diction and the gross or crude in situation and character, a type of contrast with which Chaucer was very likely acquainted in the fabliau-tradition both French and English, both written and oral.[3] And he would probably find similar effects in the fabliau-sources that we tend to assume for the Miller's and Reeve's tales. In any case, it is my primary purpose here to demonstrate that the use of would-be-elegant love-diction in ironic contexts was well established in fabliau-literature long before Chaucer's time (the extant fabliaux dating mostly from the thirteenth century); and the reader will perhaps conclude that in this matter, as in many others, Chaucer outdid his predecessors.

Some preliminary remarks are in order, for the contrast between diction and situation is merely part of that larger contrast between the sublime and the ridiculous that dominates Group I of the *Tales*—the contrast between the *Knight's Tale* and the ribald tales that follow it, between the truly aristocratic pair of lovers in the *Knight's Tale* and the merely would-be-aristocratic pairs of lovers in the

---

[1] "The Idiom of Popular Poetry in the Miller's Tale," *English Institute Essays* (1950), pp. 116–40.

[2] In F. N. Robinson's edition (Cambridge, Mass., 1933), the one used throughout this paper.

The Rev. Paul E. Beichner, "Chaucer's Hende Nicholas," *Medieval Studies*, XIV (1952), 151–53, p. 152, likewise notes that Nicholas cries for "mercy" in the courtly sense (l. 3288).

[3] Donaldson (*op. cit.*, p. 138, n. 33) suggests that it was perhaps from the French fabliau "that Chaucer got the idea of using conventional poetic idiom in ironic contexts." W. W. Heist, in "Folklore Study and Chaucer's Fabliau-Like Tales," *Papers of the Michigan Academy of Science, Art, and Letters*, XXXVI (1950), 251–58, reminds us to allow for oral versions as possible sources in the case of these tales.

fabliaux.[4] When the Miller declares that he will tell something with which to match the *Knight's Tale*, he invites us to pay attention to Chaucer's art of contrast. When, likewise, the Miller promises both to give the pilgrims "a legend and a life" and to tell how a clerk fooled an artisan, he expresses his own and Chaucer's delight in the ironic fusion of elegance and "harlotrye." In the *Miller's Tale* and to some extent in the *Reeve's Tale* also, delight in similar contrast is prominent, as when Christianity is used as a means of duping the carpenter,[5] or when Chaucer takes a most pathetic line of the *Knight's Tale* ("Allone, withouten any compaignye"—l. 2779) and uses it in the *Miller's Tale* (l. 3204) to mean "single room for male graduate student," or (the present point) when the lovers attempt high-flown love-language, and fail.

One main theme of courtly love is the necessity of secrecy; and Chaucer sounds this note early in the *Miller's Tale* by making Nicholas "ful privee" (l. 3201) and a master of "deerne love" (l. 3200). The rather striking phrase "deerne love" is used twice,[6] as if to emphasize Nicholas' quasi-aristocratic ways, and Alison, too, knows the fashion: "Ye moste been ful deerne, as in this cas" (l. 3297). Secrecy was considered necessary in any illicit love-affair, no doubt, even a bourgeois one, and indeed the lower-caste lovers of the Old French fabliaux occasionally mention the problem (one bourgeois lady, in particular, addresses a lecture on the subject to her lover[7]). At any rate, when Chaucer mentions "deerne love," he uses a term which may remind us of Criseyde and her world and seem comically out of place, or which may suggest those who would enter Criseyde's world but cannot.

Nicholas is one with Palamon and Arcite in threatening to die for love; but even as he does so, he is speeding to his goal with most uncourtly directness and speed:

---

[4] Cf. Donaldson, *op. cit.*, p. 139; and W. C. Stokoe, "Structure and Intention in the First Fragment of the *Canterbury Tales*," *University of Toronto Quarterly*, XXI (1953), 120–27.

[5] William Frost, "An Interpretation of Chaucer's *Knight's Tale*," *RES*, XXV (1949), 289–304, p. 303. Cf. various allusions to matters of religion; *e.g.*, Nicholas' anthem *Angelus ad virginem*, Alison's sealing a bargain of illicit love by swearing an oath by St. Thomas of Kent, and Alison's first coming to Absolon's attention when she goes to church on a holy day, Christ's own works for to work.

[6] See also l. 3278. The phrase is one of those studied by Donaldson, *op. cit.*

[7] A. de Montaiglon and G. Raynaud, *Recueil Général et Complet des Fabliaux* (Paris, 6 vols., 1872–90), I, 246. Hereafter, in references to this collection, the volume- and page-numbers are usually given in parentheses.

> Now, sire, and eft, sire, so bifel the cas,
> That on a day this hende Nicholas
> Fil with this yonge wyf to rage and pleye,
> Whil that hir housbonde was at Oseneye,
> As clerkes ben ful subtile and ful queynte;
> And prively he caughte hire by the queynte,
> And seyde, "Ywis, but if ich have my wille,
> For deerne love of thee, lemman, I spille."
> And heeld hire harde by the haunche-bones,
> And seyde, "Lemman, love me al atones,
> Or I wol dyen, also God me save!" (ll. 3271–81)

Absolon, too, affects high fashion. He is suffering from a love-sickness, by his own account; *e.g.*, from his speech beginning with l. 3698:

> "Wel litel thynken ye upon my wo,
> That for youre love I swete ther I go.
> No wonder is thogh that I swelte and swete;
> I moorne as dooth a lamb after the tete." (ll. 3701–04)[8]

Much to the point also is the way in which he appears to echo aristocratic love-poetry when he is about to give the "misdirected kiss." He says,

> "I am a lord at alle degrees;
> For after this I hope ther cometh moore." (ll. 3724–32)

Robinson directs our attention to the *Romance of the Rose*, where we learn that the obtaining of a kiss is a young lord's first evidence of success in the conduct of a love-affair.[9]

Turning now to the French tales, we observe first a group of clergymen. A monk,[10] who will pay money for a bourgeois lady's love and will be surprised in the act and killed by the husband, says that love of the lady has caused him to go without eating during a whole day (p. 223). Another amorous monk, offering a wife wealth in return for her love, says, "Lady . . . God save you, and give me your love . . . " (VI, 118). She refuses emphatically; and he would rather die than have her take this attitude (p. 119). A priest whom the husband will force to castrate himself calls the wife "Douce amie"; says she to the priest, "Yours is my heart, yours is my body" (V, 166).

---

[8] Cf. Donaldson's opinion (*op. cit.*, p. 135) that the last line here is Chaucer's own contribution to the language of love.

[9] And compare also, of course, ll. 3708–17, especially Alison's protesting, as if involved in courtly love, that she would be to blame if she were unfaithful to the first lover she accepted.

[10] Montaiglon and Raynaud, *op. cit.*, v, 215–42.

The butcher of Abbéville, though very forthright and practical in bargaining for love with the lady and the maid of the priest with whom he finds lodging, nonetheless has enough *savoir-faire* to promise secrecy to these paramours. To the *prêteresse* he swears "by all the saints that are at Rome" (III, 236) to speak of their love to neither man nor woman.

The aged heroine of *De La Viellete ou de la Vielle Truande* (V, 171–78), sitting alone by the side of a little-travelled road, invites to love a handsome bachelor who passes by. She was not "bele Aude" (p. 173), says the author; she was very ugly, but she primped and arranged herself, because she still wanted to be in the swim. And when she saw the handsome young man, she was so smitten with love of him "that never Blanchefleur nor Isolt the fair nor any woman of this world loved anyone so suddenly as she loved immediately" this bachelor. She said to him, "Come down sweet lover, for the love of God; and kiss me and caress me and do more if you wish" (p. 174).

In *The Friar's Breeches* (III, 275–87), the *bourgeoise*—"who was very wise and courteous" (p. 275)—and the clerk, her lover, speak the language of love. The effect is not that of the *Miller's Tale*, precisely, because the poet is in sympathy with the clerk and the wife, and does not make fun of them as Chaucer makes fun of Nicholas and Absolon; nevertheless, the love-language is in contrast with the situation. Says the clerk, "Beautiful loved one, so God help me, it behooves me now to go: he who loves ought to hide his love; for this reason I want to leave early, in order that the neighbors may not see me coming out of your house." "Handsome lover, you are right," replies the lady (p. 282).

The wife in *The Priest Who Was Carried* (IV, 1–40) finds herself in less happy case. She loves a priest "de fin cuer" (p. 6). He arrives, and bathes. The husband kills him; the wife, not knowing this, addresses her lover thus as he lies motionless in the bath-tub: "How are you, handsome sweet sir? You have been very evilly served: for would that my false villein whom I love not at all were flayed alive, for having returned at such a time! . . . Ah, God, what's the matter? Not one word? My sweet sir, my sweet lover, you are vexed because I did not return sooner . . . But I could not come to you sooner, because of my husband's presence. I am ready to serve you. I love you. Why, then, do you not speak to me, handsome sweet sir, handsome sweet lover?" (pp. 6–7). The upshot is that the body is carried about all through the night, as various persons try to dispose of it.

Similarly grotesque contrast between language and situation serves the purpose of the poet who wrote *De Constant du Hamel* (IV, 166–98). The priest, the provost, and the lord's forester want the love of Isabel, wife of Constant du Hamel. They are importunate, but she refuses. The three officials conspire to use their power to reduce the worthy couple to nothing. She, therefore, works out a stratagem. She gives the three suitors appointments for just about the same time. When the first one is with her, the second knocks at the door. "It is my husband!" says she to the first, who hides in a cask full of feathers. The second and the third find themselves in the same place, Constant himself having been the last person to knock at the door. The wives of the three rascals are summoned, and Constant does with them as their husbands would have done with his wife. He sets fire to the cask, and the three husbands flee in disgrace. Isabel retains the money and jewels that they have brought to her.

The priest, unsuccessful in his approach to Isabel, is very sad; he has been "severely wounded by the dart of love, which has pierced him to the heart" (p. 167). The forester offers the goodwife a ring, for this reason, he says: "Only in order to have leave to kiss this beautiful mouth, the sweetness of which touches me to the heart" (pp. 169–70). The effect is sardonic; and so is the moral with which the poet concludes: "May God guard us all from shame!" (p. 198).

De la Borgoise d'Orliens (I, 117–25) is called "une aventure assez cortoise" (p. 117). A very courteous clerk loves a very courteous *bourgeoise*. The husband, pretending to be the lover, comes to the garden door. She receives him in her arms, thinking that he is the lover. "You are welcome," says she (p. 119). He takes care to reply in kind, and returns her salutation: "Cil s'est de haut parler tenuz; / Se li rent ses saluz en bas" (p. 119). Recognizing the husband, the wife nevertheless continues courteously, as if talking to the lover: "Sir . . . it is very pleasant for me that I can hold you and have you . . . " (p. 120). She will hide him until the members of her household have gone to bed, and then come to him. No one will know what they are up to. "Lady," says he, "you have spoken well" (p. 120). Having put the husband out of the way, the lady receives the true lover, who "immediately sets about the game that love commands him . . . " (p. 121). Presently she proposes supper. "Lady, at your commandment" (p. 121). She sets off upon this business "moult belement" (p. 121), and speaks to her servants like one well-taught ("Si parole come enseignie," p. 122), and arranges to have them beat the disguised husband. The lady and the clerk spend the night together, under the guidance of "Amor" (p. 124). She gets out of this fix, says the poet, "like a prudent woman and a wise" (p. 125), for the husband, caring not so much as an egg for his misfortunes, is happy, and never more disturbs her, and she is free to enjoy her lover as much as she desires.

Du Prestre et d'Alison (II, 8–23) presents the rich priest Alexander, who desires the twelve-year-old daughter of a shopwoman named Dame Mahaus, a very courteous *bourgeoise*. Alexander dines at Mahaus' house, and experiences great love in his heart. He calls to the lady sweetly, and begs her to listen to his sorrows. He has kept silent for long, but must now speak. Her daughter Marion has so wrought upon his emotions that he would like, if it would not vex the mother, to have the daughter for one night; and he has a good deal of money. Mahaus refuses bluntly. "My lady," he says, "for God, have mercy on me: I will bring the money here, and you may take as much of it as you please" (p. 12). Mahaus finally appears to give in; she decides to substitute the prostitute Alison for Marion. The servant-girl Hercelot, sent to call the priest to his rendez-vous with the supposed Marion, says to him: "Sir, may you have good day from her who greets you, who is your sweetheart and your pleasure, Marion of the slender body" (p. 15); and the priest gives Hercelot gifts. Brought to Alison he says, with something of Nicholas' mixture of the romantic and the abrupt, "Marie, tell me, are you my sweetheart, beautiful sister, without any word to the contrary?" (p. 20). Presently Hercelot cries "Fire!" The neighbors arrive. Alexander is well beaten and departs in shame.[11]

We glance now at the analogues of the *Reeve's Tale*,[12] and first at *De Gombert et des .II. Clers* (Montaiglon and Raynaud, I, 238–44), in which one of two clerks loves the miller's wife and the other loves the daughter. "And I say," remarks the poet, "that love of a young girl,

---

[11] Cf. also *Du Prestre et du Chevalier* (II, 46–91), with its *prêteresse* Dame Avinée, "La preus, la courtoise, la biele" (p. 70), and the rascally knight who, when he has finished with her, dismisses her mockingly from his company with "God give you good destiny, sweet one" (p. 78).

[12] The Flemish analogue to the *Miller's Tale*, "Heile of Bersele" (printed with a translation by Stith Thompson, in W. F. Bryan and Germaine Dempster, eds., *Sources and Analogues of Chaucer's Canterbury Tales* [Chicago, 1941], pp. 112–18), has two passages resembling the wooing-speeches in Chaucer; cf. the words of the smith (who, in this version, gives the misdirected kiss and then brands his rival): " 'Ah, dear Heile, I beg you if I may this time that I may kiss your mouth' " (ll. 106–7); and " 'Heile, my love, I must come in now at last, or else I must kiss your little mouth. / One of the two things surely must be, / Or I shall stand here all night. / The Power of your love forces me to this' " (ll. 137–42).

when a noble heart is engaged in such love, is noble [gentiex] above all other things . . . " (p. 238). In *Le Meunier et les .II. Clers*,[13] the miller keeps his daughter in a bin at night, and one of the clerks, desiring both the daughter and revenge on the miller, scratches on the bin in order to get the girl's attention. "Who is it out there?" she asks. "It is he who for your body is so cast down and in such bad case; if you do not have mercy on him, he will never on any day have joy; it is he who ate with you, who now brings you a ring of gold . . . " (Version A, ll. 203–9). Similar, in the *Reeve's Tale*, is the contrast between the events of the night and the romantic sentimentality of Alan and the miller's daughter as they bid farewell to one another.

> Aleyn wax wery in the dawenynge,
> For he had swonken al the longe nyght,
> And seyde, "Fare weel, Malyne, sweete wight!
> The day is come, I may no lenger byde;
> But everemo, wher so I go or ryde,
> I is thyn awen clerk, swa have I seel!"
> "Now, deere lemman," quod she, "go, fareweel!
> But er thow go, o thyng I wol thee telle. . . . " (ll. 4234–41)

She tells him how she helped her father to cheat the clerks of their meal, and concludes,

> "And, goode lemman, God thee save and kepe!"
> And with that word almoost she gan to wepe. (ll. 4247–48)

It is of course impossible to say to what extent Chaucer found in his sources (these being unknown) the contrast between language and situation which we have been considering. We can only say that if we consider the Reeve's and Miller's tales with this point in mind, and consider the analogues of the tales and the Old French fabliaux in general, we are justified in thinking it probable that Chaucer was as usual intensifying and enriching the themes and values that he found in his sources.

GARDINER STILLWELL

---

[13] Two versions printed with comment and marginal summaries by W. M. Hart in Bryan and Demptser, *op. cit.*, pp. 124–47.

CONRAD'S DEBT TO MAUPASSANT IN THE PREFACE TO *THE NIGGER OF THE "NARCISSUS"*

BIOGRAPHERS and critics of Joseph Conrad have commented for decades on his knowledge of and respect for the writings of Gustave Flaubert and his pupil Guy de Maupassant. Edward Garnett testified to Conrad's keen interest in the "literary technique and good craftsmanship" of the two Frenchmen,[1] and Jean-Aubry recalled Conrad's frequent allusions to "characters of a third order . . . places very little known in some novel by Maupassant, or some romance by Anatole France, or some other book by Flaubert."[2] According to Conrad's sometime collaborator, Ford Madox Ford, it was their common profound admiration for Flaubert and Maupassant that, more than anything else, drew him and Conrad together in the late 1890's.

> We discovered that we both had *Felicite, St.-Julien l'Hospitalier*, immense passages of *Madame Bovary, La Nuit, Ce Cochon de Morin* and immense passages of *Une Vie* by heart. Or so nearly by heart that what the one faltered over the other could take up.[3]

During their collaboration, Ford declared, he and Conrad had striven to model their prose after that of the two French writers.

> Our chief masters in style were Flaubert and Maupassant: Flaubert in the greater degree, Maupassant in the less. In about the proportion of a sensible man's whisky and soda. We stood as it were on those hills and thence regarded the world.[4]

Conrad himself wrote in glowing terms of Maupassant's artistic integrity and impeccable craftsmanship, most notably in the well-known essay on Maupassant which he contributed as an introduction to Ada Galsworthy's 1904 translation of *Yvette and Other Stories*, and which was reprinted in *Notes on Life and Letters* (1921). He was full of praise for "the consummate simplicity of [Maupassant's] technique,"[5] and discovered in him "inherent greatness,"[6] stemming from his un-

---

[1] *Letters from Conrad* (London: Nonesuch Press, 1928), p. xxx.

[2] "Joseph Conrad," *Fortnightly Review*, CXXII (1924), 306.

[3] *Joseph Conrad. A Personal Remembrance* (London: Duckworth, 1924), p. 36. In view of Ford's decidedly blemished reputation for veracity, his testimony must always be taken *cum grano salis*. Garnett's review of this volume in the *Nation*, XXXVI (1924), 366–68, points out a host of inaccuracies, but does not specifically call into question any of the statements which are quoted in this article.

[4] *Ibid.*, p. 195.

[5] *Notes on Life and Letters* (London: Dent, 1924), p. 25.

[6] *Ibid.*, p. 26.

swerving dedication to his craft. Maupassant's diction was an element in his art that particularly impressed Conrad: "the master of the *mot juste*," he was never a mere "dealer in words." Conrad likened him to a trader in "polished gems; not the most rare and precious, perhaps, but of the very first water of their kind."[7]

There is evidence in Conrad's letters that he was especially interested in Maupassant in the 1890's, at any rate from 1894 on. In August of that year, Conrad wrote Marguerite Poradowska from the hydropathic establishment at Champel that "I am reading Maupassant with delight."[8] He was more specific in a letter which he wrote Mme. Poradowska that autumn from London:

I am afraid I am too much under the influence of Maupassant. I have studied *Pierre et Jean*—thought, method, and everything—with the deepest discouragement. It seems to be nothing at all, but the mechanics are so complex that they make me tear out my hair. You want to weep with rage in reading it. That's a fact.[9]

Writing to Garnett in 1898, Conrad referred with similar awe to another of Maupassant's novels, "that amazing masterpiece *Bel-Ami*. The technique of that work gives to one acute pleasure. It is simply enchanting to see how it's done."[10]

Since Conrad, then at the threshold of his career, was so devoted an admirer of Maupassant, it was not unnatural that he should attempt to pattern some of the imaginative writing which he was producing at the time after the Frenchman's work. Richard Curle, one of Conrad's intimate friends, stated categorically that "The Idiots," written in 1896 and published in 1898 as one of the *Tales of Unrest,* was written "consciously in the Maupassant manner,"[11] and a study of this story, its subject, its diction, its mood, seems to bear out this

---

[7] *Ibid.*, p. 28.

[8] John A. Gee and Paul J. Sturm (eds.), *Letters of Joseph Conrad to Marguerite Poradowska* (New Haven: Yale, 1940), p. 76. Most probably referring to Conrad's first visit, in 1891, to Champel, which, with a typical disregard for the facts, he calls "the hydrotherapie near Geneva where Maupassant died" (he actually died at Passy, although he had spent some time at Champel), Ford advances the intriguing, but naïve and almost certainly incorrect, suggestion that Conrad there formed the resolution to turn to writing as a career. "All to pieces as he then was he had to think of how he was going to occupy the rest of his life. For following the sea he imagined that he would no longer be fit. When he was a little better he saw on the bookstall of Geneva station those yellow volumes. The sight of them and the thought of Maupassant made him say: 'By Jove: Why not write'?" (Ford, p. 102).

[9] Gee and Sturm, p. 84.

[10] Garnett, p. 130.

[11] *The Last Twelve Years of Joseph Conrad* (London: Sampson Low, 1928), p. 116.

contention. *The Sisters*, an unfinished novel abandoned in 1896 and not published until after Conrad's death, was associated with the influence of Maupassant by Ford in the introduction which he contributed to the posthumous edition of the fragment in 1928. The story as projected by Conrad was to have revolved around the character of a zealous priest who kills his niece and her love-child in a violent manifestation of his twisted asceticism. According to Ford, Conrad abandoned the novel when he despaired of being able to differentiate his Father Ortega from Maupassant's similarly demented Abbé Tolbiac in *Une Vie*.[12]

There is, however, still another, better known, piece of Conrad's, written at the same time, which bears strong traces of Maupassantian influence: the Preface to *The Nigger of the "Narcissus"* (1897), the doctrine of which has much in common with the views Maupassant expressed on the writing and criticism of fiction in "Le Roman," the preface to *Pierre et Jean*, which we know from his second letter to Mme. Poradowska Conrad had been reading with the closest attention as recently as 1894. The most obvious resemblance between the two essays is one of function: Conrad's, like Maupassant's, codifies certain theoretical assumptions which he regarded as basic to the practice of his art, and in this respect it is virtually unique among Conrad's prefaces (as "Le Roman" is in Maupassant's *oeuvre*); for Conrad, unlike Henry James, did not habitually make his prefaces into vehicles for such disquisitions. But a number of more fundamental similarities are sufficiently striking to suggest unconscious emulation if not conscious imitation of Maupassant on Conrad's part.

Both Conrad and Maupassant insist that the artist-writer must incessantly endeavor to depict the truth, and they are in agreement that this involves a shunning of the fleeting and transitory surfaces of things. Conrad, in fact, defines art in the Preface to *The Nigger* as "a single-minded attempt to render the highest kind of justice to the visible universe, by bringing to light the truth, manifold and one, underlying its every aspect."[13] Conrad here is in complete agreement with Maupassant's dictum that art, however true to life, must rise above the level of mere photography.

Le réaliste, s'il est un artiste, cherchera, non pas à nous montrer la photo-

---

[12] Introduction to *The Sisters* (New York: Crosby Gaige, 1928), pp. 8–9.
[13] *The Nigger of the "Narcissus"* (London: Dent, 1923), p. vii. Subsequent references will be given in the text.

graphie banale de la vie, mais à nous en donner la vision plus complète, plus saisissante, plus probant que la réalité même.[14]

Nevertheless, the writer must appeal in the first instance to the senses of the reader, primarily his sense of sight. Maupassant gives credit to his master Flaubert for developing in him the visual acuity which enabled him to put his subject vividly before his reader.

Ayant, en outre, posé cette vérité qu'il n'y a pas, de par le monde entier, deux grains de sable, deux mouches, deux mains ou deux nez absolument pareils, il me forçait à exprimer, en quelque phrases, un être ou un objet de manière à le particulariser nettenent, à le distinguer de tous les autres êtres ou de tous les autres objets de même race ou de même espèce. (p. xxiv)

The vivid rendering of sense impressions is no less important to Conrad. "All art . . . appeals primarily to the senses," he says, "and the artistic aim when expressing itself in written words must also make its appeal through the senses, if its high desire is to reach the secret spring of responsive emotions" (p. ix). In what is perhaps the best-known single sentence he ever wrote, Conrad puts it somewhat more emphatically: "My task which I am trying to achieve is, by the power of the written word to make you hear, to make you feel—it is, before all, to make you *see*. That—and no more, and it is everything" (p. x). " . . . by the power of the written word": a key phrase. For to Conrad, as to Maupassant, felicitous diction, the reasoned choice and arrangement of words too often outworn and tarnished by irrelevant connotations, was an all-important means toward achieving the immediacy of presentation for which both writers strove.

Quelle que soit la chose qu'on veut dire, il n'y a qu'un mot pour l'exprimer, qu'un verbe pour l'animer et qu'un adjectif pour la qualifier. Il faut donc chercher, jusqu'à ce qu'on les ait découverts, ce mot, ce verbe et cet adjectif, et ne jamais se contenter de l'à peu près, ne jamais avoir recours à des super-cheries, même heureuses, à des clowneries de langage pour éviter la difficulté. (pp. xxiv–xxv)

And it is only through complete, unswerving devotion to the perfect blending of form and substance; it is only through an unremitting never-discouraged care for the shape and ring of sentences that an approach can be made to plasticity, to colour, and that the light of magic suggestiveness can be brought to play for an evanescent instant over the commonplace surface of words: of the old, old words, worn thin, defaced by ages of careless usage. (p. ix)

Conrad, like Maupassant, denies that the artist-writer's freedom to choose his subject should be in any way curtailed. In "Le Roman"

---

[14] *Pierre et Jean* (Paris: Conard, 1909), p. xiv. Subsequent references will be given in the text.

we read: "Lui reprocher de voir les choses belles ou laides, petites ou épiques, gracieuses ou sinistres, c'est lui reprocher d'être conformé de telle ou telle façon et de ne pas avoir une vision concordant avec la nôtre" (p. x). Such a writer, Conrad says, appeals to "the latent feeling of fellowship with all creation"; accordingly, "it becomes evident that there is not a place of splendour or a dark corner of the earth that does not deserve, if only a passing glance of wonder and pity" (p. viii). He follows Maupassant, and here there is a similarity of phraseology too striking to be entirely coincidental, in urging the writer to ignore the clamor of the multitude and to pursue his artistic aims steadfastly and with a clear conscience.

> En somme, le public est composé de groupes nombreux qui nous crient:
> —Consolez-moi.
> —Amusez-moi.
> —Attristez-moi.
> —Attendrissez-moi.
> —Faites-moi rêver.
> —Faites-moi rire.
> —Faites-moi frémir.
> —Faites-moi pleurer.
> —Faites-moi penser.
> Seuls, quelques esprits d'élite demandent à l'artiste:
> —Faites-moi quelque chose de beau, dans la forme qui vous conviendra le mieux, suivant votre tempérament. (p. ix)

Conrad, too, insists that the writer must endeavor to achieve his "creative task" undeterred by those who, "in the fulness of a wisdom which looks for immediate profit, demand specifically to be edified, consoled, amused; who demand to be promptly improved, or encouraged, or frightened, or shocked, or charmed" (pp. ix–x).

The sort of resemblances to which we have been pointing, interesting as they are in themselves, become even more significant if it is borne in mind that the fundamental theme which these two prefaces have in common is one that animated both Conrad and Maupassant, at any rate when they were at their best, as creative artists: their mutual concern for the supreme importance of craftsmanship, their mutual abhorrence of cheap, shoddy work. "Le talent est une longue patience" (p. xxiii), says Maupassant, quoting Flaubert; Conrad, similarly, stresses throughout the Preface to *The Nigger of the "Narcissus"* the supreme difficulty of the artist-writer's calling: very few attain the highest artistic success, and they only seldom, by dint of the most unremitting diligence.

GEORGE J. WORTH